Church Reform and Leadership of Change

Church Reform and Leadership of Change

EDITED BY
Harald Askeland
Ulla Schmidt

James Clarke & Co

James Clarke & Co
P.O. Box 60
Cambridge
CB1 2NT
United Kingdom

www.jamesclarke.co
publishing@jamesclarke.co

ISBN: 978 0 227 17618 4

British Library Cataloguing in Publication Data
A record is available from the British Library

First published by James Clarke & Co, 2016

Copyright © Trossamfundet Svenska Kyrkan (Church of Sweden), 2016

Published by arrangement
with Pickwick Publications

Contents

Contributors

Andreas Aarflot, Professor Emeritus, Norwegian School of Theology, Oslo, Norway; Bishop Emeritus, Oslo Diocese, Church of Norway.

Harald Askeland, Professor, Diakonhjemmet University College, Oslo, Norway.

Kjetil Fretheim, Professor, Norwegian School of Theology, Oslo, Norway.

Per Hansson, Senior Professor, Department of Education, Uppsala University, Sweden.

Isolde Karle, Professor, Faculty of Protestant Theology, Ruhr-Universität Bochum, Germany.

Karen Marie Sø Leth-Nissen, PhD student, Faculty of Theology, University of Copenhagen, Denmark.

Johanna Gustafsson Lundberg, Associate Professor, Centre for Theology and Religious Studies, Lund University, Sweden.

Bim Riddersporre, Senior Lecturer, Malmö University, Sweden.

Ulla Schmidt, Professor, Department of Culture and Society, Aarhus University, Denmark.

Hege Steinsland, MA, Norwegian University of Science and Technology, Funder/Facilitator, Relasjonsutvikling SA, Norway.

Maria Åkerström, MA, Uppsala University, Senior pastor, Vist Vårdnäs, Dean, Deanery of Stångå, Sweden.

Tables and Figures

1

Introduction

Reforms or intended processes of change appear to have become a pervasive characteristic of European Protestant churches in recent decades. These processes seem to have been spurred by a number of tendencies in society in general, as well as in religious life more specifically. Many European churches have been experiencing declining membership rates, which for many have also meant dwindling finances, reduced participation in church rituals, services and activities, and less support of traditional church doctrine. Furthermore, several churches have problems recruiting candidates for ordained ministry as well as for involvement in their democratic structures, such as parish councils. At the same time, newer forms of worship and activities, and different types of involvement and voluntarism, seem to be evolving. On the broader societal level, changed patterns of governance of religion in general and churches in particular also alter the conditions under which churches operate and which they have to relate to. In the northern region, relations between the traditional majority churches and the state have particularly been in focus and have compelled the majority churches to rethink not only their relation to the state, but also their internal organizational structures.

Much research has been conducted on the dynamics of these tendencies and their implications for institutional religion, such as churches. Less research, however, has been devoted to the ways in which churches use various forms of planned and structured institutional and organizational changes in their attempts to respond to these changes and their impact. Over the last ten years researchers have come together at biannual conferences on "Church Leadership and Organizational Change" in order to address these types of questions and further invigorate and stimulate this research field.

The fourth conference, which took place in Oslo, Norway, September 2013, focused on the topic of "Church Reform and Leadership of Change." In this volume we are delighted to present keynote lectures from the conference, as well as articles based on a selection of the presentations delivered at the conference. This also includes two articles based on Master's degree theses, exemplifying the growing interest in bringing theories and insights from leadership and organizational studies to bear on church studies.

Together, the articles address a variety of issues within the overall topic. Some deal with church reforms specifically. In the article based on her key note lecture, Isolde Karle focuses on the nature and characteristic features of pervasive reform processes in the Protestant church in Germany, and articulates some of the questions and dilemmas evoked by applying organizational reform ideas to churches. Andreas Aarflot identifies the historical background and traces the development of the recent reforms of the relations between state and majority church in Norway, revealing the various underlying ideas that played into this interesting process. Ulla Schmidt compares reforms in the Church of Norway to public-sector reforms, asking whether the former simply emulate the latter.

Another set of articles addresses the issue of how leadership of change also opens for changing patterns of leadership. Searching for new ways of fruitfully conceptualizing and understanding church leadership, Bim Ridderspore and Johanna Gustafsson Lundberg explore management of meaning, whereas Hege Steinsland discusses the idea of dual leadership. In her article, Karen Marie Sø Leth-Nissen gives an example of one prominent change which needs to be addressed by church leadership, namely that of leaving the church and the underlying stories and rationales people might have for relinquishing their membership in majority churches. Two articles deal with the more specific question of changes in leadership of ordained ministry on the organizational pastoral levels. Harald Askeland analyzes a reform in the Church of Norway to restructure leadership of local ministries through the organizational entity of the deanery and the function of the dean, whereas Per Hansson compares the Church of England and the Church of Sweden with respect to regulations and practices for clergy discipline.

A further group of articles explores how existing organizational structures in churches are used and function when it comes to governing and renewing church activities at the local level. Kjetil Fretheim uses a case study to investigate and describe the actual functions of leadership and governance of local church life undertaken by a parish council, whereas Maria Åkerström, also working with case studies, explores examples of the renewal of local church life in light of the notion of social entrepreneurship.

All in all, the articles explore the complex phenomenon of church reforms and leadership of change from a variety of angles: thematically, methodologically and theoretically.

At this point, the editors would like to express their heartfelt gratitude to all the contributors. First of all we would like to thank the authors for their willingness to appear in this book and for all the work they have laid down in developing their original contributions into articles. Secondly, we gratefully acknowledge the following institutions for their generous financial support for the original conference: KIFO—Institute for Church, Religion and Worldview Research, Oslo, Norway, Church of Norway Employers Association, Diakonhjemmet University College in Oslo, Church Research Institute in Finland, and the Peter Fjellstedt Foundation in Uppsala, Sweden. KIFO has also supported this publication. We would also like to thank the group of co-organizers of the 2013 Oslo conference: Deputy Director Marit Halvorsen Hougsnæs, Professor Per Hansson, and Professor Per Petterson. Finally, we would like to thank the editor of the Church of Sweden Research Series for including this publication in the series!

Oslo / Aarhus, March 30, 2015
Harald Askeland and Ulla Schmidt

2

Reforming Majority Churches

Possibilities and Dilemmas

ISOLDE KARLE

The Evangelical Church in Germany (*Evangelische Kirche in Deutschland*, abbreviated to EKD)[1] has been working on reform processes and discourses since 2006. In 2006 the Council of the EKD published the reform paper *Kirche der Freiheit* under the presidency of Bishop Wolfgang Huber. This is the first time that such a reform paper has been made public by the EKD. The aim of the paper was to stimulate and promote an understanding of the necessity for reforms and it has attracted a great deal of attention in Germany. Conceptually and linguistically, the paper is not oriented towards prioritizing insights from theology and sociology of religion, as would previously have been the case, but is focused on the knowledge-base of strategic management. Faced with declining financial resources, declining income from membership taxes and a critical demographic development of the population, of which the Protestant church is particularly affected because they hardly see migrants among its members, the EKD reform propagates a *Wachsen gegen den Trend*. As in a company, the attainment of ambitious overriding goals, such as higher rates of baptism or increased participation

1. The EKD association has been in existence since 1945, where all Lutheran, Reformed and United churches in Germany are associated and bound together under one roof. The Synod and the Council of the EKD assume the main responsibility for its tasks.

in services, are front and centre, where the idea is that they should be at-
tainable through good church marketing. Moreover, far-reaching changes
are also proposed, including greater centralization, a domestication of the
clergy and a significant reduction of the autonomy of local parishes.[2]

Due to its business management approach and its tendency to undermine the existing decentralized structures, the paper has provoked a great
deal of criticism in the church and in academic institutions. But actually, the
EKD is only an umbrella organization of autonomous regional churches.
This means that it cannot lay down any central guidelines or make any operational decisions. Such decisions are the responsibility of the respective
regional churches (*Landeskirchen*). In these regional churches, structural
changes, which are called reform processes, have in fact taken place over
several years. On the one hand, these processes relate to the EKD reform
paper, but on the other hand, they represent an attempt to cope with the
reconstruction of the church in a more down-to-earth way.

The reform orientation of the Protestant church should in principle be
welcomed due to the background of the Reformation and its heritage. The
Protestant church is ready to question itself. It adapts to a changing social
environment and reflects on itself in on-going discussions with the biblical
tradition and the reformatory confessions. The current reform processes
are, however, less due to the reformation heritage than part of an overall
societal development. Organizational reforms can presently be observed in
all functional systems. They are part of the giant progress project of modernity which aims for permanent optimization and acceleration, not only
in individual lives but also in modern organizations. Of course, the goal
of reform processes is self-improvement, but they are also accompanied by
self-depreciation. Reforms always presuppose that the current situation is
negative or should at least be classified as unsatisfactory and deficient.

In the Protestant church, this dynamic cannot be ignored. The EKD
discussion paper signals a clear dissatisfaction with the current work of the
church and with the ministers responsible for the main activities. The alarm-
ing picture of the future of the church that has been drawn is astonishing. It
is obvious that this has been done to illustrate the necessity of the proposed
reforms and the lack of alternatives. The decision makers are so focused on
the deficiencies that they take no account of all the work the church does
that is succeeding and worth preserving—and that all this by no means is
self-evident, namely: That many ministers preach relevant sermons Sunday
after Sunday, and that many people in many local parishes grow into faith
over the years, a faith that has fundamental importance for their lives. It

2. See in detail: Karle, *Kirche im Reformstress*.

is not self-evident that the church is still closely connected to civic commitment and the civil society, or that local choirs, child and youth work, and the religious education in church make an immense contribution to cultural education and formation. Neither is it mentioned that many people in crisis situations turn to the church and appreciate pastoral and diaconal assistance there, and that even in a secular society the church is met with high expectations, not least the expectation to be of help where no one else is willing to help.

While reforms are launched to solve certain problems, they may just as easily create new and perhaps even more serious problems. To succeed with reforms, the diagnosis must first of all be accurate when it comes to the actual opportunities for action, but also with respect to the many factors that cannot be influenced and controlled. Only a sober analysis of the situation, not enthusiasm for change in its own right, will help the church. In the following, I will not delve into the individual points of the EKD reform paper, but I will try to analyze sociologically and ecclesiologically how its main ideas have influenced the reform discourse in the church in Germany. First, I explore the assumptions underlying the problem description of the EKD reform paper. Then I deal with the question of what it means for the church when it transforms itself more and more into a modern service organization. Finally, I examine some interesting perspectives.

SECULARIZATION OR RELIGIOUS BOOM?

The intended reform efforts are based on the assumption that there is currently an extremely favorable market for religion which the church is unable to profit from because its key actors and services are too unappealing or not performing well enough. In the field of religious studies, the assumption that we are currently experiencing a religious boom has been increasingly drawn into doubt. Although studies on religion agree that there has been greater media attention on religious matters over the last few years and decades, this media attention is not identical with a religious boom.

Detlef Pollack, sociologist of religion at Münster University, tirelessly points out that the extra-ecclesial processes of religious recovery are radically overstated, and that very little religious productivity can be identified outside the churches or the religious communities: "It is simply not true that the churches are empty, but religion is booming."[3] What is claimed to be a religious boom is a religion that is largely without God. What we can observe is an esoteric searching for something that indicates a vague quest for meaning by individuals in late modernity who are unsettled in many ways.

3. Pollack, "Entzauberung oder Wiederverzauberung der Welt?" 137.

But we do not see a substantial interest in religious communication and in a lifestyle that is characterized by a religious attitude. That is why the church will hardly be able to profit substantially from the market of spiritual searching and spiritual movement within and beyond the realm of the church.

The new religiosity is to a large extent a religiosity without the church. It is "a religion without God. It is counting on cosmic energies and force fields, which we might tap spiritually, but not with a personal God who has created the human being as a responsible counterpart."[4] Not least for this reason it has become more and more preferable to talk about spirituality, which is used "as a collective term for the various types of search for meaning."[5] It includes almost everything that gives human beings a sense of importance with respect to their own existence. The sociologist Armin Nassehi assumes that religious communication becomes "increasingly independent of content."[6] Spirituality is handling the indefinable in the most indefinable way possible. The argument loses importance, while authentic speaking steps to the foreground. The trend towards a de-reification of religion is the consequence.

Spirituality is therefore not simply identical with religion. It is located on the "fuzzy edges of the religious field."[7] That is why it is questionable whether and to what extent the churches can benefit from late-modern spirituality, even if they adapt their own practice to it. We are currently not witnessing a revival of the Christian tradition outside of the church, but rather a break with the tradition which particularly affects the second and third generation of non-church members. The continuing secularization of society has to be taken into account, and a certain indifference towards religion and the church cannot be overlooked. This indifference is closely connected to the decentralization and pluralization of society.[8]

CHURCH IN THE SERVICE SOCIETY

Modern society is based on organization, and not only when it comes to the economy and transactions. In the functional differentiated society, education, religion and medical care, which of course also exist outside of organizations, are dependent on them. Organizations establish a certainty of expectations. They provide competence and professionalism and harmonize huge amounts of interactions between people. Only organizations can

4. Körtner, *Wiederkehr der Religion?* 15.

5. Ibid., 17.

6. Nassehi, "Spiritualität," 40.

7. Graf, *Die Wiederkehr*, 245.

8. Cf. Rösch, "Der Reformdiskurs."

interact with other organizations and make the functional system capable of acting in a collective way. Accordingly, as part of modernity, the church has expanded its organization. In this regard, we have observed an "organizational upgrade"[9] (*organisatorische Hochrüstung*), in particular since the 1970s, a time when the churches had many resources and were reacting to growing expectations on the one hand and to declining membership rates on the other.

Yet, as important and indispensable organization is for religion and the church, the problem with this development is that the church—and in step with other modern organizations—has increasingly developed into a service provider. However, religion and education, for that matter, are fundamentally dependent on social interactions that imply more than specific contributions or services for individuals, more than an exchange of service and return service. Religion is about an interest in the other as a person, which is why religion is reliant on informal, spontaneous social relationships where trust is crucial.

But an organization does not only come into conflict with religious communication, embedded in the trust-based community, but also with its content. A modern organization is based on decisions and lives by decisions. The more decisions have to be taken and legitimized, the more clearly their contingent character will become manifest. What has been decided in one way could also have been decided otherwise: "For religion in its function of handling contingency, it is a problem to become contingent itself through decisions, this compromises its functional compliance."[10] Basically, faith can neither be decided nor organized. The formation of faith can be promoted through organization, but faith itself eludes every organizational access. In particular, basic dogmatic self-determinations cannot easily be changed or adjusted in line with the market situation. If this were so, the church would give up on itself and cease to be a church. The problem is that "in terms of a decision . . . there is always the acknowledgement that it also could have been decided differently. Decisions undermine claims of truth."[11] When it comes to content, the church cannot simply make itself dependent on the desires of its members. But this is what the church would have to do if it is consequently thought of as a modern organization. The gospel is not anything that is amendable or replaceable. The church cannot—as Niklas Luhmann considered ironically—try to promote money instead of God.[12]

9. Geser, "Zwischen Anpassung," 46.

10. Schlamelcher, "Ökonomisierung der Kirchen," 156.

11. Luhmann, *Die Religion*, 240.

12. Luhmann, "Die Organisierbarkeit," 281.

The church is therefore not comparable with a modern (profit-making) company and nor should it want to become more like a company. If the church considers its members as customers, there is a risk that they will only use it according to rational decisions. But the church as an institution symbolizes the inaccessible and transcendent, what is not subject to any cost-benefit calculation.

THE PROBLEM OF THE COST-BENEFIT CALCULATION

Due to the financial crisis it is in, the church is trying to profit from the experiences of economic management. Neo-liberal business management strategies, such as quality management, staff development, marketing, evaluations and cost-benefit calculations, have therefore entered the Protestant Church in Germany. In the course of this development the church has also acquired an internal market form: The pressure on the ministers and other church employees is increasing. Success becomes an important indicator.

The financial crisis of the churches since the beginning of the 1990s has been caused by demographic development, tax reforms and declining membership figures, on the one hand, but, on the other hand, it has also been generated by the massive expansion of the church organization and administration in the 1970s. The organizational expansion was aimed at stopping the erosion of the institutional ties to society. However, it is quite clear that the church has not succeeded on this front. Due to the financial constraints of recent decades it is now no longer possible for the church to fund the immense expansion of positions and buildings from the seventies. The church has had no choice but to cut down on and restructure its organization: It has to become more efficient and act in a more economical way, which is why the churches are trying to gain new members, and with them new money. This combination of spiritual and economic interests is a significant part of the launched church-reform programs which have been born out of financial necessity.

This adoption of neo-liberal economic ideas affects the church deeply. The religious language is increasingly penetrated and superimposed by economic semantics. The inherent cost-benefit rationality of economics is becoming part of the religious language—and consequently of religious thinking as well. Moreover, the benefits of faith are increasingly used in church marketing: The church claims that faith makes you healthy and promises a longer life. But this choice of direction results in basic aporia. Religious belief is basically independent of success or personal advantages. This does not preclude that people who believe in God or go to church do not benefit from this; the health-promoting effects of faith should not be denied in principle. Also, the fact should not be questioned that attending a service on Sunday can be an inspiration and a place of rest and spiritual edification. But the benefit must remain *latent* in the religious field. It must not be sought purposely. Faith must not be exploited by other goals and intentions according to the motto: "If you have your child baptized, it will live longer" or: "If you are blessed in a service of healing, you will become healthy again." Or: "If you believe, you will have good luck and success in life." Happiness and salvation can never be sought directly, otherwise they will fail. This also explains why so many people are unhappy in late modernity, even though they are constantly concerned with the pursuit of happiness and seek guidance from many different advisers.

Love, art, and religion have no instrumental character, they have their meaningfulness in themselves, in their practice. The example of love highlights this: Love would not be love if an instrumental cost-benefit calculation was its prime motivation. Moreover, through the emphasis on benefits in an ecclesial context, the church is reinforcing the societal trend of the need- or demand-orientation. Everyone is constantly dealing with the question: What is useful for me? What do I need? Modern individuals cultivate their own dissatisfaction because there is still something missing; an increasing enjoyment of career or other stimulating experiences always appear conceivable and possible. "The model of church-customer orientation converges with this specific late modernist self-referentiality of the individual,"[13] and is thus lastly positioned opposite to the message of Jesus (e.g., in the Sermon on the Mount) and his way of life. Moreover, altruistic ideas are also discredited. This also hides the fact, that some people have the courage to take decisions that are based on deep feelings or convictions—decisions that may cost more than they give. The story of the Good Samaritan is an example of this. In this story, all restrictions (i.e., all external stimulations, such as money or gratefulness) are consequently hidden as a source of motivation for what the Samaritan did.

MEANS AND PURPOSE

Through scarcity of resources, particularly in non-profit organizations, a reversal of means and purpose might occur. Then the focus easily slides away from the actual function of religion or science or art to the function of economy: the acquisition of money. Money is no longer used to gain the (religious or scientific) goal of an organization. Instead, the purpose of an organization is to mobilize complementary financing sources with the help of the services it provides. This problem arises not only in the church. In

13. Preul, *Die soziale Gestalt*, 334.

universities it occurs due to the so-called third-party funding which becomes increasingly important: The attention of the scientist may then be taken away from the intrinsic value of the research work and towards managerial issues and successes.

With this development, the function of a non-profit organization is transformed into a service where the relation between organization and individual is transformed into a provider-customer relation. In this way, the orientation towards the demands of the potential customer becomes crucial. The content of the message that the church is supposed to preach is modified in the course of this shift in a sensitive way. Religion is degraded to a service which is advertised on the market. The result will then in turn be that a very vague form of religion or postmodern spirituality cannot only be found in society, but is also created by the church itself.

This description does not lead to any solutions. In fact the church has no other options than to alternate between a broad openness to all and a position with clear content. In other words, the church should welcome one and all without any restrictions on admission and at the same time keep to its own core, making clear what it stands for. The church must be identifiable as an organization and "show the difference."[14]

But a unilateral customer and service orientation leads the church into a dead-end because it makes a position independent of resonance nearly impossible. Moreover, the importance of community-based communication will be pushed to the background while the relationship between the individual and organization will come even more clearly to the fore. This is also reflected by the fact that the church as organization has developed a life of its own. It sees itself no longer primarily as a service provider for the communities and for the ministers and parishes, rather it sees itself more and more as a large company with branches in local communities, with ministers as mobile workers who are in contact with clients to attain the goals of the organization. For a church which is working in this sense, theology has mainly a legitimizing and not a guiding function in working "to achieve non-theological and non-religious goals (financial rehabilitation) with non-theological instruments (marketing)."[15]

In the EKD reform paper the future of the church is directly identified with its solvency. It is difficult to see how the church will be able to remove itself from the overriding priority of solvency, because he "who begins with money, is in danger of no longer being able to be released from the grip of the autonomy of solvency calculation, and is thus in a way dependent on

14. Nassehi, "Den Unterschied."
15. Schlamelcher, "Ökonomisierung der Kirchen?" 174.

financial considerations, that from the outset make it almost impossible to take into account any other argument."[16]

THE CHURCH AS A SYMBOL OF UNAVAILABILITY

In EKD membership polls the church members state that they do not look upon the church in the same way as any other organization. People expect the church to question processes in society critically and to be a counterpart to a world in which cost-benefit calculations, efficiency, performance and the ability to enjoy oneself are the crucial parameters. The expectations people have for the church are still supported by transcendent values that should be more or less immutable. "With the discussion about its organization shaped as a business, the church is risking exactly this ascription as an institution, from which it can win the most generalized consent."[17] The church is expected to symbolize the extraordinary, the transcendent, and not only the purpose- or goal-rationality, such as banks or agencies do. It should provide appealing services, comfort and support people in crisis situations and stand by those who are suffering within the achievement-oriented society, offering them pastoral counseling and care.

Most church members do not know much about the special ecclesial functions and hardly associate the church with the differentiated service it offers. They identify the church by the church building, through the minister, on whom they place extremely high expectations, or through other people who are involved in the activities of their local church. More than 70 percent of the respondents in the latest membership poll expect the minister to be something like a model example. At least the ministers should be convinced by the central dogma of the Christian faith. At least they should represent and live the faith authentically. A kind of vicarious faith is manifested in such an expectation.

These relatively high expectations of an "exemplary life" are not primarily a civil mission statement of respectability. Rather, they reflect the desire for "a recognizable faith, in this respect an exemplary Christian life."[18] What is expected of the parish minister is not only a specific, occupational way of behaving, but "a certain, comprehensive way of life embodied by the person."[19] This spiritual and subjective dimension of the church stands in contrast to modern organizational rationality. Inherent to the church is its sense of resistance, which is hard to grasp and does not really fit the

16. Kosch, "Kirchliches Handeln," 74.

17. Schlamelcher, "Unternehmen Kirche?" 257.

18. Hermelink, "Sind Sie zufrieden?" 132.

19. Ibid., 132.

organizational society. These resistant points to what is ultimately different or otherworldly are central to the credibility of the church.

For most of its members, the church is not an organization for which you make conscious or rational decisions. The church is rather a symbol of the inaccessible. Even the individual connection with the church has been widely recognized as having symbolic quality.

> The attention to the church, in the public, be it in mass media communication, be it in view of a church building "on-site," is apparently dominated . . . by the expectation to meet a very different tradition which stands against the horizon of the standards which the modern symbolizes.[20]

For church members, and also for many non-members, the church is a kind of contrasting principle, "an inaccessible border against the economic rationality of everyday life."[21]

It is a paradox: The church must on the one hand master the rules of the secular services, marketing and media control, while at the same time falling into a credibility trap if it actually takes them effortlessly into use. The church sees itself confronted with contradictory claims. It should be well organized and make rational decisions and, at the same time, it should be "otherworldly" (representing *das ganz Andere*) and be an opposition and contrast to the economic and rational pressures of society.

LIMITATIONS ON WHAT CAN BE ORGANIZED

The fundamental problem of the EKD reform program is that it is too reliant on the assumptions of predictability and controllability, and that it tries to organize processes that cannot be organized. For instance: It does not make sense to call for a fundamental change of mentality among ministers and to make them responsible for the crisis of the church. First, this assumes that the ministers have had the wrong mentality up to now. And second: How can an organization claim to decide over individual motivation? Intrinsic motivation cannot be controlled or commanded from the outside. If an attempt is made to do just that, individual motivation will be undermined or destroyed rather than promoted. Every parent is aware of this from educating their children.

Finally, it seems that the church authorities misjudge the basic reformational distinction of the work of God and that of human beings (*Gotteswerk und Menschenwerk*). This distinction does not highlight a dogmatic

20. Hermelink, "Die Kirche," 160.
21. Ibid.

subtlety, rather, it is essential for the understanding of the church. It means nothing other than that the most decisive factor in the church does not rely on organizing or planning: The decisive factor of the church relies on the working of the Spirit in the proclamation of the gospel, in the celebration of the sacraments, in religious education processes and in the pastoral care of people in need. Of course good sermons are better than bad ones. But, on the one hand, it is very difficult and in fact dangerous to try to improve sermons because they are closely linked to a specific (preaching) individual, and individuals are reluctant to change or change only when they themselves want to do so. On the other hand, good sermons are not always received by open ears. Even Martin Luther, a brilliant preacher, was often frustrated that his sermons had too little effect. In 1530 he even went on a preaching strike for a few months. Luther, and all the hard work and ambition he represented, stressed that the results of his actions were completely withdrawn from his own disposability because:

> I cannot go further than to the ears, I cannot reach the heart. Because I cannot pour belief into the heart, so I cannot or should not force anybody or try to penetrate their mind; for God is doing and making it all alone, making the word live in hearts. That is why we should leave the word free. . . . We are to preach the word, but the result is to be alone in God's favour.[22]

This does not mean sitting on our hands, but we need to be sensitive in the way we perceive the limits of what a person and, in particular, what an organization can work on and decide about.

There are two lessons to be learned from Luther: To him, it was a fundamental tenet that the study and proclamation of the word should be at the center of a church based on the gospel. Secondly, he was also convinced that, in addition to all the intensive efforts to make a better church, it is important to trust in God and to keep a serene distance to all human work and plans. Without such a distance and without such a sense of serenity, the church will maneuver itself into a form of activism that will lead to frustration and exhaustion, particularly among the ministers but also among other church staff.

In my view, the theological crisis of orientation and its consequences are far more significant than the financial crisis for the church in Germany. While it could be said that the organization hides this because this is an area that can hardly be organized, at the same time, the organization exacerbates the problem rather than solving it by committing itself to a unilateral expansion of formal organization. The church is not developing sensitivity for the

22. Luther, "Acht Sermone," 178.

complex interface of organization, interaction and religious communication. Such sensitivity should be strengthened instead of marginalizing the interactive and religious dimensions by favoring the organizational dimension of the church.

DECENTRALIZED STRUCTURES AND INNOVATIVE NICHES

It is difficult to understand why the Protestant Church with its deeply decentralized structures is heading now towards centralization and a further functional differentiation which is threatening its basic democratic structure. The church is not a hierarchical organization with many dependent branches. It rather exists in many congregations and assemblies. The Protestant Christian encounters his or her church everywhere, also in an extra-local sense.

The church needs both: Strong centers and at the same time many congregations in many communities, a courageous leadership sphere, and a strong basis. Deliberations on reform of the overall organization "from above" are to be combined with a large sensibility of resonance with objections and experience "from below" (subsidiary principle). Clear central requirements should mesh with the provision of enough room for local and individual variability and flexibility. If the church continues to focus unilaterally on organization, it might neglect interactive social relations which are not automatically or only partially possible to organize. Indeed, the church depends on these relations and communications—both in religious as well as financial terms.

A word or two are needed on what the church seems to be lacking most: money. Money is generated in the church when it is visible in a vivid way, where people meet their church and where they experience it as trustworthy and helpful. For most people this occurs in the local parishes. Experiences of fundraising show that in vivid local communities and in attractive central churches, representing the cultural memory of the city, people oftentimes donate high sums beyond their church tax because money that is spent for the church building or for the continuation of various congregational activities is not given to an anonymous organization, which, in case of doubt, you might not trust.

The special challenge for the ecclesial organization is that the church has to try to organize the non-organizable. The decisive cannot be changed or caused by decisions—that is by organization. The really important and "exciting things take place in practices and processes that really change something and make a difference but that elude every organization."[23] That a teacher finds the correct tone, or that a minister intuitively notes when he should keep silent, that a scientist discovers the decisive idea or works on a research question for a lifetime—"all of this is separate from what is organizable and would disappear as soon as you decide and want to organize it."[24] Armin Nassehi writes not without irony: "Perhaps the function of changing the organizable is above all to let the non-organizable take place according to its own rules."[25] But organizations are in no way unimportant: They provide the framework and the niches where the innovative and surprising can occur.

PERSPECTIVES

The Relevance of the Christian Message and the Meaning of Theological Competence

Improving church management is an important task, but it does not solve the most important problem, which is not a financial issue, but a theological crisis of orientation. This problem has affected the churches of Central Europe since the Enlightenment, and has flared up once again over the last few decades. Under the present conditions it is not easy to articulate Christian faith convincingly and self-confidently. The problem of articulation is expressed, on the one hand, in the frequently observed trivialization and moralization of the Christian message, and on the other hand, in the desire to escape in an almost time- and context-free language of dogma. What does the church really have to say to people in modern society? How can one theologically speak of God substantially and at the same time be existentially relevant, when it comes to such key terms as cross and resurrection, sin and forgiveness, grace, love and justice?

It is a major challenge to preach in a committed, understandable, and theologically substantial way, to discuss about theological and ethical issues with teenagers in their confirmation classes and with students in religious education in schools—open to criticism and skepticism. Today ministers must also be good managers. But it is even more important that they have something to say and that they are encouraged by the church leadership to look for more contact with academic theology and with continuing education that focuses on theological content. It is important that they maintain

23. Nassehi, "Die Organisation," 217.
24. Ibid.
25. Ibid., 216.

contact with the outside world and that they make themselves visible as serious interlocutors on the difficult questions of our time.

Scientific theology can provide important impulses for this process. The last century has witnessed significant shifts in theology. I think of the differentiation in the field of social ethics, the differentiated discourses on euthanasia, pre-implantation genetic diagnosis, sexuality, gender, illness and suffering. When we look at these existential themes of human life, we can see what central orientation service Protestant theology has to offer. But there has also been development in terms of central dogmatic questions. I am thinking of the changing images of God, especially in connection with Dietrich Bonhoeffer's speech about a powerless and compassionate God. I am thinking of the theology of supper, which has recently focused not only on the "sacrament of the poor sinner" but has re-discovered its communal dimension. I am thinking of the theology of justification in a society that more mercilessly than all societies before it attributes all success and especially all failure to individuals themselves.

The message of the gospel has not become indifferent. Protestants still expect of worship first of all a good homily—a sermon which unfolds the faith understandably, clearly and existentially relevant to daily life. People expect encouragement and comfort from the church, a prudent interpretation of the critical points of life such as the birth of a child or the death of a beloved. That is why the "casualia"—baptism, confirmation, marriage, and burial—are so highly valued.

Church of the Encounter: Locality in Late Modernism

The Protestant Church is a church ruled from below, it is not a top-down organization. It is a network church in need of strong centers, congregations and communities. It is not structured from above, but is rather promoted by sociable, interactive and community forms of Christian life in many different locations with a wide range of profiles, spiritualties and personalities. The opportunity of the church lies in its message and in the people who share this message, and who bear witness to it through their lives. Therefore, interactive relations are crucial for the church: Here is where religious identity is formed, here is where it is discussed. Here emotions of sadness and gratefulness can be shared, and here religious ties and lifetime loyalties arise.

The church is a place for encounters. Quite often these are floating encounters that bring people into conversation with one another. Maren Lehmann emphasizes that the church above all needs "opportunities for

encounters among people."[26] Such a church perhaps does not always have a
clear profile, it is not always uniform in the media, but all of this is not only
really a shortcoming, but rather a great strength of the evangelical church.
Such a church can tolerate discussion on controversial issues or a decision
to leave them open, it does not necessarily seek an uncompromising position for one thing and against another. It has a positive relationship with
the unknowing because some questions cannot be answered, and knowing
this honors the church. The EKD reform paper mistrusts the ambiguity of
the church. It has very clear ideas of what is sustainable and what is not, all
without knowing what the future holds. It is not relying on the church as
a community of believers and thus a loosely integrated network, "but on a
division of labor and hierarchy."[27]

A reform in a network church cannot take place in opposition to what
is happening in the parishes. The parishes are usually very well cross-linked
"to the local political, neighborhood and family structures."[28] This is "a potential that hardly can be relinquished," at least not for a church which is
looking for opportunities to come into contact with people.

> Perhaps this is the only mistake . . . of so many reform attempts
> of the church as an organization that it looks for too much order
> and too much regulation, where it would be essential to look for
> feasible disorder or (with Luhmann) for "feasible illegality." This
> important disorder can be found only at the level of communi-
> cative encounters, only at the level of the people or, to be more
> precise: only among people. . . . For it is only there, in the fleet-
> ing encounters, that the recognition, that the church is so des-
> perately looking for, can be found, where you can—perhaps in
> the smallest sums—raise the funds the church so sorely lacks.[29]

It is therefore the task of church leadership to think about how it might support ministers and other voluntary and full-time employees in the church,
to ensure that they are engaged and committed to exploring the opportunities for encounters in the many different arenas where they operate. They
are the initiators of the communities, and generally know better than dis-
tant centers what is possible and what is not. "It is not concentration that
will prove itself to be a good strategy, but a network-oriented church with
strong interdependencies with communities."[30] Although reforms might be

26. Lehmann, "Leutemangel," 125.
27. Ibid., 129.
28. Ibid., 131.
29. Ibid., 128.
30. Becker, "Die Kirche," 14.

inspired "from above," you can only be successful in the Protestant Church if such efforts come "from below," supported by and carried out by a broad base.

CONCLUSION

The church in Germany is shrinking and will probably have less financial resources at its disposal. This is uncomfortable and goes hand in hand with conflicts and tensions. That is why structural changes are necessary. One can call them reforms but they are reforms in a typical organizational mode—they will not cause a religious upheaval. In general, the church as an organization should not overestimate its possibilities. Essentially the church lives by processes, motivations, and beliefs that cannot be organized or controlled. Principally, the church lives firstly by taking its own message seriously. Secondly, it should stay in contact with the people of the communities to search for and maintain networks and a sense of communality. And thirdly, it should turn to people in life crisis through pastoral counseling and diaconal work but also through a strengthening of the civil society. These are the central ecclesial fields of action that have been addressed here. The wheel does not need to be reinvented. What is crucial is that the contact with people living under conditions of secularization should not be broken. This seems to be a delicate point for church membership. In East Germany, we see how difficult it is to get in touch with people who have never been a church member. The church must therefore see how parents, also single parents, could be encouraged to baptize their children so they can come into contact with the church. Only through the various ecclesial socialization opportunities is there a chance that they might develop an awareness of the rich heritage of the Christian faith.

BIBLIOGRAPHY

Becker, Dieter. "Die Kirche ist kein Supertanker." *Zeitzeichen* 12 (2006) 14–16.

Geser, Hans. "Zwischen Anpassung, Selbstbehauptung und politischer Agitation. Zur aktuellen (und zukünftigen) Bedeutung religiöser Organisationen." In *Institution—Organisation—Bewegung. Sozialformen der Religion im Wandel*, edited by Michael Krüggeler, et al., 39–69. Opladen: Westdeutscher Verlag, 1999.

Graf, Friedrich Wilhelm. *Die Wiederkehr der Götter. Religion in der modernen Kultur.* München: C. H. Beck, 2004.

Hermelink, Jan. "Die Kirche als Dachorganisation und Symbolisierung des Unverfügbaren. Facetten des kirchlichen Selbstbildes im Spiegel der EKD-Mitgliedschaftserhebungen." In *Kirchenreform. Interdisziplinäre Perspektiven*, edited by Isolde Karle, 143–60. Leipzig: Evangelische Verlagsanstalt, 2009.

———. ""Sind Sie zufrieden?" Die Domestizierung des Pfarrberufs durch die kirchliche Organisation." In *Religion und Ethik als Organisationen—eine*

Quadratur des Kreises? edited by Jan Hermelink and Stefan Grotefeld, 119–43. Zürich: Theologischer Verlag Zürich, 2008.

Karle, Isolde. *Kirche im Reformstress.* Gütersloh: Gütersloher Verlagshaus, 2010.

Körtner, Ulrich H. J. *Wiederkehr der Religion? Das Christentum zwischen neuer Spiritualität und Gottvergessenheit.* Gütersloh: Gütersloher Verlagshaus, 2006.

Kosch, Daniel. "Kirchliches Handeln im Spannungsfeld von Geist und Geld." In *Kirche als pastorales Unternehmen,* edited by Pius Bischofberger and Manfred Belok, 72–90. Zürich: Theologischer Verlag Zürich, 2008.

Lehmann, Maren. "Leutemangel. Mitgliedschaft und Begegnung als Formen der Kirche." In *Paradoxien kirchlicher Organisation. Niklas Luhmanns frühe Kirchensoziologie und die aktuelle Reform der evangelischen Kirche,* edited by Jan Hermelink and Gerhard Wegner, 123–44. Würzburg: Ergon, 2008.

Luhmann, Niklas. "Die Organisierbarkeit von Religionen und Kirchen." In *Religion im Umbruch. Soziologische Beiträge zur Situation von Religion und Kirche in der gegenwärtigen Gesellschaft,* edited by Jakobus Wössner, 245–85. Stuttgart: Ferdinand Enke, 1972.

———. *Die Religion der Gesellschaft.* Frankfurt: Suhrkamp, 2000.

Luther, Martin. "Acht Sermone D. Martin Luthers, von ihm gepredigt in der Fastenzeit (1522) [Invokavitpredigten]." In *Martin Luther, ausgewählte Schriften Bd. 1,* edited by Karin Bornkamm and Gerhard Ebeling, 270–303. Frankfurt: Suhrkamp, 1983.

Nassehi, Armin. "Die Organisation des Unorganisierbaren." In *Kirchenreform. Interdisziplinäre Pespektiven,* edited by Isolde Karle, 199–218. Leipzig: Evangelische Verlagsanstalt, 2009.

———. "Spiritualität. Ein soziologischer Versuch." In *Spiritualität und Medizin. Gemeinsame Sorge für den kranken Menschen,* edited by Eckhard Frick and Traugott Roser, 35–44. Stuttgart: Kohlhammer Verlag, 2009.

———. "'Den Unterschied deutlich machen.' Ein Gespräch mit dem Münchner Soziologen Armin Nassehi, geführt von Alexander Foitzik." *Herder Korrespondenz* 63 (2009) 447–51.

Pollack, Detlef. "Entzauberung oder Wiederverzauberung der Welt? Die Säkularisierungsthese auf dem Prüfstand." In *Zeitenwende—Wendezeiten,* edited by Eckhart von Vietinghoff and Hans May, 125–50, Hannover: Lutherisches Verlagshaus, 1998.

Preul, Reiner. *Die soziale Gestalt des Glaubens. Aufsätze zur Kirchentheorie.* Leipzig: Evangelische Verlagsanstalt, 2008.

Rösch, Henriette. "Der Reformdiskurs als Antwort auf das Indifferenzproblem." *Evangelische Theologie* 73 (2013) 100–7.

Schlamelcher, Jens. "Ökonomisierung der Kirchen?" In *Paradoxien kirchlicher Organisation. Niklas Luhmanns frühe Kirchensoziologie und die aktuelle Reform der evangelischen Kirche,* edited by Jan Hermelink and Gerhard Wegner, 145–78. Würzburg: Ergon, 2008.

———. "Unternehmen Kirche? Neoliberale Diskurse in den deutschen Großkirchen." In *Der neoliberale Markt-Diskurs: Ursprünge, Geschichte, Wirkungen,* edited by Walter Otto von Ötsch and Claus Thomasberger, 213–56. Marburg: Metropolis, 2009.

3

Motifs and Perspectives in the Reform Process of the Church of Norway

ANDREAS AARFLOT

The bells are ringing the death toll for the state church of Norway. Increasing pressure from a pluralistic, multicultural society has made it more difficult to advocate a politically based supremacy in the market of faiths or life philosophies/beliefs. Moreover, it has become increasingly difficult to defend a distinct political line of governance of the church of Norway as it more clearly manifests itself as a faith community, defined by modern international conventions of religious liberty and human rights. Recent decisions in Norway's Parliament have therefore opened for a juridical framework for the establishment of a self-governed church. But the road to this concession has been long and burdensome. Let us take a look at some of the main factors and ideas that have been at work in this process.

HISTORIC BACKGROUND

The theoretical or ideological foundation for the concept of "state churches" as they emerged after the Reformation, is rooted in ideas where the state and church were seen as two sides of the same coin, representing a shared set of values in a homogeneous society.

For Richard Hooker, the formative spirit of the Anglican ecclesiastical law in the sixteenth century, the essential identity of the people as a political society and the church as a spiritual assembly motivated his insistence on church and state as being two interdependent sectors of the same commonwealth, and that each national church had the right to regulate its own external forms of worship and governance.[1] "What distinguishes Hooker from his contemporaries is, first of all, his attempt to give a broader philosophical foundation . . . by treating the church as a species of "politic society," entitled to the same degree of autonomy in non-divine matters as other forms of civil society."[2] This autonomy of the church as a politic society Hooker sees exercised through the legislative power of the Parliament and the Convocations. As in a Christian commonwealth the same people constitute both church and state, so the Parliament represents them in a dual capacity. He will not exclude the clergy, "bishops and wise men," from the drafting of necessary laws to regulate church life. But

> when all which the wisdom of all sorts can do is done for devising of laws in the Church, it is the general consent of all that giveth them the form and vigor of laws, without which they would be no more unto us than the councels of physicians to the sick: well might they seem as wholesome admonitions and instructions, but laws could they never be without the consent of the whole Church, which is the only thing that bindeth each member of the Church to be guided by them.[3]

Hooker claimed that this self-government should stand under the supreme leadership of the lawful Majesty, which he regarded as the representative of the whole nation, and whose authority ultimately must be seen as derived from the consent of the people.[4] In consequence, he states the opinion:

> Happier that people whose law is their king in the greatest things, than those whose king is himself their law. Where the king doth guide the state, and the law the king, that commonwealth is like a harp or melodious instrument, the strings whereof are handled all by one, following as laws the rules and canons of musical science.[5]

---

1. For Richard Hooker, see Thompson, "Philosopher,'" with a good assessment of previous literature. The Folger Library edition of the works of Richard Hooker (1977–1998) is the indispensable source for studies in his ideas. His grand work *Of the Lawes of Ecclesiasticall Polity* (published from 1594 and onwards) is published in three parts: I–IV, V, and VI–VIII. Quoted as "Lawes" with reference to book (I–VIII), chapter, section (e.g., 2.4), and page.

2. Thompson, "Philosopher," 17.

3. Hooker, *Lawes* VIII.6.11, 403; Aarflot, *Samtidsspeil eller fyrtårn?* 212.

4. Hooker, *Lawes* VIII.6.11, 401.

5. Ibid., VIII.2.12, 342.

Johannes Bugenhagen, Luther's close co-worker in organizing the church in Wittenberg, and the great genius of practical reforms in the Lutheran church, formed the basis for church order in his insistence upon the king's authority and duties as the ruler and benefactor of the church, although the sovereign was not yet being seen as the supreme governor of the church. In the twin-monarchy of Denmark and Norway, King Christian III had emerged victorious from the civil war and had deposed all the Catholic bishops for being his opponents and conspirators. Together with a number of evangelical preachers in various parts of Denmark, he immediately began to replace the Catholic ecclesial authority with an evangelical church structure under royal supervision. In this enterprise he called Bugenhagen as the leading architect. He retained the old, medieval diocesan structure, and the new bishops who were to be appointed assumed episcopal functions but had no secular authority. Both the episcopal sees and the institution of cathedral chapters were continued. It is clear, however, that the Danish-Norwegian Church Order was also embedded in the structure of the local ruler's ecclesial authority. The king who saw himself as an evangelical prince and who confessed his evangelical faith in the preamble to the Church Order, has assumed the role of overseer, supporter and carer for the church. But there was no doubt that he thereby reserved the actual ecclesial authority for himself. And thus, in this respect, the bishops also became administrators and servants of the ecclesial authority of the royal ruler that extended to both spiritual and secular matters. There was no clear distinction between *jus in sacris* and *jus circa sacra*.[6]

For both Hooker and Bugenhagen the presupposition was that church and people constituted an entity, which could not lawfully be separated. There was a common value base, a national treasure of common religious and ethical presuppositions where the church and the political society had mutual commitments. The kings pledged to uphold the sacred traditions of the church, and the church was committed to supporting the king and the secular authorities in their duties of governing society.[7]

As we know, this uniformity, and especially its ideological basis came under pressure from ensuing events. In the twin states of Denmark and Norway the political theory more and more leaned towards the concept of "absolute monarchy," where all sectors of society were seen as part of the exclusive power of the king, granted by God as a divine authority belonging to the monarch alone, without any reference to the will of the people. The king represented God's own power both in secular and spiritual matters. As

---

6. Aarflot, "Det teologiske og statsrettslige grunnlag," 12–13.
7. Further: Aarflot, "Das bischöfliche Amt," 512–15. See also Aarflot, "Bugenhagen."

supreme proprietor of the territory, the king was not bound to any special loyalty to the national church, but it served his purpose as ruler to keep up the traditions and values that the church stood for. The national church increasingly became a state church, and the king exercised his authority through the clergy, which were seen both as civil servants and ministers for the congregations. In the legislation for Denmark and Norway in the 1680s this was expressed through the so-called prerogative of the king in church matters:

> The King also has the sole authority over the whole clergy, from the highest to the lowest, to order and arrange for all public church and liturgical service, all meetings and assemblies concerning religious matters, consistent with the Word of God and the Augsburg Confession, to allow or prohibit according to his judgement.[8]

In the wake of the Enlightenment, the principle of absolute monarchy was abandoned, giving way to the principle of the sovereignty of the people. For Norway this took place in 1814, but the Church of Norway was still left with the principles of royal supremacy as the basis for ecclesiastical law. The paragraphs dealing with religion in the National Constitution from 1814, which until recently were still in force, stated that "the Evangelical-Lutheran religion remains the official religion of the state" (§ 2), and the earlier principle of royal supremacy was expressed in § 16, which said that "the King ordains all public church services and public worship, all meetings and assemblies dealing with religious matters, and ensures that the public teachers of religion follow the norms prescribed for them." The logical and corresponding consequence of this was drawn in § 4 of the Constitution, stating that "the King shall at all times profess the Evangelical-Lutheran religion, uphold and protect the same." Until recently this has meant that both the *ius liturgicum* and the *ius ecclesiasticum* were regarded as matters to be decided by royal decree or general legislation.

Through the introduction of parliamentary government in 1884 the real power in ecclesial matters was, however, transferred to the government emerging from the elected constituency in the Norwegian Parliament, called the Storting. The distinction between the so-called prerogatives of the king and the legislative power of the political administration became blurred. The church was seen and treated as one sector of society, the clergy

---

8. The basis for this concept was already set down in the so-called "Kongelov," dealing with the supremacy of the Majesty (1665), and fully expressed in The Norwegian Law of 1687, Second Book, entitled "Of the Religion and the Clergy."

were counted as civil servants, and the parishes were treated as part of the municipal pattern.

CRITICAL ASSESSMENT OF THE PAST

For more than a century political governments in Norway, seconded by conservative lawyers in the departmental administration, developed a kind of ideology of *democratic supremacy* over the church. The presupposition was that the will of the people in all internal national affairs was expressed through the process of free elections. The real governing authority for the church rested therefore in the hands of the minister for church affairs. Instead of the absolutism of the king there came the absolutism of the person in charge of dealing with church matters. To use the imagery of Richard Hooker, the minister took the role of the master-musician who alone played the harp, using the separate strings to create music accommodated to the political score. This person was bound to be a member of the church, as was until recently half of the ministers of the government, in order to keep up the charade of representing the church as its highest decision-making body. One of the major obstacles for a change in the relationship between church and state has been the fact that this ideology has not been seriously questioned by lawyers and political thinkers.

In the German churches, this principle was abandoned after the Weimar Constitution of 1919. New juridical agreements were developed, recognizing both the supremacy of the state in civil affairs and the autonomy of the churches in all matters pertaining to their organization and work. The pattern developed in the German churches presents an interesting model for the further efforts to clear the ground between church and state in Norway.[9] The German expert on church law, Axel Frh. von Campenhausen, briefly explains this achievement as follows:

> The right of churches to self-government is the *lex regia* of church-state law and the core and centre of the church political system created by the Weimar Constitution. It applies to all religious communities regardless of whether they enjoy the rights of a corporation under public law, are private-law associations, or completely lack legal capacity. The Basic Law does not accord them a kind of self-government law, but recognizes the churches' right to govern themselves and thereby their freedom from government oversight and paternalism.[10]

9. See also Aarflot, "Aktuelle forfatningsprinsipper."
10. von Campenhausen, "Churches' Right."

The constitutions of the German churches are based upon a principle where the state recognizes the role of the churches as important contributors to the common good of the people, while the churches, for their part, are free to develop their own identity and independence, accepting the overall responsibility of the state for the communal life. As a result, the concept of the state became more clearly defined in secular terms, and the concept of the churches became more theologically founded. The basic understanding of state church legislation was that it constituted a secular framework for religious freedom, a frame also seen useful to support the development of the common welfare of the people.[11]

In Norway, however, the supremacy of the state in the governance of the church has been strictly adhered to by political authorities and juridical consultants right until the present day. The main problem with the present state of affairs is that it has become more and more difficult to defend a practice where the actual government (frequently changing due to unstable political party constellations) has felt both constrained constitutionally to deal actively with ecclesiastical law, and at the same time inclined by political preferences to make decisions that are more in line with general public opinion than with the expressed, biblically based opinion of the church.

The idea of a national church with political authorities as arbitrator is difficult to claim in a society of religious and moral pluralism. In this respect one may agree with the Anglican bishop and long-time proponent of greater independence for the Church of England, Eric Kemp: "There is still a feeling that the State has a responsibility to "hold the ring" and ensure that no one group or party acquires control of the Church. The changes that have taken place in the last half century have made this responsibility more difficult to exercise."[12] In Norway, both individuals and groups have advocated the idea that the minister of church affairs might serve as a "referee" in matters under discussion in the church, but this idea has been strongly opposed by representatives of church reform, and the latest events show that the political authorities see the necessity of retracting from such a role and pave the way for a self-governing church with freedom to organize its life and work according to its own standards.

11. Link, *Kirchliche Rechtsgeschichte*; Heckel, "Kirchliche Rechtsgeschichte in neuerer Sicht."

12. Kemp, "Legal Aspects," 49.

GUIDING PRINCIPLES IN THE PROCESS
OF CHURCH REFORM

The process of reform has moved one small step at a time over a period of more than a hundred years. Pages by the thousands have been written and countless proposals have been forwarded with only a smattering of results. One of the milestones is the comprehensive report of an official commission delivered just over a century ago, in 1911. Established in an era of social, religious and political unrest, the majority of the commission concluded that very few changes were needed, while a minority laid out a detailed proposal for a church structure with elected councils, from the parish level, including the establishment of a church assembly as the top of a pyramid.[13] The political interest was lukewarm, and the political will even colder, but after an extended deliberations process the government presented a proposal establishing for the first time a parish council in all congregations (1920). The main issue for debate was the criteria for election and eligibility to this organ. The conservative faction wanted restrictions by way of demanding personal expressions of commitment for those voting or being nominated as eligible, while the more realistic view was that every baptized member of the church with electoral rights in the civil society should be accepted. This view prevailed and has been a main ecclesiological principle ever since. The parish councils were, however, commissioned with very distinct tasks of a spiritual kind, which has safeguarded the churchly character and confessional loyalty of the work of the councils.[14]

Later, small changes indicated a step by step approach, which over the course of a hundred years pointed towards the present stance of the church: 1933 saw the establishment of a diocesan council in each diocese. Elected by parish council members, the main task of the council was to nominate candidates for the appointment of bishops. But the diocese took on a more important role as the organizer of regional meetings for the voluntary movement for church reform through its leading organ the national council of church affairs (*Det frivillige kirkelige landsråd*), which later became the prime mover in the process for further independence of the church.

---

13. *Kirkekommisjonen av 1908. IV.*

14. With minor amendments the present wording of this paragraph runs like this: "The parish council shall be concerned with everything that may be done in order to awaken and nourish the Christian life in the parish, especially that the word of God may be abundantly proclaimed, and also provided for the sick and dying, that those being baptized may receive Christian instruction, that children and young people be called together for good purposes and corporeal and spiritual need be met." *Kirkeloven*, § 9a. In § 28 it is stated that the church councils and boards shall act in loyalty to the Lutheran confession.

The situation during the Second World War called for consolidated efforts to keep the church united in the front against Nazi infiltration. The Bishops' meeting under the eminent leadership of Bishop Eivind Berggrav in Oslo joined with leaders of the strong lay movement of Norway and representatives of the other denominational churches in the country and established a solid basis for church resistance. The church of Norway severed its organizational ties with the Nazi state and established a kind of independent church led by a few leaders known as "The temporary church government." This form of church structure fit well into the pattern advocated by Bishop Berggrav, who, based upon certain philosophical principles of law and order and an elitist concept of society envisioned a future church organization led by a handful of strong persons with specific leadership qualifications.[15] What he felt was most at stake was whether the church order should be according to political or Christian principles: "The organs of the church must be construed according to the principle that the church is a spiritual brotherhood, organized through entrusted authorization."[16] In a letter from 1932, he already wrote: "My ideal is the few, the most responsible, those representing the broadest contact with reality—these are called to govern. I will add: the most independent ones." Consequently Bishop Berggrav voiced his skepticism to the idea of democratic structures in the church: "Introducing democracy in the church will never overrule the fact that the congregation is no sovereign assembly of the people, but a flock of disciples. No one in this group holds an authority in himself or by the will of the majority."[17] Accordingly, he vehemently opposed the idea that church affairs might be subject to a vote in a representative synod. The reform movement has not pursued this line of thought.

Notwithstanding these principles, Berggrav joined the government appointed commission set up after the war to chart the future order of the Church of Norway. The recommendations included an item proposing the establishment of a national church council with some elected and some called members.[18] In retrospect it seems clear that the functions of this structure were more along the lines of Berggrav's concept, described as a deliberative meeting with no decision-making power.[19]

15. Aarflot, "Eivind Berggravs kirkeforståelse," 115.

16. Berggrav, *Kirkens ordning i Norge*, 61.

17. Ibid.

18. Kirkedepartementet, *Innstilling til Lov om Den norske kirkes ordning*, 21.

19. The proposed composition of the council was this: three bishops with the bishop of Oslo as permanent member and the other two elected by the Bishops' Conference; one representative of the clergy from dioceses not represented by a bishop, plus one extra from Oslo: two lay representatives from each of the larger dioceses, and one from

In the following debate, the Norwegian Storting, dominated by the Labour Party, rejected this and most of the other recommendations from the commission. One small point should, however, prove to be the opening for future development in the process of the reform of the church. The diocesan councils were given the opportunity to convene once in the election period of four years to discuss matters of interest for the church at large. After a few years this assembly made the decision to elect a permanent council, which in due course led to the formal establishment of an official church council, legally based in a revision of the Church Act (1969).

In the meantime, the initiative in the reform process had been assumed by the voluntary movement for church reform and its national council. At its national convention in 1965 it authorized a commission to deal with several topics regarded as important for the renewal of the church, such as the church's answer to the challenge from the changes in society and the need for a more flexible pattern of vocational service in the church. A special focus was to be placed on the relationship between different structures of governance in the church, which led the commission to specifically address the relationship between church and state. The recommendations in the final report signaled a clear preference for a complete national structure of the church, including a national assembly, a synodic structure based on indirect elections by the members of the parish councils. The existing diocesan councils were seen as the core of the assembly, but an equal number of delegates should be elected in separate elections.[20] The commission did not make explicit reference to the question of how these reforms would affect the status as a state church, but expressed hope that several of its recommendations might be realized without breaking the formal bonds with the state. By a narrow margin the following national convention in 1969 voted to appoint a follow-up commission to specify some of the proposals in more detail and deal more explicitly with the relationship between church and state. The report of the new working group, headed by the Bishop of Oslo, Kaare Støylen, was published in 1973 and laid down more significantly the program of the reform movement.[21] In a more persuasive way this report pointed out the discrepancy between a modern concept of both state and church and the existing pattern of church governance with its more and more obsolete historic roots. The political implications of the work obvi-

---

each of the smaller; one representative from each of the two theological faculties and one lawyer as legal advisor—a total of twenty-five members. The council was granted status as a consultative or advisory organ in various matters where the government or the Storting claimed the final decision.

20. *Reform av Den norske kirke.*

21. *Den norske kirke og staten.*

ously had an impact on the government, which in turn appointed an official commission led by the former Labor minister for church affairs, Helge Sivertsen. Largely to the surprise of many, this commission tabled a clear majority recommendation advocating the disestablishment of the church, much along the same lines of argument as those promoted by the reform movement.[22] Most compelling was the reference to international principles of religious freedom, a factor which should prove to be a dominant trait in later discussions and lead to an erosion of the political support for upholding the state church system.[23]

But the immediate follow-up of the report from the socialist government did not give many indications of a change in the attitude towards the church on the part of the administration. The former ideology of a strong political management of the church still prevailed in the proposed regulations of the Church Act.[24] In many parts of the presentation a strong animosity against the program for church reform could be discerned, and the idea of an independent church organization once again lost ground. On the other hand, the document expressed positive considerations about the role of religion and the values represented by the church as a formative power in society. But the main message was that these elements were best safeguarded when they remained under the control of the state. However, when the revision of the Church Act was finally passed by the Storting, one important achievement was gained for the reform movement through the establishment of the General Synod, designed as the highest representative organ of the Church of Norway (1984).

Later developments saw new initiatives to investigate the burning questions of further relationship between church and state, first initiated by the Church of Norway National Council on behalf of the General Synod, whose study commission issued its report in 2002,[25] and later by yet another official commission, appointed by the government, whose report was published in 2006.[26] Both reports advocated by a substantial majority the

22. Kirke- og undervisningsdepartementet, *NOU 1975:30. Stat og kirke.*

23. Ibid., 143, 154. This was in line with important principles laid down in the commission working on the foundation for the earlier Act related to religious communities (1969), which was a cornerstone in legislation for religious communities in Norway. Justisdepartementet, *Innstilling til lov om trossamfunn.*

24. Kirke- og undervisningsdepartementet, *Stortingsmelding nr. 40 (1980–81) Om stat og kirke.*

25. Kirkerådet, *Samme kirke—ny ordning.*

26. Kultur- og kirkedepartementet, *NOU 2006:2. Staten og Den norske kirke.*

separation of church and state and the establishment of a juridical frame-work for an independent church, however with close links to the people.[27]

The Official Norwegian Report from the Government's church/state Commission, aims to establish a new government policy on religious matters. This new policy should provide freedom of religion for individuals and religious communities, as well as active government support for religious communities on an equal basis. The need for a revision of the present acts and regulations of the church structure is based on the following considerations: The Church of Norway is partly governed by a state that administers pluralism, religious freedom and equality between religious and life stance communities. The State is responsible for securing the rights and interests of its citizens, while at the same time ensuring that the Church of Norway serves as the official religion. These two tasks may lead to a conflict of interest for the government. The commission therefore recommended that the formal bonds between the state and the church of Norway should be cut. But the political processing of the proposals seemed rather to fortify than to loosen the bonds of the state. The political parties were divided, with the Labour Party majority forcefully pushing towards the status quo. But following a strong plea from an almost unanimous opinion expressed by the church, the parties finally struck a deal triggering the changes in the Constitution which opened for a new development towards independence of the church.[28] It had become increasingly clear that the commitment to international conventions on human rights and equality are at odds with the idea of any church appearing as "the official religion of the State."

The most recently revised text of the constitution, following up on the political deal, introduces the idea that the Church of Norway remains as "Norway's folk church" (*Norges folkekirke*). This political "truce" had its shortcomings. It takes a lot of explaining to demonstrate the difference between the formula "the official religion of the state" in the old § 2 of the Constitution and the expression "Norway's folk church" in the new § 16.[29]

27. It is interesting to note that several of the commission members, representing a variety of political positions, who formerly were advocates of the status quo in church-state relations, became clear proponents for disestablishment of the state church.

28. Kultur- og kirkedepartementet, *Stortingsmelding nr 17 (2007–2008) Staten og Den norske kirke*, 67–68. Agreement April 10, 2008 between all political parties represented in the Storting.

29. The new paragraph runs like this: "All inhabitants of the realm shall have the right to free exercise of their religion. The Church of Norway, an Evangelical-Lutheran church, will remain the Established Church of Norway and will as such be supported by the State. Detailed provisions as to its system will be laid down by law. All religious and belief communities should be supported on equal terms." (Passed by the Storting May 21, 2012).

The term carries the notion of a national church, but falls short of stating what the nature of such a church is meant to be and what is seen as the relationship between "folk" and "church." Moreover, the deal did not give any overriding directions for the future organization of the church, but by removing the "royal prerogative" from §16, which substantiated the idea that the state retained the final authority over the church, it made clear, for the first time, that this political claim, based upon the two-hundred-year-old paragraphs of the constitution, had been abandoned, and the last vestige of the prerogative of the king (i.e., the state) was removed.

ECCLESIOLOGICAL BASIS FOR REFORMING THE CHURCH

By and large there has been general agreement on the theological understanding of the church in the documents of the reform movement. The principles were most clearly summed up in the report delivered to the national assembly of the reform movement in 1973. The structures and organizational system of the church cannot be defined only by general sociological or community-related criteria. Church governance must take its orientation from a theological understanding of the church. This fundamental ecclesiological basis for the self-understanding of the church has been confirmed, developed and honed through a series of decisions in the General Synod and the Bishops' Conference over the last decades. It has been the point of departure for all work dealing with strategies and structural proposals for the Church of Norway to the present day.

Based upon a comprehensive concept of the identity and self-understanding of the church, the General Synod, as the representative body of the Church of Norway, has coined the description of the church as "a confessing, missionary, diaconical, open folk church." In general terms this theologically based understanding of the church is rooted in the conviction that the church finds its existence as a fruit of God's plan for the salvation of mankind, linked with the commission that Jesus gave his disciples to deliver the gospel to the whole world. According to the New Testament, the church is founded by Jesus Christ and commissioned by him to be an instrument for the divine salvation. The passage in Matt 28:16–20 shows that Jesus selected the small band of disciples and empowered them as the core of his church, the new people. By following his designation they put themselves under his authority, and pledged obedience to his commission. To this mixed group of individuals, among whom according to the narrative there were some who doubted, Jesus gave the calling to impart his teaching to the world and bring forth the gifts he had prepared in the gospel and the sacrament of baptism. The church is characterized by the dual movement: *gathered* to meet the Lord in worship and faith, and *sent* to the world to call people into his discipleship. The church is rooted in God's plan for salvation. The great commission, proclaimed by Christ, is the constitutive principle for all church organizations, all structures and administrative regulations and all constitutional and juridical rules for the church. The Christian church bears its true mark in being a church under the gospel and for the gospel.

Sensitive to the guidance of Jesus Christ, the church and those who are called to serve it, regardless of what functions they are entrusted, should be responsible for organizing the communal life in faith. Collectively they share the responsibility for developing the instruments of leadership that are necessary for the church to function as an instrument for God's mission in the world. It is in this context one should read the passage in 1 Pet 2:9 talking about what is commonly called "the priesthood of all believers." The main concern of the saying is to ascertain the fundamental principle that all believers bear a common responsibility and accountability for the commission of the church. This vouches for the legitimate spiritual basis for all the elected members in the various boards and councils sharing in the governance of the church. They are part of representative structures of authority and leadership reflecting the collective responsibility for the church and all its members. They give a visible confirmation of the fact that the people of God take the responsibility for the world in earnest. Bearing this in mind, one may conclude that elected councils and other representative organs in the church are legitimate and necessary expressions of the God-given task to contribute to the growth of the church as the body of Christ.

From this basic conviction it becomes clear that the elected representatives of the councils and governing boards of the church are functioning from an authority which is different from what is framed by general democratic principles. We are talking about baptized members of the church placing themselves at the disposal of the church for qualified ecclesiastic tasks and purposes. They may be regarded as having been "chosen" and "called" for this assignment, in the biblical sense of the words,[30] even if the nomination and election processes have been ordered in accordance with general public elections in society. Sitting on a church council, being elected to serve in the general assembly or holding another office in the church means carrying the confidence of the church at large, the communion of the baptized, and thus also being entrusted by the church as the body of Christ. The election process is an expression and representation of the church as the "communion of saints." This gives reason to believe that those who are

---

30. Rom 1:7 "To all God's beloved in Rome, who are *called* to be saints . . ."; 1 Cor 1:26 "Consider your own *call*, brothers and sisters."

elected may count on the blessing of God, equipping them for the spiritual service in the governing organs. There is a need to reinforce this kind of biblically based self-confidence in the members of the elected church boards.

The structures of leadership in the church are founded on a general principle of cooperation, shared responsibility and representation, where lay people, based upon their baptism, and ordained ministers, based upon their pledged loyalty to the church, are working together in mutual respect towards a common goal. This principle is not identical with a political concept of democracy, which is based upon the sovereignty of the people. The representation of laypeople in the church, emanating from the status as baptized member, is qualitatively different from the political democratic representation based on secular rights of civil citizens. But the church may be free to apply appropriate principles of human rights, oriented from international law and guided by the belief in God's creative will, and thus have a positive regard for the principle of democracy and recognize many justified biblical concerns in its program. The church has both a spiritual and a sociological nature, and the task of ordering the structures and work of the church as a community in this world is a legitimate and necessary part of church leadership. The official position of the church is that it welcomes the process of democratization that has taken place in recent years in the organizational structures of the church.

But the general concept of democratic structures in the reform process has consistently supported the understanding of a fully shared responsibility between lay people and representatives of the ordained ministry. The Lutheran Confession describes the ministry of word and sacrament as a constitutive element for the church.[31] The means of grace create communion in the church. In the same manner one may say that the ordained ministry, serving in the office of word and sacrament, is constitutive for the church in so far as the Holy Spirit, actively imparting the effect of the gospel, is brought forth to men through this ministry. The Lutheran Confession further underlines the prerequisite that a person who is assigned the ordained ministry must be "lawfully called" (*rite vocatus*).[32] Through such a lawful procedure it is safeguarded that at all times a permanent, regular and public service of preaching and administering the sacraments will be provided in order that persons may be called and led to the salvific faith. The orderly calling into this ministry may take different forms, but it signifies that the appointed minister has been entrusted with the authority needed for his work through lawful and valid procedures by recognized governing bodies

31. *Augsburg Confession*, art. 5.
32. Ibid., art. 14.

or persons in the church. Essentially the ordained ministry of the church represents a uniform service, but within this singular ministry there is room for a differentiation between the office of a minister in a local parish and the office of bishop in a regional community of congregations, a diocese. Church leadership and administration are elements designed to deal with practical issues which are in need of a certain degree of recognized power. In this context the office of the bishop is also the bearer of a genuine authority from the church, provided it has been granted through a recognized and accepted procedure.

The question of representative leadership and legal authority of governance in the church may be seen from different perspectives. In Norway the general attitude, also in documents from the reform movement, has been that the General Synod, constituted by both lay members and clergy on an equal basis, is the ultimate decision-making body of the church in all matters, including issues of doctrine and liturgy. But the concern for the greatest possible unity in the whole church has led to acceptance of a demand for a qualified majority on certain doctrinal issues and a requirement of consensus between the Bishops' Conference and the General Synod in such matters. It is also worth noting that in the decision-making bodies of the church of Norway, the representatives of the clergy have the same voting rights as the lay members.

THE ISSUE OF THE FOLK CHURCH

In the concept of the reform movement, the church is commissioned by Jesus to dedicate its work to the people and all mankind. Its aim is to draw as many as possible into the attraction of the gospel and offer every human being the possibility to enter into the fellowship with Christ in faith. The church stretches beyond its boundaries to encompass the civil society, the neighborhood, the country. This intentional program lies at the root of the idea of the folk church. From the very beginning the church appeared with formative elements to ensure its physical existence in the world, thus showing forth sociological traits and characteristics. There is no fundamental contradiction between the spiritual nature of the church and its outward appearance as a community. The reform movement is not advocating a spiritualistic concept of the church which does not see the visible church as a proper church. Throughout its history the leading spokesmen for church reform have distanced themselves from the idea that the real church is limited to the number of true believers, and that the organized church only functions as "a scaffolding to stand on while we are building the true church," as one of the critics of the state church once formulated his opinion.[33] But, on the other hand, the reform movement has not been inclined to give the outward organization and the democratic structures of the church as a folk church constitutive legitimacy for the identity of the church. It is not the people that constitute the church, but baptism and the gospel. The church is not a fruit of creation, but of salvation. One might hardly claim conformity with the Reformation's concept of natural man in an effort to ascribe a certain quality to human nature or the people at large in the definition of the nature of the church. Ecclesiology, according to Luther, is basically derived from soteriology and eschatology, and not from the concept of creation. This does not mean a spiritualization of the church. The church as the body of Christ also has the marks of an outward, bodily form in this world. The nature of the church, however, is decided from within, from the gospel, and not from outside, from the people as a sociological entity.

The church is there for the people. But the true sociological legitimacy of the church lies in its identity as a communion of a different kind than the civil society. The church is not and cannot be a melting pot for various expressions of a privatized, civil religion. It is a creature of the Spirit, a pilgrim people. From this point of view there may be reason to question the tendency to describe the church mainly in terms and vocabulary taken from a sociology of business administration or corporate enterprise structures. But admittedly the future establishment of the church as a self-governing legal personality calls for structural forms that may sustain it in a context of common law and corporate regulation.

DECISIVE ELEMENTS IN INTERNATIONAL
CONVENTIONS ON RELIGION

The documents of the reform movement, confirmed in large part by the General Synod, have increasingly underscored the nature of the church as a faith communion, or a "community of believers" as defined in the declaration of human rights.[34] This identity of the church has also been increasingly accepted in recent public documents from the government dealing with the relationship between church and state. Most explicitly this tendency is apparent in the follow up to the latest report from a public commission dealing with the role of religion in society.[35] The commission report struggles with the restrictions given in its mandate to deliver proposals and recommenda-

33. Hope, *Kyrkja og Guds folk*, 240.

34. See Conference on Security and Cooperation in Europe, *Concluding Document*, § 16.

35. Kulturdepartementet, *NOU 2013:1 Det livssynsåpne samfunn.*

tions without jeopardizing the present stance of church/state relations. But taking a natural starting point in the international conventions of religious liberty, the commission felt constrained in posing critical questions about the practice of political influence in the work of churches and religious societies. The dominating focus of the report is on the implementation of guidelines for individual religious freedom, and the safeguarding of equal conditions for the various groups of both religious and philosophical life view communities. But in dealing with the Norwegian church as an historic, national church, the commission fails to see the extent of the positive impact of this church in society, and the need for a wider implementation of the collective freedom for the church, bearing in mind the increasing stress on this issue in international human-rights organizations. The commission underestimates important elements of popular adherence to the church and other religious communities in our country. Only little regard is taken of the *de facto* influence of the church as a sustaining institution in society through social and diaconal initiatives, educational enterprises and its function as a binding factor, a glue in the local society. The important contribution of the evangelical revival movements for the liberation of lay people and the development of democratic elements in our social and political culture is largely overlooked. The role of the church as a socializing factor and inspiration of cultural expressions in art and music deserves greater appreciation.

In the view expressed by proponents of church reform, the holy traditions and rites of the church do not serve solely as the foundation for the faith of the church, but may also serve as inspiration and guidance for a moral life and right decisions by those in power in our society. They serve as a reminder of fundamental norms that have to do with the sacredness of life as created by God and protected by God's will. The churches are convinced that by presenting this concept of life they are offering something which is to the benefit of all human beings. The common welfare and the shared good life are gifts from a God who loves people, and the churches are called to be stewards of this divine blessing.

The fact that the conventions of human rights have their main focus on the freedom of the individual may lead to certain conflicts in relation to the freedom of collective structures. This may also be seen in the jurisdiction and decisions made in the treatment and practice of international courts dealing with issues of human rights. While the conventions are mainly concerned with safeguarding the freedom of the individual citizens when it comes to their political, social and religious rights against the *state*, the jurisprudence in the courts is often dealing with complaints forwarded by individuals or groups as to violation of their freedom caused by *churches or religious societies*. The material from the case decisions indicates that considerations in favor of religious pluralism are dominant. This may prove important as a protection against a religiously based intolerance. But the danger is that the courts consolidate pluralism as a superior principle taking on almost religious characteristics. This may lead to an intolerance based on secularism, where political authorities demand conformity from the religious societies according to political or opinion-based positions. "Religious intolerance gives a religious dogma the status of law of the state. Secular intolerance claims the law of the state as a religious dogma."[36]

Some of the directives from the international commissions and courts give perspectives and possible guidelines for the future legal basis that needs to be established for the church of Norway, the main precondition being the recognition of the church as a self-governing body, with legal status as a juridical personality. A summary comment on international law and jurisprudence from one of the leading writers on church law in Europe points out important issues. They also have bearing for the Norwegian church and may serve as appropriate guidelines for the future efforts on establishing an independent church:

> At the Convention level after initially refusing standing to churches, the European Commission of Human Rights accepted that it was artificial to distinguish between rights of the individual members and of the religious body itself. It is now clearly established that a Church or a religious body may, as such, exercise on behalf of its adherents the rights guaranteed by Article 9 of the Convention. Moreover, it has been recognized that protection of collective religious liberty may require the giving of legal status or personality to religious organizations. This enables them to hold property (important for establishing premises in which to meet and to fund-raise), to employ staff, to enter binding contracts, and to sue and be sued. . . . Since religious communities traditionally exist in the form of organized structures, Article 9 must be interpreted in the light of Article 11 of the Convention, which safeguards associative life against unjustified State interference. Seen in that perspective, the right of believers to freedom of religion, which includes the right to manifest one's religion in community with others, encompasses the expectation that believers will be allowed to associate freely, without arbitrary State intervention. Indeed, the autonomous existence of religious communities is indispensable for pluralism in a democratic society and is thus an issue at the very heart of the protection which Article 9 affords. . . .

36. Martínez-Torrón, "(Un)protection of Individual Religious Identity."

The way in which national legislation enshrines this freedom and its practical application by the authorities reveal the state of democracy in the country concerned. . . . In this key passage the ECtHR endorses a vision of religious organizations free of state interference, allowed to take their place in civil society as one of the building blocks of pluralism.[37]

BIBLIOGRAPHY

Aarflot, Andreas. "Aktuelle forfatningsprinsipper for en nyordning av Den norske kirkes rettsgrunnlag i lys av tyske lutherske kirkeordninger." In *Mot en selvstendig folkekirke*, edited by John Egil Bergem and Andreas Aarflot, 58–87. Bergen: Vigmostad & Bjørke, 2007.

———. "Das bischöfliche Amt—unter besonderer Berücksichtigung der norwegischen Kirche." *Zeitschrift für evangelisches Kirchenrecht* 51 (2006) 505–33.

———. "Bugenhagen und die Kirche in Dänemark und Norwegen." In *Verpflichtendes Vermächtnis. Ökumenisches Bugenhagen-Gedenken in Greifswald*, edited by Norbert Buske and Christoph Ehricht. Greifswald: Evangelische Landeskirche Greifswald, 1985.

———. "Eivind Berggravs kirkeforståelse. Om kirken som "fellesbasseng" og "føderativ organisme"." In *Eivind Berggrav. Brobygger og kirkeleder 1884–1984*, edited by Per Voksø, 104–23. Oslo: Land og Kirke/Gyldendal Norsk forlag, 1984.

———. "Richard Hooker—den engelske reformasjons store rettsteoretiker." In *Samtidsspeil eller fyrtårn*, Andreas Aarflot, 205–33. Bergen: Eide forlag, 2008.

———. "Det teologiske og statsrettslige grunnlag for kirkestyret i Danmark-Norge på reformasjonstiden." *Tidsskrift for teologi og kirke* 41 (1970) 1–31.

Augsburg Confession. Online: http://www.iclnet.org/pub/resources/text/wittenberg/wittenberg-boc.html#ac.

Berggrav, Eivind. *Kirkens ordning i Norge*. Oslo: Land og Kirke, 1945.

von Campenhausen, Axel Freiherr. "The Churches' Right of Self-Government in the Church-State Legal Order of the Basic Law of the Federal Republic of Germany." Paper presented at Forum for Church Law. Oslo, January, 2005.

Conference on Security and Cooperation in Europe. *Concluding document of the Vienna meeting 1986*. Online: http://www.osce.org/mc/40881?download=true.

Den norske kirke og staten. Innstilling fra Det frivillige kirkeråds utredningskommisjon av 1969. Stavanger: Nomi, 1973.

Heckel, Martin. "Kirchliche Rechtsgeschichte in neuerer Sicht—eine Leseempfehlung zu Christoph Links Lehrbuch." *Zeitschrift für evangelisches Kirchenrecht* 57 (2012) 1–56.

Hooker, Richard. *Of the Lawes of Ecclesiasticall Polity* I–IV, edited by Georges Edelen, 1977; V, edited by W. Speed Hill, 1977; VI–VIII, edited by P. G. Stanwood, 1981. Cambridge: Harvard University Press.

Hope, Ludvig. *Kyrkja og Guds folk*. Bergen: A/S Lunde, 1948.

Justisdepartementet [Ministry of Justice and Police]. *Innstilling om lov om trossamfunn, avgitt av dissenterlovskomiteen av 1957*. Oslo: Ministry of Justice and Police, 1957.

37. Ibid.

###

Kemp, Eric. "Legal Aspects of the History of Church and State." *Ecclesiastical Law Journal* 7 (2003) 47–49.

Kirkedepartementet [Ministry of Ecclesiastical Affairs]. *Innstilling til Lov om Den norske kirkes ordning*, 1948. Oslo: Ministry of Ecclesiastical Affairs, 1948.

Kirke- og undervisningsdepartementet [Ministry of Church and Education]. *NOU 1975:30. Stat og kirke*. Oslo: Kirke- og undervisningsdepartementet, 1975.

———. *Stortingsmelding nr. 40 (1980–81) Om stat og kirke*. Oslo: Kirke- og Undervisningsdepartementet, 1981.

Kirkekommisjonen av 1908. IV. Indstilling angaaende den norske kirkes organisation. Kristiania, 1911.

Kirkeloven [Church Act]. *Lov 7. juni 1996 nr. 31 om Den norske kirke*. 1996.

Kirkerådet. *Samme kirke—ny ordning. Om ny ordning av Den norske kirke, med særlig vekt på forholdet mellom kirke og stat*. Oslo: Kirkerådet, 2002.

Kulturdepartementet [Ministry of Culture]. *NOU 2013:1 "Det livssynsåpne samfunn"— en helhetlig tros-og livssynspolitikk*. Oslo: Kulturdepartementet, 2013.

Kultur- og kirkedepartementet [Ministry of Culture and Church Affairs]. *NOU 2006:2. Staten og Den norske kirke*. Oslo: Kultur- og Kirkedepartementet, 2006.

———. *Stortingsmelding nr. 17 (2007–2008) Staten og Den norske kirke*. Oslo: Kultur- og kirkedepartementet, 2008.

Link, Christian. *Kirchliche Rechtsgeschichte*. (2nd edition). München: Beck Verlag, 2010.

Martínez-Torrón, Javier. "The (Un)protection of Individual Religious Identity in the Strasbourg Case Law." *Oxford Journal of Law and Religion* 1 (2012) 363–85.

Reform av den norske kirke. Innstilling fra Det frivillige kirkeråds Reformkommisjon av 1965. Stavanger: Nomi, 1969.

Thompson, W. J. Cargill. "The Philosopher of the "Politic Society." In *Studies in Richard Hooker*, edited by W. Speed Hill, The Folger Library edition, 3–76. Cleveland: Case Western Reserve University, 1972.

4

Church Reforms and Public Reforms

ULLA SCHMIDT

REFORM WAVES: A COMMON FEATURE OF CHURCHES AND PUBLIC SECTOR?

Over the last ten to fifteen years the Church of Norway has gone through a whole range of reforms in such areas as church order and structure, Christian education, relations to the state, church democracy, and liturgy, to mention just a few. This phenomenon is far from exclusive to the Church of Norway, rather it appears to have become a hallmark of the majority of Protestant churches throughout Europe.[1]

Reform and renewal strategies are obviously not new to the Church of Norway. But what seems unprecedented over the last two to three decades is the sheer volume and pervasiveness of the reforms that are being implemented, more or less simultaneously or following rapidly one upon the other. To mention just a few, in 2003 the Christian education reform was introduced, in 2004 a reform to restructure the administration of the local ministry (the "deanery reform"), in 2008 a creation and sustainability reform, and in 2009 a liturgy/worship reform. In 2008 it was decided to change the basic relations between church and state, which not only included a reform of church democracy, but also a subsequent reform of the basic church order and organizational structure, still in the preparation phase.

---

1. Community of Protestant Churches in Europe, *Ecclesia semper reformanda*.

Moreover, several plans and programs have addressed renewal in specific areas, such as diaconia, church and culture, and Sami church life.

Three features of the broader context seem particularly relevant for an understanding of this intense reform period. First, it coincided with the Church of Norway becoming more autonomous in relation to the state. As a result of a lengthy political debate on church-state relations, authority over a number of internal matters has been delegated to the church. This has entailed the development of a church structure and church agencies to deal with this delegated authority, foremost a church synod (1984), but also a new Church Act (1996), which established the local parishes as legal entities. Among other things, the church has now become responsible for developing its own national strategies, plans and work programs. Second, church reforms evolved at a time when demographic changes began to alter the Church of Norway's position in society. The proportion of the population joining the Church of Norway began to drop, mainly due to immigration, and has dropped relatively steadily by 1 percentage point a year since 2000. And, third, the church members' relations to the church have also begun to change. Participation in church rituals, in particular church weddings, has been dropping among church members, as has participation in church services and support for the church's core beliefs and doctrines. In other words, the church reforms evolved at a point in time when the Church of Norway was becoming more independent and responsible for its own profile and operations, but was also beginning to experience a noticeable decline in membership, support, and participation.

Conceptually, reform can be defined as "an active and intentional attempt from political or administrative agents to change the structural features of organizations,"[2] or as intentional and planned changes of the structures and processes of public organizations with the aim of improving their functioning.[3] Applied in a church context, the concept of "reform" easily invites associations with reexamining roots, sources, and traditions of the church to find renewed and more relevant, but also faithful and authentic ways of communicating and practicing Christian faith in changing circumstances and contexts. This article takes a different approach. Inspired by studies of reform processes in organizational contexts in general, it analyses church reforms in terms of their potential connection to a surrounding context, asking whether they can also be interpreted at least in part as the effects of external pressure.

2. Christensen et al., *Organisasjonsteori*, 149.
3. Klausen, "Fra Public Administration," 49.

There are two reasons for taking this approach, one theoretical and one empirical. The empirical reason is related to the fact that this period of comprehensive church reforms coincides with or follows even more wide-ranging reform processes in the public sector, not only in Norway but internationally. This has often been labeled under the general and somewhat imprecise heading of "new public management" and then "modernization of the public sector." This coincidence itself calls for explorations of possible connections between the two reform waves. Furthermore, theoretical explications of public reform and reform processes in the public sector, based on comparative studies, suggest that reform processes should also be understood in terms of interaction with and influence from a larger surrounding organizational context. This invites the question of whether church reforms can be interpreted along these lines. First, are there similarities between church reforms and public sector reforms? And second, if there are, how can these similarities be explained theoretically?

Two church reforms, the Christian education reform and the so-called "deanery reform" are analyzed in-depth with respect to possible similarities with and influences from or exchange of ideas with public-reform processes. Material for the analysis mainly involves various forms of official documents describing the background, intentions, and key elements of the reforms and their implementation. Furthermore, the article applies theory on organizational reform processes, and in particular theory on how organizational ideas are transferred between different organizational contexts. This includes transformative theory explained in relation to internationally comparative studies of public reform processes, and translational theory in studies of organizational ideas and how they "migrate" between organizational contexts.[4]

TWO CHURCH REFORMS

In 2003 the Norwegian parliament adopted a Christian education reform for the Church of Norway with the objective of developing and providing baptismal education for all baptized children and young people. Its wider background was the understanding that a large group of children and young people who had been baptized in the Church of Norway received little or no further education in the Christian faith and were not acquainted with the life of the church. There were several combined reasons for this development.

---

4. Christensen and Lægreid, "Introduction"; Lægreid and Verhoest, "Introduction: Reforming Public Sector Organizations"; Røvik, *Trender og translasjoner*. I am indebted to Helge Hernes for making me aware of the relevance of K. A. Røvik's work on translation-theory.

The church's existing programs and activities only reached a small proportion of the baptized children and young people, there were huge variations between parishes and dioceses, and the activities for the children and young people were traditionally offered by Christian laymen organizations facing the challenge of declining participation.

The aim of the reform was to confront this situation and provide a renewed Christian education for all baptized children and young people between zero and eighteen years of age. This is underlined in the national curriculum on Christian education adopted by the Church of Norway national synod in 2009, stating that Christian education "must be aimed at the whole breadth of the age groups concerned." Two more specific implications followed from this objective. First, Christian education must "make provisions for children and young people with different interests, abilities, and prospects."[5] Based on the premise that the Christian faith is "a resource both for interpreting and encountering life's many aspects and for developing one's own identity," Christian education must relate to the situation, experiences, and interpretations of life of children and young people, and communicate faith "in such a way that they can understand their past life and their present situation in the light of faith and God."[6] Second, the national curriculum also underlines how children and young people should not simply be considered as recipients of teaching. Instead they should be involved in developing and shaping Christian education and have the right to influence decisions and processes relating to its programs and activities and also the life of the church in a wider perspective.

A core element and ideal of the reform was that Christian education should be locally developed and shaped. This was underlined in the preparatory white papers and reports, as well as in the national curriculum adopted by the church synod after the initial five-year trial and development period. It should be a "national reform with a local foundation," with considerable space and flexibility for local adaptation.[7] The national curriculum should serve as a framework, resource, and guidelines for the local parishes, but not as a regulatory text or overriding directive.

This curriculum was implemented organizationally by making each parish responsible for developing its own curriculum for Christian education, to be decided by the parish council and approved by the bishop. Funding for the reform in each parish would be allotted by the deanery, with the joint parish council as the administratively responsible body, and in order

5. Kirkemøtet, *Plan for Christian Education*, 18.

6. Ibid., 14.

7. *Innst. S. nr. 200 (2002–2003)*, 3, 5.

to utilize resources effectively, the parishes were encouraged to cooperate with other parishes when it came to activities, resources, and personnel. The Church of Norway national council would provide various support functions, course material, and other resources, and would be responsible for overseeing and reporting to the government ministry on development and performance of the parishes and dioceses with respect to the reform.

The importance of this last point was related to the funding scheme for the reform. The total annual budget frame when the reform was expected to be fully implemented in 2013 was set at NOK two hundred and fifty million (adjusted to the 2013 price index, according to the Church Council). Like other allocations, the national budget sets certain objectives which the reform is expected to promote and realize. The Church Council is therefore required to provide an annual report on the church's performance on these objectives and goals. All local parishes have to report to the diocese and the Church Council on specific variables which are considered to be relevant parameters and indicators of the success of the overriding objectives. Reports on activities were provided (types and hours), as were participation figures (number of participants) in these activities, but more recently information on learning outcomes has also been especially requested by the ministry. These reports serve different purposes. One purpose is auditor general's control and overview of public funding being spent according to parliamentary, democratic decisions. Other purposes are to monitor how the reform develops, to ascertain the degree to which its objectives are being realized, to improve performance and to rationalize spending on resources.

The second reform being discussed here, the "deanery reform," or more precisely the reform relating to the restructuring of the local ministry, was an administrative reform introduced by the government ministry, which was and still is the employer of the local clergy in the Church of Norway.

This reform was intended to solve two kinds of problems: lack of flexibility in the clergy workforce and lack of leadership. The first allegedly impeded collaboration and specialization and made effective administration of vacancies and vacations more difficult and unmanageable, whereas the second allegedly exacerbated the reported dissatisfaction of local ministers with their working conditions. Apparently supervision, support for young and/or newly appointed clergy, and motivation and encouragement of employees received little attention and priority. This was also considered to have a detrimental effect on the recruitment of ministers and on the operation of the parishes and the services, including the activities they offer members of the church.

The "deanery reform," or reorganization of the parish ministry, launched under the official heading "new directive on the employment of deans and changes in employment procedures for the clergy," was introduced in 2004 to counteract these problems.[8] According to the circular from the Ministry of Culture, the main objectives were to strengthen the role of the dean as leader of the ministry in the deanery, and to stimulate collaboration between ministers. Several initiatives were implemented to achieve these objectives. In order to free a sufficient amount of working hours for leadership tasks, deans would no longer be appointed as ministers in a local parish but would only perform more limited duties and services as parish ministers. Furthermore, stronger priority would be given to developing the deans' leadership abilities.

Changes in organization meant that the deanery was made the district of employment for ministers rather than the local parish. Ministers should primarily serve in one specific parish, but could in addition also be assigned to services in other parishes. The aim was to strengthen teamwork and reduce a sense of isolation. But personnel could also be assigned for services in neighboring parishes in cases of vacation, vacancies, or leaves of absence, although this was not explicitly stated in the circular.

The deans were also provided with a number of tools they could apply to improve working conditions and provide support for ministers, such as specific early career supervision programs, opportunities for further education, and life-course adjusted working conditions.

However, as mentioned above, the Church of Norway is certainly not the only arena for reforms. For nearly three decades extensive reform processes have also occurred in the public sector, not only in Norway, but throughout the entire OECD area, and, according to some, even more or less globally. Bearing in mind how church reforms might at least partially be understood in terms of influence from reform processes in a larger organizational and societal context, this invites the question of whether these described church reforms are similar to the public reforms. If they are, how can these similarities be interpreted theoretically? To answer this question, an overview of the characteristic features of this broader movement of public reforms is needed.

PUBLIC REFORMS

Public reforms are even less of a novelty than church reforms. In a Nordic context the welfare state developed during the decades following World War II and well into the 1970s through comprehensive reforms of health care, education, social services and benefits, pension schemes, infrastructure,

8. Stifoss-Hanssen et al., *Ny organisering av prestetjenesten.*

and so on. Since the 1980s another "mega-reform cycle"[9] has evolved. It is often referred to under the label "new public management" (NPM), not only in the Nordic countries, but internationally, particularly within the OECD area. New public management is not a distinct or clearly defined reform process, but rather a mixed bag of numerous reform elements, implemented and transformed in quite different ways in various sectors, as well as in different countries.

Not all reforms in the public sector, in Norway or elsewhere, can be categorized under this heading. Johan P. Olsen has identified three reform waves over the last four or five decades that have addressed a number of challenges in the Nordic public sector. Throughout the 1970s a red wave of reforms was inspired by values of social solidarity, criticism of dominant power structures, and universal welfare rights, equality, and participation. A "green" wave, emerging in the 1970s, ebbing throughout the 1980s and early 1990s, but reinvigorated from the mid-1990s and now a more or less self-evident component in political programs and public administration, emphasizes environmental sustainability as a necessary profile of public administration.[10]

What Olsen identifies as the third "blue" wave largely coincides with what has more generally been termed "new public management." Generally speaking, one basic feature of this wave has been the idea that the public sector should be governed and operated along the same lines and principles as the private sector and businesses. Internationally, it has often been associated with the impact of neoliberal ideology, which spread from the 1980s onwards into ever more forms of organizational life, subjecting them to the rationality of economic efficiency, commodification, and consumerism.

Recent studies discuss whether this wave has evolved into a "post-NPM" set of reforms to compensate for the problematic consequences of NPM reforms, and if so, whether these post-NPM reforms have surpassed or rather supplemented the previous NPM reforms.[11] Either way, this discussion suggests that new public management is neither a distinct clear-cut category, nor an exhaustive category for describing public reforms in general. That said, it still makes good sense to speak about new public management as a set of reforms which, although not distinct in the sense of being sharply delineated, share a core of features which set them aside from other types or sets of reforms.

9. Klausen, "Fra Public Administration," 51.

10. Ibid., 51.

11. Christensen and Lægreid, "Introduction," 1–2; Christensen and Lægreid, "Increased Complexity"; Lægreid and Verhoest, "Introduction: Reforming Public Sector Organizations," 17–18.

According to ideals and principles from the private business sector, new public management, or the modernization of the public sector, is often described as consisting of two pillars. The first pillar is economism, emphasizing concerns and ideals related to economic rationality. The second is managerialism, linking to organization and leadership theory.[12]

The core element of the first pillar of economism, making the public sector more economically efficient, was based on the contention that long-term expansion had rendered it exceedingly bureaucratic and economically inefficient. To combat this tendency and improve the public sector's economic efficiency and sustainability, it was compelled to make far more efficient use of resources in its production and supply of services. Furthermore, it should be more inclined towards the preferences and choices of citizens. To put it in another way, the public sector organizations were expected to consider and approach users and receivers of its services more as if they were customers or consumers. Public goods and services, at least some, were exposed to competition in the expectation that this would stimulate more efficient production and improve their quality in terms of satisfying the preferences and interests of citizens who were expected to act in the same way as consumers in a market. Outsourcing and contractual agreements rather than bureaucratically regulated political decisions increasingly regulated relations between producers and the end users. In short, the production and exchange of services within the public sector were increasingly envisioned as part of and structured according to the market and market terminology.

The other pillar, managerialism, can be viewed as the basic principle of economism applied to leadership and organization theory. One important aspect is the distinction between politics and political decision-making, on the one hand, and bureaucracy and administration on the other. Political decisions define overriding objectives and allocate resources to public sector entities and agencies, whose leadership is then responsible for pursuing and realizing these objectives as efficiently as possible within the frames of the allocated resources. These overriding principles for organizational structure have implications for management, frequently described in general terms as "management by objectives." Organizations and organizational entities and agencies are essentially managed by monitoring how these predefined objectives are realized, identifying impediments to more efficient achievement, remedying these, and improving performance. Correspondingly, public organizational leadership becomes relatively autonomous and has the main responsibility for how the organization performs according to its

12. Klausen, "Fra Public Administration," 53; Røvik, *Trender og translasjoner*, 36.

politically and strategically defined objectives, and for organizing the flow of resources optimally for attaining these objectives.

A related dimension of managerialism is therefore focusing more attention on leadership and its role in optimizing organizational performance. In its "softer" version this took the form of emphasizing its social dimensions and human interaction as essential ingredients of organizational performance. Motivating and stimulating employers through supervision, incentives, opportunities for further education, support structures, and caring for professional and personal well-being became important. In its "harder" versions, however, the human and interactional dimensions of leadership were subordinated to the overriding strategic philosophy of economic efficiency and rationality as a means of realizing the organization's overarching objectives. This approach is also exemplified by the prolific use of the term "human resources" about employers and personnel.

More recent developments, often referred to as post- or second-generation NPM, have two features that are particularly prominent and relevant in this context. First, post-NPM reforms emphasize and pursue cross-sectorial coordination and integration, whereas NPM reforms allegedly created disintegration and fragmentation. This includes top-level as well as local-level integration with a view to promoting consistency of policies and providing seamless services to citizens. Second, post-NPM reforms imply reasserting and strengthening central political and administrative capacities and control of the public sector to put an end to and reverse the decentralization and devolution tendencies typical of the NPM reforms. This is visible through the presence of measures of control and regulation, and formal structures of authority and decision-making that are also present in public reforms.[13] In contrast to the allegedly decentralizing tendencies of NPM reforms, post-NPM reforms are "re-centralizing" and "re-regulating."

CHURCH REFORMS: PRODUCT OF EXTERNAL INFLUENCE?

This presentation of key elements of public reforms already suggests that there are similarities between the church reforms and public reforms. The adaptation of Christian education to the needs and interests of children and young people, and involving them in decisions on the programs and activities of Christian education, resembles the emphasis on participation and listening to the preferences of clients and users in the production and supply of public services. The governance and management of the Christian

13. Christensen and Lægreid, "Introduction," 11–13; Christensen and Lægreid, "Increased Complexity."

education reform follows some of the same principles and ideas as public reforms when it comes to management by objectives. Furthermore, both church reforms presented here reveal a similar combination of the centralizing and decentralizing tendencies as the public reforms do. Finally, the deanery reform exhibits managerial elements, soft and hard.

These similarities will be analyzed in more detail below after outlining the theoretical understanding of how organizational ideas might be transferred between organizational contexts, which will then be applied in the discussion.

Comparative studies of public-reform processes in various countries, including Norway, offer valuable perspectives that might have a bearing on and help explain and interpret the relation between more general public-reform elements and the specifics of the two church reforms analyzed above. These studies have applied a combination of transformative and translational theoretical approaches. The first, the transformative approach, concentrates on how reform ideas can affect and transform the system where they are implemented. More specifically, it identifies factors which are likely to affect and condition the possibility of having a political and administrative leadership that designs and redesigns an organizational system by implementing reform ideas. It suggests that there are three kinds of factors: First those dealing with political-administrative structures and decision-making and governing systems, second, those related to external pressure, either based on assumptions regarding the technical efficiency of the reform ideas or of their ideological hegemony, and lastly factors dealing with history and culture of the institutional context in question.[14] A translation-theoretical approach, on the other hand, recognizes not only how the introduction of reform ideas might affect the context into which they are introduced, but also how reform ideas themselves might change and be modified as they encounter and are implemented in a new context.

How are these theoretical descriptions of transferring and translating organizational ideas between different contexts able to explain and interpret the dynamics of the described church reforms and their relations to public reforms?

The process of translating organizational ideas into new settings can, according to Røvik, follow different modes which imply different degrees of change and revision of the ideas. These modes are: reproduction, more or less directly copying organizational ideas into a new setting; modification, which implies either some form of addition or subtraction from the ideas as they are translated into a new setting; and radical alteration, which, needless

---

14. Christensen and Lægreid, "Introduction," 4–8.

to say, implies that the organizational ideas undergo a more comprehensive revision and change as they are inserted into a new setting.[15]

This typology of translation of organizational ideas can also be used to understand and explain the dynamics of how public reform ideas relate to a church setting. The specific translational mode used when an organizational idea is inserted into a new context depends, according to Røvik, on features of the idea as well as the relation between the contexts it is translated between. This might help explain the process through which the above-mentioned organizational ideas flow between the contexts of public reform and church reform.

As mentioned above, the Christian education reform underlined the need to pay attention to the experiences and interests of children and young people and to involve them in the development of Christian education. A relevant Christian education program adapted to the "breadth" of the needs of baptized children and young people should focus on what children and young people and their families consider significant, and adapt to children and young people with different interests, talents, abilities, and backgrounds. This emphasis clearly resembled the more widespread idea of user orientation and involvement in public reforms, and adapting to the preferences and interests of public services clients or customers.

For example, healthcare reforms have emphasized customer preferences and satisfaction as an important indicator of the quality of services. Thus, the idea that children and young people should be involved and participate in the development of programs and activities for the Christian education given in the local parish resembles basic principles of new daycare and preschool legislation. The latter refers to the UN Convention on the Rights of the Child to justify this idea of involving children and young people. The curriculum for Christian education contains a more general reference to the way the participation of children and young people in matters relating to their upbringing, education, and living conditions has been put on the agenda and how this also affects the way the church relates to children and young people. A second reform document refers more explicitly to the Norwegian Kindergarten Act and to the UN Children's Convention.[16]

Nonetheless, both documents are careful to also offer justifications and explanations taken from theological understandings and perspectives of church identity and tradition. Prominent in this context is the fact that the New Testament testifies to how Jesus welcomes children and includes them fully in the community he is forming, and offers a Lutheran understanding

---

15. Røvik, *Trender og translasjoner*, 305–318.

16. Styringsgruppa, *Når tro deles*, 35.

of baptism as being embedded in the grace of God and the community of faith, regardless the age of the baptized person. Even though the reform idea, or the principle itself, namely to include children and young people as participants in the forming and developing of the activities and programs, is prominent in the public reforms, it is also given its own specific justification in the church setting, explaining and demonstrating its place as an authentic ingredient in a church reform.

Furthermore, the idea of involving children and young people in developing programs and activities related to Christian faith and practice is not a novelty in the Norwegian church context. Several Christian youth organizations have a longstanding tradition of offering leadership programs for young people to prepare and give them leadership tasks and responsibilities for activities and programs for younger participants. The principle of participation of children and young people in the development of church activities and programs is therefore not due entirely to the arrival of public reform ideas in the church setting.

Finally, this idea of involving children and young people and relating to their interests and needs is expanded through another different but related point, namely that Christian education should relate to children and young people's life experiences, approach the children and young people on their level, and provide them with resources to interpret their daily lives and situations. But this element is not present in the public reform setting in the same way as the other two elements are. It appears as an addition to the public reform idea of the "user- or customer-orientation" of public services. Moreover, this is justified by referring to how experiences can be a way of gaining insight into and understanding of doctrines of Christian faith, such as the meaning of baptism. The content, meaning, and significance of Christian tradition and doctrine, so goes the argument, are explained and grasped by relating to human experiences. But this is a theological point concerning justification of Christian teaching, rather than deriving from general public reform thinking.

The other element in the Christian education reform resembling public reform processes is the emphasis on management by objectives as the approach for leadership and governance. This element seems at least to arise in part from external pressure, exerted through the legislative and administrative requirements, along with funding via national and municipal budgets. This funding system carries with it the requirement that the Church of Norway should develop the reform in accordance with politically defined objectives and reports on the performance of these objectives. But these ideas are not only implemented in the government ministry's relation to the Church of Norway, as a part of public governance and administration.

They are also introduced by the church itself for its internal governance of the reform.

This does not mean that the governance and leadership of the Christian education reform is limited to a management-by-objectives approach. The reform, its development, and content are is also regulated by the Plan for Christian Education which, for example, defines its core content as well as its three basic aspects and the various dimensions which ought to be included in Christian education programs and activities. The reform is not exclusively, not even primarily, governed through the definition of objectives and allocation of responsibility for pursuing and realizing them. Yet, even though the reform is certainly not exclusively governed according to "management by objectives," this approach is clearly present, and in a way which impacts the content of the reform. It is visibly present in the way the orientation of the reform towards the breadth of baptized children and young people has been implemented. "Breadth" is not only understood in terms of quantity and how large a proportion of the age group should participate, but also in terms of quality, in the sense that it should include children and young people with different social, cultural, ethnic, and ability backgrounds. This objective comes to play a key role in governing and forming the reform locally as well as nationally, as the potential for attaining broad participation also influences and conditions the development of programs and activities. For example, it affects how national and regional church authorities advise local agents with respect to which kind of activities should and should not to be included in the local curriculum. When an activity does not appear to reach out to the breadth of the baptized people in the age group, it should not to be included, according to national recommendations and guidelines. One consequence of this has been that many of the previous traditional activities offered to children and young people, especially those offered by the Christian laymen organizations, such as Sunday school, have not been included in the local curricula for Christian education.

Furthermore, defining "breadth" as the reform's main objective means that the responsible agents must report annually on participation, i.e. on performance regarding the overriding breadth objective. The government ministry requires that these reports are given at the national level so that it can control that public funding is being spent according to the parliamentary decisions and as a basis for political decisions regarding future allocations. But as mentioned above, the reports on results and performance are also included in the church's own governance of the reform, and are addressed in the annual administrative dialogs. Bearing this in mind, management by objectives has not only been implemented in the church context in terms of defining objectives and goals, but also in the more strictly economic sense of measuring performance and results, and using this information on performance to adjust the activities in the reform (i.e., as an instrument of managing the reform).

But there are also indications of a much more resistant and highly modified implementation of this idea of management by objectives in the reform. For one thing, the national curriculum for Christian education and other national agencies only defines a limited set of objectives, and only on the general level. The local parishes are given the authority and responsibility for deciding not only objectives for each specific activity in their program, but also the more comprehensive and general objectives for Christian education in the parish. Unlike the typified "management-by-objectives" model, local entities, such as parishes, are not simply presented with centrally defined objectives and assigned responsibility for achieving them in the most effective way possible. Instead they are entrusted with the task of defining and formulating what they see as adequate and relevant objectives for Christian education in their parish.

The reform idea of management by objectives that is prominent in a number of public reforms is thus also quite visibly present in the Christian education reform, but in rather different ways. Its translation into a church setting implies various forms of modification, where it is predominantly implemented in terms of defining general as well as more specific objectives for the local Christian education, and using these as tools to shape programs and activities. The part of the original reform idea which deals with measuring results and performance as a basis for correcting and improving activities is to a large extent omitted in this translation. The very important exception is the overarching breadth objective. Not only is this objective centrally defined and entities at various levels in the church structure are given an independent responsibility for achieving it, the entities are also required to measure and report results and performance regarding this objective, not only for governmental control and auditing purposes, but also for shaping local programs and activities and regulating what forms of activities should and should not to be included in the local curriculum for Christian education. In other words, the translation of the idea of management by objectives is modified in terms of which elements are implemented: first with respect to whether the element for measuring results and performance as an ingredient of management is included or not; second the level at which objectives are decided, and in particular the relatively wide range of discretionary freedom local parishes have in defining objectives for Christian education in their congregation.

The deanery reform and its similarities with public reform reveal further dimensions of the dynamics of transferring the reform ideas between different organizational contexts and settings. As mentioned above, these similarities mainly come under the second pillar of public sector reforms, managerialism. In the deanery reform, increased attention has been directed towards the leadership competencies of the deans and the initiatives to improve them, but also on heightening professional and personal well-being and job satisfaction among employees through such initiatives as further education, life-course adjusted working conditions, support for early career employees, and programs for supervision. This resembles an element within what some have labeled a "soft" version of managerialism, with focus on support, encouragement, and motivation of employees as an essential ingredient of leadership.

But unlike the public sector reform, these ideas were not implemented in a setting previously dominated by bureaucratic management of employees by means of directives, regulations, and hierarchically structured decision-making routines. They were embedded in a context where ministers had traditionally worked very independently, with very little regulation, directives, and hierarchical leadership and management. Roughly speaking, the reform seemed to introduce rather than to change leadership in relation to the local ministry.

This is further underlined by the second element of the deanery reform which resembles public reform in terms of the "hard" version of managerialism. The key component here, as mentioned above, is the decision to employ local ministers in the deanery and with the deanery as their service district. The explicit intentions were to achieve a more evenly distributed workload and to improve cooperation, collegiality, and opportunities for specialization.[17] But the ministers have also perceived this as a way of using resources more effectively, for instance coping with vacations and vacancies without relying on extra resources.[18] In other words, measures to strengthen leadership at the same time also subjected leadership to concerns of efficiency and overriding strategic, organizational objectives. Thus it not only represented a previous concern in public reform often described as a turn from managing to leadership, but also the more recently identified turn from leadership to management.[19]

Making the deanery rather than the local parish the district of employment is also similar to the tendency to centralize leadership. Nonetheless, this is combined with an emphasis on how ministers will continue to have specific responsibility for one parish in the attempt to convince ministers

17. Stifoss-Hanssen et al., *Ny organisering av prestetjenesten*, 20.

18. Ibid., 36–37.

19. Røvik, *Trender og translasjoner*, 146–147.

as well as parishes that the ties between one minister and one parish have not been cut and the local parishes continue to be related to one minister in particular. This could be seen as a translation of the original reform idea of centralization that is modified in accordance with the deep-seated tradition in the Lutheran church, namely the combined idea of the local parish and the worshipping community as the basic entity of the church, and the basic autonomy of the office of preaching. According to Røvik's typology of translational strategies, this represents a rational-strategic addition.[20] A local version of an organizational reform idea is modified by deliberately attuning it to decisive elements in the self-understanding and traditional operations of the organization. This is expected to make it more acceptable to or congruent with existing traditions, yielding a less radical change and transformation of the organization.

Based on these observations it is possible to extract more general insights regarding the translation of reform ideas as they move between different organizational contexts, insights which also shed light on the relation between church and public sector more broadly. These insights can be explained in part according to the above-mentioned transformative and translational theories regarding the transference of organizational ideas, but can also add to these theories.

At a general level they demonstrate how the translation of public reform ideas into a church setting implies modifying them to reduce conflicts with the key elements of church identity and history. One such key element, which reform ideas are modified according to, is the position and constitutive role of the local parish in the organizational structure of the church. This becomes visible in the translation of the principle of management by objectives, where the key "breadth" objective, according to the principle, is defined centrally with each local entity being responsible for realizing it. But a number of other objectives for Christian education and the specific activities for this are defined locally and used for local management, but hardly for a centralized governance of the reform. But this modification is better described as partial transference or implementation, compared to Røvik's suggested forms of addition or subtraction.

A similar modification used to avoid conflict with the key principle of the local parish as the church's basic entity is found in the deanery reform and its attempt to balance between centralizing the local ministry by employing ministers to the deanery, and still reaffirming its local basis by asserting that it will continue to be responsible for one parish in particular.

20. Ibid., 313.

Both elements testify to the translation of public reform ideas and the modification of them to the position and importance that the local parish has in the organizational structure, as well as in the self-understanding and identity of the Church of Norway.

However, at a different level this can also be viewed as a manifestation of a tension between two opposite ideas that are each present in the public reforms, namely a centralizing as well as a decentralizing tendency. Another interpretation concerning the translational process thus is that different and potentially contrasting or opposing elements from public-reform elements are both transferred into the church setting, but to different parts of it. If this is the case, this could rather be seen as organizational ideas being filtered through and tested for compatibility with the organizational structure.

Another important dimension of the translation revealed in the above analyses is how the translation of public reform ideas into a church setting might also involve providing them with a justification congenial to church history, identity, and theology. The original reform idea, in the above analysis most clearly demonstrated in terms of the participation of users and clients, and orientations towards their interests, preferences, and experiences, is transferred quite directly and without extensive modifications to the setting of the church reform. But it is provided with a justification and basis inherent to the identity, theology, and history of the church.

CONCLUSION

These analyses show how church reforms, like public reforms, are best understood as a multifactorial process than explained in terms of one, single factor. This implies firstly that it is as misguided to view church reforms solely as the outcome of isomorphic processes of adapting to external pressure from a surrounding context, as it is to view them as the result of intended and designed plans developed and implemented by church leadership. Instead they are the result of a complex mixture of external and internal forces and factors.

Public reform ideas influence church reforms through legislative and administrative regulations, especially associated with funding, and through an ideological hegemony of certain organizational ideas disseminating into new sectors. But these ideas are not simply passively accepted and accommodated into a church setting. They are translated into a new organizational setting or "language" and thus to a smaller or larger extent transformed and changed. This is typically done to avoid conflicts with key points in existing church identity and self-understanding, whether they are organizational, theological, or historical. This may occur, for example as illustrated above, through a partial or discriminatory transferring of public reform ideas, or through more wholesale transference, where the public reform idea has been provided with a justification congenial with the identity and history of the church.

BIBLIOGRAPHY

Christensen, Tom, and Per Lægreid. "Introduction—Theoretical Approach and Research Questions. In *Transcending New Public Management. The Transformation of Public Sector Reforms*, edited by Tom Christensen and Per Lægreid, 1–16. Farnham: Ashgate, 2007.

Christensen, Tom, and Per Lægreid. "Increased Complexity in Public Organizations— the Challenges of Combining NPM and Post-NPM." In *Governance of Public Sector Organisations. Proliferation, Autonomy and Performance*, edited by Per Lægreid and Koen Verhoest, 255–75. Basingstoke: Palgrave Macmillan, 2010.

Christensen, Tom, et al., *Organisasjonsteori for offentlig sektor. Instrument, kultur, myte.* Oslo: Universitetsforlaget, 2009.

Community of Protestant Churches in Europe. *Ecclesia Semper Reformanda. Reform and Renewal within the Life of European Protestant Churches*, 2012. Online: http://www.leuenberg.net/sites/default/files/Ecclesia%20semper%20reformanda%20-%20Final%20version%202012.pdf.

Innst. S. nr. 200 (2002–2003). Recommendation to the Storting no. 200 (2002–2003).

Kirkemøtet. *Plan for Christian Education.* Oslo: Church of Norway National Council, 2009.

Klausen, Kurt Klaudi. "Fra Public Administration over New PA til NPM—en fortolkningsramme for reformer." In *Modernisering av offentlig sektor. Trender, ideer og praksiser*, edited by Tor Busch et al., 48–61. Oslo: Universitetsforlaget, 2011.

Lægreid, Per, and Koen Verhoest. "Introduction: Reforming Public Sector Organisations." In *Governance of Public Sector Organisations. Proliferation, Autonomy and Performance*, edited by Per Lægreid and Koen Verhoest, 1–20. Basingstoke: Palgrave Macmillan, 2010.

Kirke-, utdannings- og forskningsdepartementet [Ministry of Education, Research and Church Affairs] NOU 2000:26 ". . . til et åpent liv i tro og tillit." *Dåpsopplæring i Den norske kirke.* Oslo: Kirke-, utdannings- og forskningsdepartementet, 2000.

Røvik, Kjell Arne. *Trender og translasjoner. Ideer som former det 21. århundrets organisasjon.* Oslo: Universitetsforlaget, 2007.

Stifoss-Hanssen, Hans, et al., *Ny organisering av prestetjenesten ("Prostereformen"). Evaluering.* Rapport 2013/2. Oslo: Diakonhjemmet høgskole, 2013.

Styringsgruppa [Steering committee for the Christian Education Reform]. *Når tro deles.* Report from the trial-and-development phase of the Church of Norway Christian education reform 2003–2008. Oslo: Church of Norway National Council, 2008.

5

Church Leadership and the Management of Meaning in Times of Change

Notes from the Inside

BIM RIDDERSPORRE AND
JOHANNA GUSTAFSSON LUNDBERG

After its separation from the Swedish state in 2000, the Church of Sweden is formally a confessional actor among others. The former state church is still the largest religious community, but increasing secularization, a constant member pin and the fact that Sweden has become a multicultural country have forced the former hegemonic church to make decisions and to have discussions of a new kind, such as on different theological and sometimes even political and worldwide issues.[1] From taking for granted its status as a state church with about 80 percent of the population as members, these changes have actualized a reinterpretation of the church's identity, whereby some theological actors would claim that (pro-)activity and a larger emphasis on participation in society are important elements for the future of the church.[2]

---

1. Zuckerman, "Danes and Swedes."
2. cf. Hagman, *Efter folkkyrkan*; Modéus, *Mod att vara kyrka*.

Parallel to these changes and challenges, the Church of Sweden has also undergone a structural change on the organizational level, whereby formerly small parishes have joined to become larger units. This restructuring is ongoing and, as all major changes, has caused hope, frustration and confusion. All these contextual and internal changes pose new questions not only to church identity but also to different concepts of church leadership. As stated in Hanson and Andersen, "This calls for leadership with a propensity to manage change."[3] Thus in this chapter, we focus on how ministers in the Church of Sweden who are interested in leadership issues reflect upon leadership and narrate their experiences as co-workers.

The overriding aim of this study is to gain access to recent, experience-based pictures of church leadership in times of organizational change in a Swedish Lutheran context. Additionally, we are interested in the thoughts and beliefs as regards improving organization and successful leadership in times of change. In this chapter, we use the theories of post-heroic leadership[4] and of leadership as the management of meaning.[5] Our research questions focus on the experiences and the impact of leadership in times of organizational change as well as on suggestions for improvement.

RESEARCH ON CHURCH LEADERSHIP AND CHANGE

Earlier studies of church leadership show ministers wrestle with problems concerning their managerial tasks. Among several areas of experienced ambiguity is the division between the minister and the parish council in decision-making, which leads to unclear responsibilities and roles.[6] Since the disestablishment from the state in 2000 and the last reorganization mentioned initially in this article, there are a large number of new managerial tasks and responsibilities that need to be implemented. These changes are a challenge to the minister's possibility and capacity to take responsibility and face the consequences of the organizational changes.

An important but less explored issue is the psychosocial work environment. Different approaches of leadership tend to enhance or diminish conflicts.[7] Unclear organizational structures, an experience of being different, stressful working conditions and destructive communication patterns could cause psychosocial problems. Informants in Ann-Sofie Hansson's study de-

3. Hanson and Andersen, "Vicars as Managers," 108.

4. Alvesson and Spicer, *Metaphors We Lead By*.

5. Smircich and Morgan, "Leadership"; Fairhurst, "Reframing"; Alvesson and Spicer, *Metaphors We Lead By*.

6. Stålhammar, "Some Reflections."

7. Hansson, "Psychosocial Work."

scribe underlying non-communicated conflicts as important. Additionally, towards the end of the 1990s, the Church of Sweden reported a larger number of occupational injuries due to psychosocial and organizational work environmental causes than any other occupational group, related to the number of employed.[8] An aggravating circumstance is the expectation of goodness that people tend to direct towards the church and its employees. This can be frustrating both for the individual minister and for the whole place of work, which becomes depicted as an ideal working place where everyone is friendly and where there are no tensions.[9] Because of expectations like these, there is a risk that real conflicts are suppressed and disregarded.[10]

Another interesting aspect of church leadership is the sometimes presupposed uniqueness. Does church leadership differ from leadership in other contexts? In a comparative study by Hansson and Andersen (2008) on capacities to initiate and implement organizational change, the ministers stood out as a special group. Only 1 percent of the ministers in the Church of Sweden managed to work successfully with change. The study indicated that ministers had a lower capacity than other groups of civil servants, such as principals and social insurance officers, in initiating and implementing organizational changes in their parishes. While principals and social insurance officers were more oriented to change and development, the ministers were predominantly relationship-oriented. Hansson and Andersen differentiate between the professions and pastoral work, which is founded in relations but also in the pastoral training and a so-called weight of history. According to the authors, another explanation could be that many ministers are perceived to have a "helping approach" to leadership, and this might also be highlighted through the personalities attracted by the call to priesthood.[11] Overall, this kind of leadership research is oriented towards identifying and denominating different leadership styles whereby the leaders' interests and/ or capacities in different areas provide the basis for creating leadership.

MANAGEMENT OF MEANING AND POST-HEROIC LEADERSHIP—THEORETICAL PERSPECTIVES

Compared to the kind of research presented above, our study has a quite different focus. We discuss, rather, the ambiguity and the context dependent aspects of the so-called post-heroic leadership: considering leadership as co-constructive and as framed by language and discourse. From a discursive

8. Hansson, "Psychosocial Work."

9. Pettersson, *Kvalitet i livslånga relationer.*

10. Hansson, "Psychosocial Work."

11. Hansson and Andersen, "Vicars as Managers."

perspective, reality is constituted rather than mirrored by language,[12] and leaders can be transformative agents. As agents of change, they are viewed as having the ability to co-create the contexts to which they and others must respond—just as they might shape any other "social reality" such as identity or legitimacy that, in turn, often vary based on how the context is being constructed in and through discourse.[13] To understand organizations and leadership, one has to consider leaders, co-workers and the specific context as a whole.[14] This confirms a perception of leadership as oriented to meaning-making, which, in turn, is considered as a co-construction between leaders and co-workers; in this article, this is also conceptualized as a management of meaning.[15]

The attention to leadership and related issues is of a fairly late date in a church context. In Sweden the separation of the church from the state put the issue on the agenda. Organizations that traditionally have been seen as being professional and needing little leadership—such as the church, schools and academic institutions—have become targets for improvement through leadership.[16] But how can leadership be understood and communicated in such an organization, and how could we evaluate the aspirations to improve it? Relating leaders, followers and context is, of course, vital in any understanding of leadership. This is self-evident, but surprisingly rarely done.[17] The perspectives above are well established in a wider leadership research discourse but are quite new in the research area of church leadership. Therefore, we take the opportunity to give a wider yet brief introduction to these theories. The different ways in which people understand and construct leadership opens up significant space for ambiguous interpretations, understandings and experiences of leadership. However, ambiguity and incoherence are still neglected aspects in the study of leadership. There is a "comparative lack of recognition given to the possibility that "leadership" can encapsulate a diverse range of meanings and multiple frames of reference."[18] Stressing these aspects of leadership is a way of deconstructing and criticizing more essentialist and non-contextually anchored ideas of leadership. There are a number of preconceived, "ideal," ideas about leadership.

12. Fairhurst, "Considering Context."

13. Ibid., 1608.

14 Alvesson and Spicer, *Metaphors We Lead By*.

15 Smircich and Morgan, "Leadership."

16. Alvesson and Spicer, *Metaphors We Lead By*, 30.

17. Ibid., 28.

18. Bresnen, "All Things," 496.

Alvesson and Spicer argue that the variation, incoherence, and com-plexity need to be taken seriously; this involves a greater sensitivity to cultural contexts and different meanings attributed to leadership.[19] They stress the importance of "listening to people in organizations and finding out when and why they talk about leadership, what they mean by it, their beliefs, values and feelings around leadership and different versions and expressions of it."[20] How people discuss leadership is indicative of wider cultural patterns in an organization, and we need a range of different ideas to understand leadership. We think that among other tools, metaphors are a way to approach an understanding of organizations. There is a correlation between a common understanding in an organization and the emergence of spontaneous metaphors, in this study labeled as metaphors-in-use.[21]

An important aspect of leading processes, especially in times of crises, is how the organization or enterprise deals with change (i.e., the communi-cation of potential problems and solutions and steps to take the organiza-tion further in a longer journey of changes). Instead of looking at leadership as a one-way maneuver, from the leader towards more or less receptive sub-ordinates, a contemporary focus is increasingly turning to processes where one discusses leadership and employee-ship by implicitly/explicitly pictur-ing leadership as a process of meaning-making which rests upon a dialec-tical relationship between the leader and the employees, denominated as co-constructors.[22] Linda Smircich and Gareth Morgan claim groups where leadership emerges spontaneously tend to attribute leadership to those who structure the experiences of the group in a meaningful way:

> They emerge as leaders because of their role in framing experi-ence in a way that provides a viable basis for action, e.g., by mo-bilizing meaning, articulating and defining what has previously remained implicit or unsaid, by inventing images and meanings that provide a focus for new attention, and by consolidating, confronting, or changing prevailing wisdom.[23]

Through the ability of framing the situation or the process, a shared meaning of what is at stake is established in the group. Interaction and the idea that meaningful leadership always operates dialectically between the leader and the co-workers are important concepts in this kind of leadership approach.

19. Alvesson and Spicer, *Metaphors We Lead By.*

20. Ibid., 10.

21. Oswick and Grant, *Organizational Development.*

22. Smircich and Morgan, "Leadership"; Fairhurst, "Reframing"; Alvesson and Spicer, *Metaphors We Lead By.*

23. Smircich and Morgan, "Leadership," 258.

Alvesson and Spicer depict this emphasis on interplay and dialogue as a post-heroic leadership.[24] We assert this is based on a collaborative learning and a continuous calibration between managers and employees.

Metaphors

Metaphors are linguistic figures of a certain kind. They offer a dense image of human experience. An often-discussed feature of metaphor is its generative function, its inherent potential to create new ways of seeing the world.[25] In the influential work *Metaphors We Live By*, George Lakoff and Mark Johnson suggest "the essence of metaphor is understanding and experiencing one kind of thing in terms of another."[26] In reality, as viewed through the lens of a metaphor, some aspects are highlighted while others are obscured. One of the most powerful lenses is culture. By studying the use of metaphors, we begin to understand our physical and cultural experiences.[27] In that respect, the use of a joint metaphor can contribute to a common understanding of a phenomenon. Shared metaphors could also reinforce collaborative learning in an organization. Language is, under normal circumstances, spontaneously enriched by metaphors-in-use, also called metaphors-of-the-field.[28] A low prevalence of metaphors in the language used in a specific context can reveal a lack of a common discourse or frame of reference in the actual group of people. Within a common frame of associations or experiences, it is, in contrast, possible to create and share metaphors as a way of heightening a joint understanding of an aspect of reality. Leadership is a field with the potential to be more deeply understood or reframed through metaphors.[29] In this chapter, we create some metaphoric pictures with the intention to share a deepened understanding with our readers; some discursive themes are unveiled and explored. The interpretive frame is the post-heroic leader, struggling together with her co-workers in meaning-making processes.

MINISTERS' NARRATIVES OF LEADERSHIP

The material for our analysis consists of one hundred and twenty-five student papers (with a span from approximately one thousand to three thousand words) written in a course on Church leadership given in cooperation

24. Alvesson and Spicer, *Metaphors We Lead By.*

25. Tietze et al., *Understanding Organizations*, 35.

26. Lakoff and Johnson, *Metaphors We Live By*, 5.

27. Hogler et al., "Meaning."

28. Oswick and Grant, *Organizational Development*, 217.

29. Morgan, *Images of Organization.*

between Lund University and Malmö University. This course has been offered since autumn 2010 but became compulsory for all ministers who aim
to apply for positions in 2013. In this course, the students write a paper in
which they analyze one of the professional teams they are part of in their
congregations. Part of the task also includes suggestions for improvements.
Our chapter is based on these texts, with a focus on two research questions:

1. What experiences and impact of leadership in times of organizational change are expressed?

2. What suggestions for improvement are formulated?

We consider the ambiguous and discursive aspects of professional life,
where individual mental maps are as important as common organizational
identities. Our theoretical point of departure is that organizations, leadership and followership can be understood through language and linguistic
artifacts.[30] With a linguistic and discursive approach, we regarded these
papers as kinds of narratives or narrative descriptions. Through their texts,
our aim was to collect authentic information retrieved from the ministers'
life worlds. However, the impact of our own interpretation must be taken
seriously within this methodological approach; in this regard, we could be
considered as co-creators of meaning.

Initially, we treated the entire material as a whole, reading through all
125 texts, creating a sense for variance as well as similarity in these narrative
descriptions. Through this, we formed a strong impression of a number of
common denominators related to our research questions.

Therefore, a further step was to re-read the papers with the clear purpose of identifying common denominators and differences between individuals or groups of authors. A brightened image of a few major themes,
each divided into variants, emerged. We mapped these observations and
collected relevant quotations (published with a written permission from the
respective authors) from the papers to illustrate them.

Regarding our first research question about how experiences and the
impact of leadership in times of organizational change are expressed in the
student texts, we used *metaphors* to capture our findings. These metaphors
came quite naturally and were equally relevant for both authors of this
chapter. Additionally, we considered the concept of *professional role* to be of
central importance in understanding how these ministers perceived leadership and organization. In this context, we tried to use the role concept as a
central part of a theatre metaphor. The main part of the results section is
devoted to the first question.

30. Tietze et al., *Understanding Organizations*.

The participants in the church leadership course were asked to suggest improvements as part of the analysis of leadership and organization in their congregation, the focus of our second research question. To identify these suggestions, we made yet another reading of the entire material. This part of the material showed a diverse picture. We conceptualized the suggestions in a small taxonomy on the title "leadership in change", touching on questions about handling contemporary challenges, as well.

To make use of a motley collection of ideas outside the taxonomy, we end our analysis by quoting and commenting on some of the ideas of improvements that came up in different papers. Here, one finds a visionary grounded idea of the good leader, which is not always consistent with experiences from a daily working context.

METAPHORS AND PICTURES OF LEADERSHIP

The analysis starts with the first research question concerning experiences and impact of leadership in times of organizational change, followed by suggestions for improvements. Finally, a reflection in the discussion and conclusions section highlights three phenomena as central for development and change in organizational settings.

The use of metaphors can give access to a more discursive and complex way of understanding organization and leadership. Highlighting a phenomenon could give a deeper understanding by describing its similarities with another. When sorting out and structuring comments and statements on various kinds of leadership experiences in the material, we created metaphors which captured and highlighted the students' experiences in an explanatory way. Through the metaphors, we also captured the complexity in the interplay between leader and co-worker in view of the generative function, whereby the metaphor sometimes brings forth new and unexpected perspectives of a certain phenomenon.

Leadership and employee-ship, as well as the professional context, are relevant aspects to answer our first question, on the experiences of leadership in the material. In accordance with Mats Alvesson and André Spicer, we consider metaphors a useful tool for understanding organization and professional life.[31] Some metaphors closely related to the students' texts emerged. Through these metaphors, we sampled a pattern of different reactions and experiences triggered in the interface between leaders and employees. The preferences and capacities of the employee, together with the professional context, evoked different interpretations of a certain kind of

31. Alvesson and Spicer, *Metaphors We Lead By*.

leadership. This interplay between the needs and offers from the leader and the co-worker, frames our understanding of leadership as co-constructive.[32]

Leadership as Parent's Arms

The first metaphor of leadership was conceived as *the parent's arms*, and this generated two other metaphors: *the open arms leadership* and *the closed arms leadership*. The open arms leadership and the closed arms leadership are, so to speak, the two sides of the coin. Depending on what the leader puts into a certain leadership approach (e.g., the parent's arms strategy) and on how the co-workers respond to this approach, the reactions are colored differently.

The parent's arms metaphor is what Alvesson conceptualizes as a first-level metaphor, which then is developed into sub-set of metaphors, called second-level metaphors.[33] Such second-level metaphors yield more precise insight and are more useful for organizational analysis, which is a way of working and analyzing; Alvesson calls this to "look for the metaphors within metaphors." The metaphoric picture of a leader and leadership as a parent offering his or her arms to a child was the result of an interpretive reading of the student texts. It gave an impression of dependency, emancipation and abandonment as principal themes in the workplace narratives. The second-level metaphors derived from our material divide into two different ways of approaching leadership visualized as an open respectively a closed arms strategy. A parent could give a child access to his/her arms in an open manner with a possibility for the child to move and act freely. Conversely, the same open arms could cause another scenario, for example, an experience of abandonment. A parent's arms may as well be perceived as closed, holding the child tight and solid. This could be experienced as a tight and suffocating hug or as a secure frame for a child. Both of these strategies, (open and closed) could thus be experienced as either desirable or undesirable by the child/employee. Again, the experiences vary depending on what the leader places into his/her assignment and how the co-workers receive this kind of leadership.

Some students perceived the open arms leadership, characterized by a great amount of freedom for the employees, as a *holding capacity* of the leader, where the leader was considered engaged and confident in giving the co-workers space for action and decision-making. By contrast, and in relation to the same kind of leadership, some students expressed that the leader

---

32. Barge and Fairhurst, "Living Leadership."
33. Alvesson, "Play of Metaphors."

abandoned the co-workers and was unengaged. The degree of security on the part of the employee is essential for how leadership is received.

An example of a holding capacity approach characterized by a mutual trust between the leader and the co-workers is given in the following quotation:

> Due to our extensive assignment related to a relatively small team our professional roles are intertwined. Also our minister works together with us in different team constellations as a co-worker on equal terms. But there is however no doubt on who is the responsible leader in critical situations.

Here, the leader is experienced as a co-worker who both takes part in the different teams and takes responsibility when needed.

On the other hand, in other texts, the students describe this open arms leadership as insecure and abandoning: "The leader considers the team as something that is supposed to work automatically without his actual engagement. In problematic situations the leader withdraws and presupposes the team to take full responsibility."

Leadership like this could be understood positively as a leader who gives a large amount of freedom to his/her co-workers. However, in this quotation, the leader is not considered as someone who, in an engaged way, trusts his/her co-workers and therefore affords them a lot of space. On the contrary, he/she seems to be a less engaged leader who does not care enough about the co-workers and their commitments, and, in times of trouble, he/she withdraws. The open-arms metaphor—which, in its descriptive meaning, brings forward associations of security, confidence and, to some extent, autonomy—at the same time runs the risk of "concealing" the kind of leadership whereby the leader abandons the co-workers in certain situations.

The uniting aspect about these citations is that the leader does not attend all aspects of the daily activities in the parish in an active, conscious way. This kind of leadership strategy can be more or less conscious in the sense that the leader decides not to interfere too much. An important insight is that this leadership can be experienced in extremely different ways, showing the leadership/co-worker relation is co-constructive and interactive.

The experiences connected with the other second-level metaphor—the closed arms leadership—consider a kind of *micromanagement* whereby the leader is involved in, and sometimes experienced as, controlling everyday details, which is described in the texts both negatively and positively.

A micromanagement approach could be experienced as a lack of creativity and professional free. "The minister has an authoritarian leadership style with a great amount of control. He has problems to delegate and trust the co-workers. Instead he gets involved in details."

The co-workers experience that they are controlled and that the leader lacks confidence in his/her way of running the parish. The leader is also perceived as authoritarian. With a kind of "forced grip," the leader gets engaged in details concerning daily activities, which frustrates the co-workers.

In another setting and context, this same kind of leadership approach is experienced as a secure base. The minister is experienced as clear and well structured, which is exemplified in his/her creation of different teams that are considered as well functioning. "Our assignment is given by the minister who, based on the regulations for our different professions, has put together our team. . . . These guidelines prescribe, in a clear way, the competences needed for a well-functioning team."

The examples above, both positive and negative, illustrate quite traditional views in terms of depicting the leader as the one to blame or to acknowledge. At the same time, and in different ways, they illustrate what Bresnan describes as an ambiguity or ambivalence concerning leadership experiences.[34] As shown above, one kind of leadership encapsulates a diverse range of meanings and multiple frames of reference. Depending on what the co-worker and the leader expect and prefer and how they interpret the situation, experiences vary.

Moreover, a leader who ultimately has his or her co-workers' trust is allowed to fail, while the leader who is experienced as controlling or as someone who abandons employees in difficult situations does not have the space to fail. In other words, from the discursive perspective employed in this article, a leader who has the capacity to frame the processes at stake in a meaningful way, who masters leadership as a management-of-meaning, creates a climate of co-construction as well as co-responsibility together with co-workers.

In describing a well-functioning leadership, one student refers to her minister who makes use of a well-known metaphor in the leadership management field: "Our team meetings are regularly used for spiritual growth. The minister talks about the team and the parish as a green house, a place for individual as well as common growth where we get spiritual guidance and community."

In the material, there is a relative lack of so-called metaphors-in-use, that is, naturally occurring metaphors formulated by the students in their texts. The greenhouse metaphor is one of few. This might be explained by the students trying to avoid such painting with words when writing an academic text. From our theoretical perspective, it might also highlight that

34. Alvesson and Spicer, *Metaphors We Lead By.*

the discourse of church leadership is vague and hard to capture. In earlier research on church leadership, one discourse has been quite problem-oriented.[35] Another interesting aspect of church leadership discourses is the balance between a management-oriented focus and an emphasis on the minister as a spiritual leader. These positions are not necessarily incompatible but are a question of focus and interest.[36]

Professional Roles and Stable Roles

In this chapter we continuously intend to turn our eyes towards ambiguous aspects of leadership. Depending on leader and co-worker characteristics, a situation could be interpreted in different ways, revealing leadership as a result of co-constructive processes. One important issue is the distribution of professional roles. The issue of profession and the emphasis on developing professional tools in the organizational changes of the church raise questions of professional identity and professional boundaries. Since teamwork has become a frequent element in everyday life in the parish,[37] the risk for role conflicts is enhanced.

The team analyses processed in this article also reveal problems concerning responsibilities connected to different professional roles. In a parish, different teams are constructed whereby ministers, deacons, musicians, and youth educators are mixed in different constellations. These professions have different roles, different areas of responsibility and different expectations due to specific skills. At the same time, there are activities in the parish that could be carried either by, for example, the minister or the deacon, depending more on personality and suitability than on professional residence.

Therefore, it is natural that the descriptions of teamwork on different levels and in different constellations also include reflections on how these different professional roles might come, or actually have come, into conflict. Power relations and traditional hierarchies are also made visible in these analyses.

The first-level metaphor in analyzing experiences of the interplay between the professions within the parish is borrowed from the theatre (i.e., roles and role stability).[38] The various professional assignments are acted out in an arena where they interact according to partial pre-set patterns. The stability and correspondence of such patterns differ, as well as the individual perception of them. As in the former analysis, this role metaphor is also

---

35. Hansson, "Psychosocial Work"; Hansson and Andersen, "Vicars as Managers."
36. Huse, *Prosten.*
37. Grundy, *What's New.*
38. Goffman, *Presentation of Self.*

divided into two second-level metaphors: a stable, "strict-script" role and an unstable, improvising role. While the stable roles in a "strict-script" team are characterized by a predetermined role content, the unstable or improvising roles are characterized by flexibility and context dependency. Another kind of aspect of flexible roles is of a more subjective character, such as personality factors, managing interpersonal relationships and power relations.

Both these ways (stable or unstable) of allocating professional roles could be perceived in a positive or in a negative way. A stable role perspective is exemplified in the following quotation, in which stable professional roles are appreciated as something that brings clarity and structure to the team. "Flexibility in roles runs the risk of becoming vague, but in our team this is not the case, because the distribution of tasks is often obvious, relating to our specific professions."

On the other hand, another student described this orientation around a strict script for each professional role as a disincentive:

> For the time being, we are stuck in the traditional professional roles and activities. Does it have to be the minister who teaches the adult groups when you have a competent and trained educator? And why must the deacon lead the excursions if the youth assistant has the gifts in managing these kinds of activities?

To continue our theatre metaphor, one is here given the impression the director has decided a stable content for the different roles in advance, without framing or communicating his/her thoughts to the actors. In this quotation, the student asks for more flexibility, inferring those professional boundaries sometimes need to be crossed.

It is exactly this kind of flexibility that could be either experienced as desirable or uncomfortable, which becomes clear in the student essays. In the following quotation, the student expresses her appreciation of the effectiveness that flexibility offers in her team context: "The team has a flat structure. We mainly work together in creating an open environment with the individual person in focus. . . . In practice the roles are inevitably intertwined. I think that the assignment actually needs this."

Here, it seems that the team is very content oriented rather than being guided by preconceptions of traditional professional identities.

Even flexibility is a mixed blessing. A similar flexibility in handling professional roles is experienced as a source of conflicts by another student, where one of the main issues becomes unclear leadership: "Our experience shows how unclear structures and role definitions create conflicts and concern in the team. Unclear structures in the team also make it more difficult to identify who is the real leader."

Apart from the vagueness in roles and leadership that is expressed in the quotation, this kind of unclear structure also risks leaving room for informal claims to power. A way of handling the ambiguous character of organizational life is the proposing of frames for common understanding, sometimes described as the most important part of leadership.

The Importance of Framing

Looking closer at the content in these quotations on stable versus unstable roles, it is interesting to note the negative reflections on both variants express a need for a distinct and common frame of reference for the assignment and the approach to professional roles versus personal gifts and interests. The leader has a major responsibility for this so-called *framing*. According to Gail T. Fairhurst and Robert A. Sarr, framing is a quality of communication that causes others to accept one meaning over another. The main tools in framing are language, thought and forethought. As a leader's most powerful tool is language, it is reasonable to take a linguistic perspective and consider leadership as a language game.[39]

Framing provides the map for interpreting action; for example, one can frame a difficult situation as a problem or as an opportunity. "Framing is the way that leaders describe the present or future purpose of the group or organization. It is the contextual frame in which specific rhetorical techniques are employed."[40]

Framing is an important cornerstone in the successful management of meaning. Therefore, a lasting lack of framing also ironically (since the assignment ought to be helping other people creating meaning of their lives) risks creating disorientation and a lack of meaning, as the students' experiences illustrated in the above quotations indicate.

LEADERSHIP IN CHANGE

Although it can be difficult and challenging enough to run a group of people and cooperate under normal circumstances, things could get even more difficult to maneuver in times of organizational change. Some of the student texts describe congregations that were recently appointed a new leader or that were waiting for a new one. We designated these kinds of reflections "leadership in change," which works not as a first-level metaphor but which pinpoints aspects of time, position and contextual knowledge in processes of change. The kind of second-level metaphors emerging out of the

39. Fairhurst and Sarr, *Art of Framing*.
40. Tietze et al., *Understanding Organizations*, 136.

leadership-in-change concept is pictured as "stand-by" leadership and "out-of-phase" leadership. Finally, in one of the texts, there is also an example of what we describe as the kind of leadership focusing on the management of meaning, where the leader has managed to frame the process of change in a successful manner.

The idea of a "stand-by" leadership is probably not that unusual in organizations where the leader holds his/her position until retirement. In such cases, the leader's amount of energy, willingness to lead or just manage, and openness or reservation to change may provide special challenges. Even if the situation in the following case seems peaceful and not particularly challenging, "stand-by" leadership is exemplified in the following quotation:

> But now a status of peace and tranquility has appeared, in waiting for the minister's retirement in a couple of years.

The team is waiting for new, more eventful times to come. Nevertheless, this position of calm waiting also contains an aspect of expectation, where the co-worker anticipates a coming change. What seems to be static is, in fact, already in mental process and is, thus, affecting the situation. The importance of the relationship between mental and external changing processes must be added to individual and contextual aspects.

In this context, "out-of-phase" leadership is exemplified by a leader who, for different reasons, is not in phase with co-workers. The organization in this example has gone through a major change, and the new leader has to catch up with an organization that is already far ahead in the new arrangements.

> We have recently got a new minister. We experience that he still is out of phase, trying to catch up. A new organization was implemented before he got his position and we don't perceive him to be in charge of the organization yet.

There were also examples given of a leader who, despite being new in the position, manages to handle the organizational change in a meaningful way.

> Before, the work with the two groups of children and youths were like two isolated islands, with an impassable bridge in between which caused a vast amount of problems. Then the parish council decided to employ a minister with full responsibility for both groups, which was a very good decision resulting in a very engaged team creating wonderful venues for the parishioners.

In this parish, the parish council has sorted out a problem by employing a new minister. Here, both an organizational change and the employment of a new minister become a successful solution.

To summarize, some additional aspects of framing leadership in change, except for time, position and contextual knowledge in our study seem to be the following: sequence, process and ambiguity. Further, from a meta-perspective, the need for learning appears important in organizational change. Entering a new situation and organization requires replacing old knowledge and understanding in favor of an updated picture. An awareness of these kinds of re-learning processes could enhance analysis of conflicts and misunderstandings related to transitions from the well-known to the unknown.

Proposals for Improvement

As stated initially, the students were asked to articulate ideas for organizational and leadership improvement in comparison to the actual experience, focused on in our second research question. In these proposals, one finds many statements of a general nature.

Some of them concern better leadership structures and clear delegation, which is in line with what Hansson points out in her article on conflicts and socio-psychological problems within the Church of Sweden: "The more clarity the better organization."[41] Other general, but frequently recurring, themes concern the importance of a leader who is both present and involved in everyday matters. Straight communication is also highlighted as an important aspect together with a clear goal: "With a clear assignment and a clear goal, the roles in the team could be easily reallocated." A clear assignment gives space for a more creative allocating of tasks in the team. In many of the texts, there is a positive attitude towards interdisciplinary cooperation: "The more participation and cooperation between different professional categories the better."

We can make an overall comment on these ideas of an ideal leader: on the one hand, these proposals are *contextually dependent*, and, on the other hand, they are *quite general* and sometimes decontextualized in the texts. The character of suggested improvements tended to be influenced by the amount of prior working experience on the part of the ministers. Those with more experience tended to be more context-specific in their reasoning, while the less- experienced ministers rested upon more unspecific, even idealized, or "heroic" leadership descriptions of good leadership. Another aspect related to this reasoning is the generic character of the proposals and the sometimes clichéd way of denominating leadership phenomena. From our theoretical perspective, these kinds of general statements do not capture the idea of leadership as co-constructed, ambiguous, and discursive.

41. Hansson, "Psychosocial Work."

To capture these aspects of leadership, we must transcend these general descriptions and idealized leadership traits.

CONCLUSIONS: LANGUAGE, LEARNING AND MEANING

This study is a qualitative analysis of one hundred and twenty five student papers in which we have identified patterns concerning experiences of leadership and suggestions for improvement. Although every paper was written individually, they were also analyzed as a coherent entity by an inductive process. The primary advantage of this approach is the rich variety of experiences expressed in the ministers' own words, doubtless unlike the answers one would get through questionnaires or structured interviews. The main disadvantage is that the material in its richness could be perceived as unfocused.

Nevertheless, where earlier research sometimes tends to focus on normative concepts such as functional and less functional church leadership, we have tried to gain access to authentic experiences in a diverse range of contexts. Diversity contains complexity that unfolds the ambiguities specific to this organizational setting. The emphasis on strong heroic leaders in organizational change is challenged by our theoretical choice, with a post-heroic leadership underlining a dialectical relationship between leaders, followers and the context.

Instead of bracing against idealized leadership styles, in this chapter we have argued for the importance of leadership practices such as framing and management of meaning, which to be successful are deeply dependent on the leaders' contextual knowledge. A successful framing requires a leader who understands the contextual/organizational premises and who is able to articulate proposals for common interpretations accepted by co-workers—a manager of meaning.

Considering our results and conclusions, we would finally like to make some brief methodological reflections for further research in the theoretical field of post-heroic leadership. We believe there is a need for research that deepens the understanding and complexity in church leadership. A proper approach for such research could be field studies with observations combined with interviews. Through access to the everyday activities in an organization it would also be possible to study spontaneous metaphors (i.e., metaphors in use). To capture the processes of organizational change, longitudinal studies would be necessary. These methods would also enable the analysis of learning processes, de-learning and re-learning. A multidisciplinary approach could also be a creative way to handle the richness of perspectives as regards issues of organizational change.

In this study, we got insights from within a large number of congregations in the Church of Sweden. Our main focus was leadership and organizational change and the conditions to create meaning. In concluding the results, we want to highlight three important prerequisites for processes of change to be fruitful and functioning.

First, we want to highlight the central importance of *language* for understanding as well as exercising leadership—in general, and particularly in times of change. What is expressed is possessed, and we could hardly imagine an organizational change without linguistic explanations, negotiations and agreements. To handle change, the organization needs a frame for common understanding. One of the most influential aspects of leadership is the capability to offer proposals and meaningful frames accepted by a leader's followers as a common entrance for further negotiations and agreements. A sufficient level of joint understanding in an organization also serves as a basis for the creation of spontaneous metaphors-in-use. In this way, language can serve to connect leaders and co-workers in agreements, negotiations and discussions, the reason leadership can be considered as a language game. Therefore, a qualification of leadership in change is a heightened awareness of linguistic tools.

Second, the most crucial prerequisite for a change to be successfully implemented is the experience of *meaning*. The management of meaning is perhaps the hub of leading people towards a common goal (i.e., a shared understanding of different situations and a shared responsibility to emerge). In this study, we used the concept of framing to describe the art of making meaning in organizational change.[42] As noted above, in organizational change, meaning is created both as social and individual processes. Sustainable change rests upon framing both.

Finally, we point to the need for *learning* as a vital aspect of change, although this is only indirectly traced in our material. Some things one already knows and applies have to be replaced. The first step is a phase of de-learning (i.e., to make space for new insights, knowledge and behavior). Then re-learning begins to meet the new claims and possibilities emerging in the change process. The learning aspect of change applies to leaders and to co-workers. To understand what is happening in organizational change, knowledge of de-learning and re-learning processes is of vital concern. When not brought to consciousness, being in different phases or "out-of-phase" can cause tensions and misunderstandings.

---

42. Fairhurst, *Art of Framing.*

BIBLIOGRAPHY

Alvesson, Mats. "The Play of Metaphors." In *Postmodernism and Organisations*, edited by John Hassard and Martin Parker, 114–31. London: Sage, 1994.

Alvesson, Mats, and André Spicer. *Metaphors We Lead By: Understanding Leadership in the Real World*. New York: Routledge, 2011.

Barge, J. Kevin, and Gail T. Fairhurst. "Living Leadership: A Systemic Constructionist Approach." *Leadership* 4 (2008) 227–51.

Bresnen, Michael J. "All Things to All People? Perceptions, Attributions, and Constructions of Leadership." *Leadership Quarterly* 6.4 (1995) 495–513.

Fairhurst, Gail T. "Reframing the Art of Framing: Problems and Prospects for Leadership." *Leadership* 1.2 (2005) 165–85.

————. "Considering Context in Discursive Leadership Research." *Human Relations* 62 (2009) 1607–33.

Fairhurst, Gail T., and Robert A. Sarr. *The Art of Framing. Managing the Language of Leadership*. San Fransisco: Jossey-Bass, 1996.

Goffman, Erving. *The Presentation of Self in Everyday Life*. New York: Doubleday, 1959.

Grundy, Malcolm. *What's New in Church Leadership?* Norwich: Canterbury, 2007.

Hagman, Patrik. *Efter folkkyrkan. En teologi om kyrkan i det efterkristna samhället*. Skellefteå: Artos, 2013.

Hansson, Ann-Sophie. "The Psychosocial Work Environment in the Church of Sweden." *Non Profit Management and Leadership* 16.3 (2006) 329–43.

Hansson, Per, and Jon Aarum Andersen. "Vicars as Managers Revisited. A Comparative Study." *Nordic Journal of Religion and Society* 21.1 (2008) 91–111.

Hogler, Raymond, Michael A. Gross, Jackie L. Hartman, and Ann L. Cuncliffe. "Meaning in Organizational Communication. Why Metaphor is the Cake, not the Icing." *Management Communication Quarterly* 21 (2008) 393–412.

Huse, Morten. *Prosten. Ansvar, arbeidssituation og ledelse*. KIFO rapport nr. 10. Trondheim: Tapir akademisk forlag, 1998.

Lakoff, George, and Mark Johnson. *Metaphors We Live By*. Chicago: University of Chicago Press, 1980.

Modéus, Fredrik. *Mod att vara kyrka*. Stockholm: Verbum, 2005.

Morgan, Gareth. *Images of Organization*. Beverly Hills: Sage, 1986.

Oswick, Cliff, and David Grant. *Organizational Development: Metaphorical Explorations*. London: Pitman, 1996.

Pettersson, Per. *Kvalitet i livslånga relationer: Svenska kyrkan ur ett tjänsteteoretiskt och religionssociologiskt perspektiv*. Karlstad: Karlstad University Studies, 2000.

Smircich, Linda, and Gareth Morgan. "Leadership: The Management of Meaning." *Journal of Applied Behavioural Science* 18 (1982) 257–73.

Stålhammar, Bert. "Some Reflections Concerning the Vicar as a Leader of Three Organizations in One." In *Church Leadership*, edited by Per Hansson. Uppsala: Tro & Tanke, 1997.

Tietze, Susanne, Laurie Cohen, and Gill Musson. *Understanding Organizations through Language*. London: Sage, 2003.

Zuckerman, Phil. "Why are Danes and Swedes so Irreligious?" *Nordic Journal of Religion and Society* 22.1 (2009) 55–69.

6

Church Leadership and Congregational Change

Staff, Volunteers, and the Parish Council

KJETIL FRETHEIM

A number of initiatives to change the organization and working methods of the Church of Norway have been launched in recent years. The institutional ties between church and state have been weakened[1] and there are on-going reforms to strengthen church democracy,[2] to change the organizational structure of the church,[3] and to renew its liturgy[4] and religious education.[5] A key element in the efforts to strengthen the democratic governance of the church is the initiative to improve and increase the participation in elections to the parish council. The role and function of the parish council is also questioned and under consideration.[6]

In this chapter I present a single-case study from a parish in the Oslo area where I have observed parish council meetings and interviewed council

---

1. Plesner, *Skal vi skilles?*; Bergem and Aarflot, *Mot en selvstendig folkekirke*; Kultur- og kirkedepartementet, *Staten og Den norske kirke.*

2. Schmidt, "Demokrati"; Schmidt, "Evaluering av demokratireformen."

3. Askeland, *Reform av den lokale kirke.*

4. Aarflot, *Guds hus og himmelens port*; Kirkerådet, *Saman for Guds andlet.*

5. Hauglin, Lorentzen, and Mogstad, *Kunnskap*; Hegstad et al., *Når tro skal læres*; Kirkerådet, *Gud gir.*

6. Aadland, *Ledelse i menighet*; Hegstad, "Parish under Pressure"; Schmidt, *Menighetsrådsmedlemmer.*

members as part of a larger study on the relationship between staff and volunteers in congregations in the Church of Norway.[7] With a particular focus on the relationship between staff and elected members of the council I will describe the role of the parish council and how it functions. Analyzing how the division of roles and responsibilities between staff and elected council members is interpreted within the parish council, I will discuss how this impacts on the understanding of the council and its ability to function as a governing body.

The parish council is a statutory governing body of the Church of Norway. Still, standing for election to the parish council is voluntary. Although both real and perceived pressure makes people stand for election, they are not forced to do so. In this sense, the elected members can be seen as volunteers who commit to doing a task in a similar way to other church volunteers: in Sunday school, the youth choir, social service etc. Accordingly, the parish council can also be seen as an activity where staff and volunteers interact with each other. Below I will argue that there is a tension and ongoing negotiation between these different ways of understanding the role of the elected parish council members and that this impacts on how the parish council functions as a governing body in the church. I conclude that the ongoing negotiation of the relationship between staff and elected council members seems to inhibit the ability of the parish council to give a constructive contribution to church leadership and to address and handle congregational change.

THE PARISH COUNCIL

The Church of Norway is a majority Lutheran church with close ties to both the state and the people of Norway. Traditionally it has been a state church. Parish ministers have been (and some still remain) civil servants and bishops have been appointed by government minister of church affairs. In 2012 the church-state relationship was reconfigured and the Church of Norway is now defined as a national *folk*-church.[8] This loosened the formal ties between church and state, but the close relationship between the church on the one hand and state and society on the other persists. The Church of Norway continues to receive and rely on public funding and approximately three quarters of the Norwegian population are members of this church.

---

7. For a more comprehensive presentation of this case study, including more on its methodological and theoretical approaches, see Fretheim, *Ansatte og frivillige*.

8. *Grunnloven*, § 16.

The Church of Norway sees itself as called to proclaim the Gospel of Jesus Christ and to work for justice and compassion.[9] To fulfill this mission, the church has a dual structure. On the one hand it has an episcopal structure going from the local parish ministers to the twelve bishops. On the other hand, it has a democratic, synodic structure from the local parish council to the national General Synod of the church. In the following I will focus on the local parish level of this democratic, organizational structure. The parish council in the Church of Norway was established by law in 1920 and is a statutory governing body in the Church of Norway at parish level. At the municipality level these parish councils are represented in and by the *joint parish council*. While the joint parish council is responsible for administrative and financial issues, coordination between parish councils, as well as employer liability for most of the church staff members (though normally not ministers),[10] the parish council has an overall strategic responsibility for "the Christian life" of the congregation. As the life in and around the congregation changes, the parish council's role is to give direction, determine priorities and provide leadership to address and handle this kind of congregational change. The Church Act states that:

> The parish council will have their attention focused on all that can be done to awaken and nourish the Christian life of the parish, especially that the word of God may be preached, the sick and dying serviced by it, the baptized given religious education, children and youth gathered for worthy causes and bodily and spiritual distress remedied.[11]

Members of the Church of Norway (above eighteen) are eligible to the parish council and bound to accept election. If elected they remain in office for four years.[12] Accordingly, becoming a parish council member implies taking an office in a law-mandated governing body of the church.

A recent survey study on parish council members finds that there are more women (58 percent) than men (42 percent) in the parish councils, most parish council members are over forty-five years old and they are relatively well-educated, have a high level of professional and social participation and strong local roots.[13] In general the parish council members are characterized by relatively frequent participation in the Sunday church service and

9. Kirkemøtet, *Den norske.*

10. *Kirkeloven* § 14

11. *Kirkeloven* § 9, author's translation

12. *Kirkeloven* § 6.

13. Schmidt, *Menighetsrådsmedlemmer*, 9.

strong support for classic Christian beliefs and dogma.[14] In addition to these elected parish council members the parish minister or the bishop's representative attends the parish council meetings ex officio.[15] Often they are also supplemented by one administrative staff member. Accordingly, the council is a venue where staff and representatives of the church members meet and interact with the common task of governing the Christian life of the congregation.

CONFLICT AND AUTHORITY

A range of activities run by the Church of Norway would not be possible without the involvement and commitment of both staff and volunteers. In this sense the two groups seem largely dependent on each other and cooperation between them is often portrayed as a key to success in churches, in civil society organizations as well as in the public sector. Still, conflict between different groups of professionals and between staff and volunteers is a well-known phenomenon.[16] The partnership between staff and volunteers thus not only facilitates synergies and opportunities, but also implies a potential for conflict. The two groups might, for example, disagree on how they perceive the current challenges of the church as well as the aims and goal of church work.[17]

The potential for these kinds of conflicts can, of course, manifest itself also in the work of the parish council. As Harald Hegstad notes in his discussion of the increased professionalization of the Church of Norway, an

> . . . aspect of this development is that the staff and the staff meeting take over parts of the function of the parish council as the central forum for planning and consultation. The real guidelines are made by the staff, even if the parish council in several cases has to approve what the staff has decided.[18]

Max Weber's ideal types of authority can shed light on such conflicts and issues of legitimacy and authority.[19] In a church context *charismatic authority* makes itself known both as personal and institutionalized charisma, and given the long-standing status of the parish minister and the role of

14. Ibid., 32.

15. *Kirkeloven* § 6.

16. Heitmann, "Ansatte og frivillige i lykkelig forening?"; Askeland, "Menigheten som organisasjon og trossamfunn."

17. Grimstad, *Konflikter i kirken.*

18. Hegstad, *Kirke i forandring*, 128, my translation.

19. Weber and Parsons, *Theory of Social and Economic Organization.*

the Bible as being authoritative in doctrinal issues, there is an element of *traditional authority* too. As the Church of Norway is an established major- ity church and the parish council a part of its governing structure, Weber's third category, that of *legal authority*, plays an important role too. Three subcategories of this latter kind of authority seem particularly relevant in this context.[20] Staff members can be said to represent a *bureaucratic* kind of legal authority based on formal laws and rules. This applies, however, primarily to the administrative staff members, while the parish minister to a larger extent can make use of a *professional* authority based on her extensive academic training and exclusive privilege of baptizing and ministering Holy Communion. The parish council in general and the majority elected mem- bers of the council in particular, on the other hand, enjoy a *democratic* form of authority. Their role as lay parish council members is also legitimized theologically through the egalitarian doctrine of the universal priesthood. Accordingly, and despite the low turnout at church elections in relation to church membership, parish councils can be seen as an expression of a democratic governance of the church.

Having *democratic authority* is, however, not the same as having ac- tual influence on the issues discussed in the council or of relevance to local congregational life. It seems though that parish council members generally find that they have a say in matters important to them and/or the church. Approximately half of the parish council members say they do have an in- fluence in matters important to the church, while only 15 percent find that the parish council has little influence on important questions.[21] In general they do not, however, relate much to other levels in the synodic structure: the diocese council and the national general synod.[22] In terms of how they prioritize their time, parish councils tend to spend most of their time dis- cussing finances, management and personnel, followed by worship and strategy and planning.[23]

CONGREGATIONAL CHANGE

There is a long tradition of volunteering both in Norwegian society in gen- eral and in the Church of Norway in particular. The increased pressure on the welfare state and the (perceived) need to find more cost efficient ways of maintaining the welfare state have, however, made politicians, researchers

20. Hougsnæs, "Legitimitet som leder i kirken," drawing on Repstad, *Religiøst liv i det moderne Norge*. See also Carroll, *As One with Authority*.

21. Schmidt, *Menighetsrådsmedlemmer*, table 7.2.

22. Ibid., 51.

23. Ibid., 39.

and others look to civil society and voluntary organizations for further support and innovative solutions. When the Church of Norway today turns to
volunteers as a resource group to support and run activities in the congregations of the church, this therefore parallels suggestions to increase voluntary
engagement in for example the public health sector.[24] In both cases the turn
to voluntary organizations and volunteers can be seen as a response to a
financial challenge and a need to find new ways of delivering services.

The way the parish council deals with congregational change must be
understood in light of the specific history, conditions and role of the Church
of Norway in society. The history, organization and popular understanding
of the church define the particular position of the church and how it can deal
with change and new challenges. This is not to say, however, that the church
is isolated from wider society. On the contrary, and in line with insights
from neo-institutionalism,[25] it is important to recognize the contact with,
and lines of continuity between, different institutions and social spheres in
society. Institutions such as the Church of Norway are only relatively independent from their surroundings and when dealing with congregational
change these links can be highly important, not least in a situation when
different institutions are confronted with similar challenges.

Further, it can be assumed that different parish councils and their
members deal with such challenges in different ways. In his discussion of
leadership roles in the local church, sociologist Harald Askeland distinguishes between four kinds of roles.[26] This division reflects how church
leaders place themselves with regard to internal and external orientation
on the one hand, and stability and change/development on the other. The
administrator emphasizes stability and combines this with an internal orientation. His or her emphasis is on shaping and maintaining structures. The
producer shares the emphasis on stability, but has a stronger external orientation. Thus production and goal achievement become important aspects
of leadership. The *integrator*, however, shares the internal orientation, but is
more focused on change. His focus is therefore on integration and relationships. Finally, the *entrepreneur* has an external orientation and focuses on
change, making adaption to on-going change his primary focus.

---

24. See Helse- og omsorgsdepartementet, *Mestring*; Kultur- og kirkedepartemenet,
Frivillighet for alle; Helse- og omsorgsdepartementet, *NOU 2011:11, Innovasjon i
omsorg*.

25. Meyer and Rowan, *New Institutionalism in Education*.

26. Askeland, *Ledere og lederroller*; Grimstad and Askeland, "Den lokale kirkes
styrmenn og -kvinner."

CONTEXT AND METHODOLOGY

The main concern in the following is to explore the ways in which local congregational leadership is interpreted and performed within the changing context of the local congregation. As limited (recent) research has been done on this topic, the methodological approach adopted here is the qualitative, singular case study. This approach does not allow for statistical generalization, but rather offers an in-depth study of one single case and thus insights from the particular, so that a theoretical generalization is possible. If the findings in this study find resonance with the readers, practitioners' experiences or other researchers' studies and thus can be transferred from one particular context to other, this kind of generalization takes place. This can then become a platform for further research and for developing more comprehensive theories in the field.[27]

The parish council I have studied is situated in one of Oslo's outer suburbs. It holds regular Sunday services and the church building is frequently used for cultural events, confirmation classes, children's and youth ministry, diaconal work, etc. In the sense that it organizes activities for almost all age groups, the church appears resourceful and vibrant. The parish council has eight members, including one chairman and one deputy chairman. Both the parish minister and another (administrative) staff member attend these meetings, the latter functioning as the secretary for the council.

In the autumn of 2011 and the winter 2012 I observed three meetings of the council and interviewed four of the council members. The semi-structured interviews lasted on average one hour and I interviewed three men and one woman. Two of them were church staff members (the parish minister and secretary of the parish council) and the other two were elected parish council members (the chairman and one parish council member). The interviewed staff members have extensive experience in church work through being employed in the church, but also in terms of various forms of volunteer involvement in the church context. One of the elected parish council members has several years of experience from serving on the parish council, while the other has been part of the parish council for only a short period. These informants describe themselves and each other as relatively active church members. When asked how they experience working in and for the church, both staff and elected members emphasize their good experiences. One of the informants emphasizes the joy of experiencing fellowship in the church; another highlights the positive challenges of being a part of the parish council's work.

27. Flyvbjerg, "Five Misunderstandings."

Parish Council Meetings

The parish council meetings I observed lasted on average approximately three hours. Prior to the parish council meetings there was an amicable and cheerful tone between the council members and meetings began with a short devotion.

A number of practical issues related to the implementation of specific events, the hiring out of the church, the organization of volunteer work, etc. are discussed in the parish council meetings. Reflecting on the work of the parish council, one of the interviewees ranks work with personnel matters among the most important issues in this parish council. However, there seems to have been some discussion about the kind of issues the parish council should spend their time and effort discussing. One of the elected council members explains: "Some have wanted us to take a broader look and think more about strategy and the direction we should go." She has a feeling that the focus has been "pretty much on the daily running of things, not so much strategy work." The elected council members I interviewed tend to understand the task of being church council members primarily as taking part in the parish council meetings, while the staff secretary of the parish council explains that her main task is to prepare the documents for the parish council meeting. The parish minister, however, emphasizes her responsibility to have an overall perspective and to be visionary and strategic.

It varies how the parish council members engage in discussions at the parish meeting. Some talk a lot; others remain silent. Some issues stir debate, but controversy does not seem to be deep or fundamental. One of the informants puts it this way: "As a rule, we reach a unanimous decision. But there have been a few times when we have voted." In fact, other studies have shown how parish councils in general seem, to a large extent, to be driven by consensus. Forty-four percent of the parish council members report that they rarely or never vote on issues in the parish council meetings.[28]

In this particular parish council it seems that in most cases it is the staff secretary who gives the oral presentation of the issues to be discussed. Most often, it is the secretary and the elected chair (or deputy chair) that ensures progress in the meeting. Occasionally there is disagreement between some of the elected council members and the secretary and in some cases the parish minister suggests a compromise and helps to curb or stop the run-up to conflict. In fact, the key role of the staff is emphasized both in the parish council meetings and by the informants when interviewed individually. One of them says: "The staff runs the church. And they've got lots of ideas

---

28. Schmidt, *Menighetsrådsmedlemmer*, 44.

about what they want to achieve and stuff." Another says "the employees are important to the meeting because they have a lot of information." This indicates not only the key role of staff members in the life of the congregation, but also that there is space for bureaucratic and professional authority.

From the secretary's perspective a good parish meeting is a meeting where "people have read all the documents I have sent out and that they have made up their minds on the issues so that we can have few rounds of discussion . . . and pretty quickly arrive at a proposal for a conclusion and a decision." However, the secretary experiences "that not everyone is interested in reading all the documents." This makes her question the way the parish council works. She says: "Sometimes I think it is better that someone just decides rather than having four or five sit around a table and discuss it. Also we spend a lot of time and so we don't reach out to the grassroots the way we should. . . ." From her point of view the parish council has two main areas where they have a particular influence: finances and guidelines. This corresponds to some extent with the formal responsibilities of the parish council, but also with those of the joint parish council, as this is stated in the Church Act. This secretary understands, however, the voluntary parish council members' motivation primarily related to their desire to do something practical in the church: "I think that when someone enters a parish council, they think that they contribute with something practical in the church." In this way she seems to attribute to the elected members a motivation that primarily relates to practical tasks, as opposed to more strategic and overarching tasks. Put differently, the role of the elected council is seen to be on par with other volunteers in the church, rather than as elected representatives of the church members with a governing function.

NEGOTIATING TASKS AND RESPONSIBILITIES

A major challenge for this parish council is finding financial resources to cover current expenses. One issue that was discussed at the parish council and which exemplifies this issue of financial (and human) resources is the hiring out of the church. This is an important source of income for the church, but requires follow-up, for example in the form of a health and safety officer being present when the church is hired out. Previously the staff took care of this, but recently volunteers have taken over. Now, however, this is again up for discussion and the question is whether there are enough volunteers for this task. A sense of reluctance among the volunteers in the church to do this is articulated in the meeting. At the same time it is the parish council's responsibility to hire out the church and organize health and safety checks. The discussion also indicates that a list of volunteers who can assume this task exists, but there is some uncertainty regarding how this list is managed. It seems unclear who has the primary responsibility for the administration and organization of church hire. Can it again become a staff responsibility?

A similar challenge appears when a church service in the near future is discussed. A worship team for this particular Sunday has not been set up and this now needs doing. The staff secretary of the parish council puts it this way: "Is it our task in the staff to set up these lists, or is it the parish council? Or the minister?" After a long discussion the parish minister finally asks if the elected council members will take on the tasks associated with this specific worship service and, in the end, they agree. Similarly, in connection with a church concert the questions of who will be involved in preparing for and cleaning up after the concert become a matter for the parish council. In this case too, the elected members of the parish council end up taking on these tasks. In this way, the parish council seems to accept that the work of the council leans towards implementation rather than strategy and organizational governance.

Another issue concerns an event for young people in the church. Again, it is the expectation of staff members that volunteers or elected parish council members take on practical tasks. The options initially outlined are either to get volunteers to cook or to buy food from a catering company. The discussion moves in the direction of the latter option. But then one of the staff members emphasizes the social aspects of the event: "You forget something important: Now, adults can come and be where the young people are. I really think about the diaconal dimension here." Thus, the challenge is sent back to the elected council members again. Towards the end of the discussion, however, one of the employees said: "We take this at the staff meeting . . . and we will ask volunteers." Accordingly, this case seems to suggest that various tasks and responsibilities can be taken care of by volunteers, while it is clear that the elected parish council members are not willing to do this. The responsibility for these tasks therefore remains with the staff. In this case, the elected council members thus seem to insist that their role is one of governance, in contrast to one of volunteering. Similar discussions take place regarding the church's website. Previously, a volunteer has been the web-editor for the church. More recently this has been taken care of by a staff member. As the staff has "more than enough to do," can this again be maintained by a volunteer? Again, the administration asks for assistance, but in this case the parish council shows limited willingness to make it a voluntary task and sends the issue back to the administration.

To sum up, the division of tasks and responsibilities between staff and elected members seems to be an unresolved question in this parish council.

In effect this challenges the democratic authority of the council. On several occasions the expectation that the elected members of the parish council must or should become more involved and take on more voluntary tasks and responsibilities is articulated. Questions like "Who asks the volunteers?" and "Does anyone know someone who can . . ." are repeated in the meeting. It seems they plan for more than staff resources permit and thus the church activities rely on the efforts of both staff and volunteers. Largely the elected council members seem to be regarded as resources to solve relatively simple practical tasks such as making phone calls, cooking food or the like.

THE VERGER AND THE CHURCH STRUCTURE

One of the questions that the parish council members spent a lot of time discussing concerns the role of the verger or, more precisely, the lack of a verger. In the Church of Norway this is a paid position with a longstanding tradition. The verger was traditionally responsible for the practical organization of the service. He or she would make sure that the church is open for worship and that the service is conducted smoothly and in an orderly fashion. The parish council I visited is faced, however, with the fact that this position has been reduced by the joint parish council. The congregation can no longer assume that a paid verger will perform these tasks at all the services in the church. This is, in other words, an example of external pressure or expectations put on the congregation that represent a task and challenge to the parish council.

The consequences of this change are described as extensive and severe. The secretary stresses that the premises will be cleaned less frequently: "There is no-one to clean tables and chairs anymore. Now the volunteers have to take more responsibility for everything, to keep order here. . . . If there has been a church choir rehearsal, you must take away the equipment you use yourself." The question at hand is how the parish council should respond to this changed situation: Who shall do these tasks? One of the elected council members suggests splitting up the task of the verger into many subtasks. This becomes the consensus of the meeting, and some of the council members take on specific tasks themselves as voluntary vergers.

The lack of a verger has further implications, for example in relation to who it is that makes sure there are enough wafers and altar wine for communion. In the discussion about alternative ways to take care of these tasks, one of the elected council members highlights that "this is the duty of the joint parish council." Also others in the parish council argue that the parish council risks "taking on the tasks of the joint parish council." In fact, such examples of disagreement and conflict between the parish council and the joint parish council were articulated on several occasions Many of the parish council members find the organization of the Church of Norway to be an exceedingly "complex structure." The ecclesial structure seems to create a frustration over the lack of power and authority of the parish council in contrast to that of the joint parish council, implicitly highlighting a congregationalist dimension of the Church of Norway. One of the informants said: "I think the parish council is the highest authority in the church, in a way. But as a rule we have no final word in minister appointments and other appointments."

EXPECTING PROFESSIONALISM

Disagreements related to the ecclesiastical governance structure and parish council's position, role and responsibilities are also related to other frustrations concerning the relationships between staff and elected members in the parish council. Some of the council members call for a greater degree of professionalism. When asked about the frustrations associated with the work of the parish council, one of the interviewees said:

> It is about the governance structure. There are some matters that are trivial matters that end up there [in the parish council]. Because the environment is uncertain . . . concerning the expertise and authority . . . in particular financial issues. . . . Even the smallest amounts, will those staff . . . think it is okay to make a decision on the parish council, but I think it should be much clearer so that when one has passed a budget, they have to have the different responsibilities of a budget to deal with and to operate within it. In that way, we would not have to spend time on that again.

Similarly, another of the elected members said:

> When the church staff is supposed to be the secretary of the parish council, I would have really expected him . . . if there are questions about what kind of decisions you made earlier, that he has the energy or resources enough to find out what we have adopted in the past. We sit there time and time again and make a new decision, and we do not know properly what has been decided before. That's not good.

The perceived problem is that the framework for the parish council's work, including the planning and implementation of parish council meetings, does not match this elected member's expectations. She says: "It is normal that the church staff follows up the council's decisions. It is the administrative staff who records and keeps the overview. But this has not worked well." The parish council is thus not only an arena where expectations of the staff are aired, but also those of the elected members.

In a discussion on a staffing issue, this criticism becomes tangible. Some of the elected members complain that the documents they have been provided with do not offer enough information. Additional documents are requested and some ask to see the relevant agreements and other supporting documents. It seems that some of the parish council members want to be involved and take responsibility for the decisions they make and it is clear that the council's elected members possess considerable competence and experience that is relevant to their role as parish council members. In contrast to the notion that the elected members are primarily interested in practical tasks, they use their professional expertise to highlight the issues, as well as to challenge the bureaucratic authority of the staff.

The Parish Council and Church Leadership

In contrast to staff members who are paid for their work, elected council members and church volunteers are not. In other words, financial compensation is a key criterion for this distinction.[29] Another, though related, distinction is between *amateur* and *professional*.[30] The *amateur* is a person without special skills, often with tasks that do not require much experience, expertise or education. The professional, however, has a high degree of knowledge and skills, through his or her formal and specialized education.[31] This distinction is therefore not based on compensation, but competence.

Traditionally these distinctions between staff and volunteers, as well as between professionals and amateurs, have been relatively clear cut. Professionals have been understood in contrast to idealistically motivated volunteers, and while the term *amateur* can have somewhat negative connotations, being *professional* often designates quality and responsibility. The observations and interview statements from this case study indicate, however, that the understanding of roles and responsibilities of staff and elected parish council members are not a given, but something which is negotiated through their discussions and interaction. In particular, there seems to be an ongoing negotiation of the role of these elected members, from viewing them as members of a statutory governing board to volunteers

29. Pearce, *Volunteers*; For studies on volunteering in the Norwegian context, see Wollebæk, Selle, and Lorentzen, *Frivillig innsats*; Wollebæk, Selle, and Strømsnes, *Endringsprosesser i norsk frivillighet*.

30. Taylor, "Amateurs."

31. Burrage and Torstendahl, *Professions in Theory and History*.

just like other volunteers performing various church activities. In fact, this unresolved negotiation seems to blur the very distinctions between staff, volunteers and the parish council.

The division of roles and responsibilities is challenged, negotiated and changed in the interaction between staff and the elected council members. Some of the latter come across as highly competent, and there are tasks taken care of by paid staff members that are transformed into responsibilities for volunteers. The cooperation between staff and council members is, accordingly, quite multifaceted: both harmonious and with elements of tension and conflict. Staff members are expected by elected members to be professionals, but also to engage in recruiting and involving volunteers. Elected members are expected by staff members both to contribute with strategic considerations and to use their professional qualifications in their role as parish council members, as well as to take on practical responsibilities. Consequently, the division of roles and responsibilities between staff and elected members is both complementary and overlapping.

The parish council I have observed seems to deal with this unresolved relationship between its paid and unpaid members on an ad hoc basis, making the issue of clarifying this relationship a recurring issue in the council. There seems to be no formal or given guidelines for dealing with these issues. At the same time, these on-going negotiations implicitly recognize the positive contribution of both groups in the life of local congregational life in the Church of Norway. Within the parish council neither staff nor elected members use their respective positions or authority to challenge the legitimacy of the other group or to claim primary authority. On the contrary, both groups seem to recognize the competence, role and responsibility of the other, and both groups contribute with insights and experiences from their respective backgrounds in their on-going discussions.

Further, the parish council repeatedly deals with issues related to ongoing changes in and around the congregation. Some of these changes have a financial character. As there are no longer funds to pay the verger, the parish council needs to find alternative ways of having the tasks of the verger taken care of. This implies restructuring the organization of the congregation and renegotiating the relationship between staff and volunteers. The challenge of recruiting volunteers and involving them in a constructive and efficient manner in the running of church activities, is similarly a recurring issue that reflects financial changes, but also a changing attitude to voluntary work in (and around) the congregation.

It seems that some of the challenges related to the unclear relationship between staff and elected council members are associated with a weak organization of the voluntary work in the church. In part, the organization of voluntary work seems to be considered a voluntary task or the responsibility of the elected parish council members; partly it seems to lie with the staff. In some cases, it seems it is the administrative employees who are in charge of making sure that "things work," even when the volunteers do not follow up the tasks they have assumed. In the end responsibility therefore seems primarily to be ascribed to staff members, although this is not necessarily made explicit.

Changes in the organizational structure of the church have transferred governing functions from the parish council at the congregational level to the joint parish council at the municipality level. This has weakened the parish council of its governing function and seems to contribute to these unresolved negotiations on the role of the elected parish council member and their relationship to the staff members. Largely, the elected parish council members seem to be seen more as volunteers than members of a governing board. The parish council largely seems to be perceived as a possible resource for solving issues, such as making lists of participants, calling volunteers, baking cakes, etc. The *democratic authority* of the parish council is in effect reduced from an authority to govern to an authority to implement. In this way the parish council also seems to become geared more towards stability than change, and more towards an internal orientation rather than an external orientation. As a whole, the parish council thus seems primarily to adopt the role and functioning of an *administrator*.

CONCLUSION

The understanding of the parish council as a governing body to provide strategic leadership for the development of the local church is articulated formally in the Church Act, but also in the parish council meetings and in individual interviews with parish council members. In this study, however, this understanding is challenged and limited by the unclear relationship between staff and elected council members, as well as recurring expectations relating to practical tasks, the implementation of decisions already made and to relieving staff members of their work load. The elected members of the parish council—officials in a law-mandated council—thus experience their role and responsibilities as sliding in the direction of those of volunteers responsible for various practical tasks.

In this way, the disputed relationship between staff and volunteers and the tendency among both staff and elected council members to regard the parish council as an implementing body rather than a strategic governing body, seems to inhibit the ability of the parish council to give a constructive contribution to church leadership and to address and handle congregational change. When the parish council focuses primarily on administrative and practical tasks, this is time consuming and diverts attention away from strategic considerations. This is contrary to the role of the parish council as described in the Church Act and the guidelines for parish council members. The findings from this case study therefore suggest not only a need for more explorative and theoretical research in the field of local church leadership, but also a need to reconsider the role and functioning of the parish councils in the Church of Norway.

BIBLIOGRAPHY

Aadland, Einar. *Ledelse i menighet: Rapport fra et forsøks- og utviklingsprosjekt.* Oslo: Diavett, 1997.

Aarflot, Andreas. *Guds hus og himmelens port: På vei til nye gudstjenesteformer.* Oslo: A. Aarflot, 2010.

Askeland, Harald. *Ledere og lederroller: Om ledelse og lederroller i den lokale kirke.* Oslo: Stiftelsen kirkeforskning, 1998.

———. "Menigheten som organisasjon og trossamfunn. Organisasjonsteoretiske grunnperspektiver og forståelsen av menighet i endring." In *Menighetsutvikling i folkekirken. Erfaringer og muligheter,* edited by Erling Birkedal, Harald Hegstad, and Turid Skorpe Lannem, 115–36. Oslo: IKO-forlaget, 2012

———. *Reform av den lokale kirke: Kontekst, prosess, utfall.* Oslo: Stiftelsen Kirkeforskning, 2000.

Bergem, John Egil, and Andreas Aarflot. *Mot en selvstendig folkekirke.* Bergen: Vigmostad & Bjørke, 2007.

Burrage, Michael, and Rolf Torstendahl. *Professions in Theory and History. Rethinking the Study of the Professions.* London: Sage, 1990.

Carroll, Jackson W. *As One with Authority: Reflective Leadership in Ministry.* Louisville: Westminster Knox, 1991.

Flyvbjerg, Bent. "Five Misunderstandings About Case-Study Research." *Qualitative Inquiry* 12.2 (2006) 219–45.

Fretheim, Kjetil. *Ansatte og frivillige. Endringer i Den norske kirke.* Oslo: Prismet Bok, 2014.

Grimstad, Frank. *Konflikter i kirken: En artikkelsamling om forståelse, håndtering og forebygging av konflikter.* KA-Perspektiv. Oslo: Kirkelig arbeidsgiver- og interesseorganisasjon, 2002.

Grimstad, Frank, and Harald Askeland. "Den lokale kirkes styrmenn og -kvinner— Sitter de ved roret?" In *Kirken, lekfolket og presteskapet,* edited by Marit Halvorsen Hougsnæs, 40–58. Oslo: Kirkens Arbeidsgiverorganisasjon, 1999.

Grunnloven [The Constitution]. *Kongeriket Norges Grunnlov, gitt i riksforsamlingen på Eidsvoll den 17. mai 1814.* 1814 (and later amendments).

Hauglin, Otto, Håkon Lorentzen, and Sverre Dag Mogstad. *Kunnskap, Opplevelse og tilhørighet: Evaluering av forsøksfasen i Den norske kirkes trosopplæringsreform.* Bergen: Fagbokforlaget, 2008.

Hegstad, Harald. *Kirke i forandring: Fellesskap, tilhørighet og mangfold i Den norske kirke.* Oslo: Luther, 1999.

———. "The Parish under Pressure: New Ways of Organizing the Local Church in the Church of Norway." In *The Second International Conference on Church Leadership*, 47–53. Uppsala: Uppsala University, Faculty of Theology, 2005.

Hegstad, Harald, Olaf Aagedal, and Anne Schanche Selbekk. *Når tro skal læres: Sju fortellinger om lokal trosopplæring*. Trondheim: Tapir akademisk forlag, 2008.

Heitmann, Jan H. "Ansatte og frivillige i lykkelig forening?" In *Sammen i forandring. Refleksjoner om menighetsutvikling i folkekirken*, edited by Eling Birkedal, Harald Hegstad, and Turid Skorpe Lannem, 185–202. Oslo: IKO-forlaget, 2012.

Helse- og omsorgsdepartementet [Ministry of Health and Care Services]. *NOU 2011:11 Innovasjon i omsorg*. Norges Offentlige Utredninger. NOU 2011:11. Oslo: Helse- og omsorgsdepartementet, 2011.

———. *Mestring, muligheter og mening: Framtidas omsorgsutfordringer*. Nr. 25 (2005–2006), Oslo: Helse- og omsorgsdepartementet, 2006.

Hougsnæs, Marit Halvorsen. "Legitimitet som leder i kirken." In *Ledelse i kirken*, edited by Harald Askeland, Frank Grimstad, Marit Halvorsen Hougsnæs, and Gunvor Lande, 77–92. Oslo: Kirkens Arbeidsgiverorganisasjon, 2003.

Kirkeloven [Church Act]. *Lov 7. juni 1996 nr. 31 om Den norske kirke*. 1996.

Kirkemøtet [Church of Norway General Synod]. *Den norske kirkes identitet og oppdrag: Uttalelse fra kirkemøtet 2004*. Oslo: Den norske kirke, Kirkerådet, 2004.

Kirkerådet [Church of Norway National Council]. *Gud gir—vi deler. Plan for trosopplæring*. Oslo: Kirkerådet, 2010.

———. *Saman for Guds andlet: Planlegging av det lokale gudstenestelivet*. Stavanger: Eide forlag, 2011.

Kultur- og kirkedepartementet [Ministry of Culture and Church Affairs]. *Frivillighet for alle*. Oslo: Kultur- og kirkedepartementet, 2007.

———. *Staten og Den norske kirke*. Nr. 17 (2007–2008), Oslo: Regjeringen, 2008.

Meyer, Heinz-Dieter, and Brian Rowan. *The New Institutionalism in Education*. Albany: State University of New York Press, 2006.

Pearce, Jone L. *Volunteers*. London: Routledge, 1993.

Plesner, Ingvill Thorson. *Skal vi skilles?* Oslo: Forlaget, 2006.

Repstad, Pål. *Religiøst liv i det moderne Norge*. Kristiansand: Høyskoleforlaget, 2000.

Schmidt, Ulla. "Demokrati og valgordninger i Den norske kirke." In *Mellom prinsipper og pragmatisme*, edited by Hans Stifoss-Hanssen and Inger Furseth, 31–60. Trondheim: Tapir akademisk forlag, 2008.

———. "Evaluering av demokratireformen i Den norske kirke. Sluttrapport." Oslo: Stiftelsen Kirkeforskning, 2011b.

———. *Menighetsrådsmedlemmer og menighetsråd i Den norske kirke*. Notat. Oslo: Stiftelsen Kirkeforskning, 2011a.

Taylor, Brian. "Amateurs, Professionals and the Knowledge or Archeology." *The British Journal of Sociology* 46.3 (1995) 499–508.

Weber, Max, and Talcott Parsons. *The Theory of Social and Economic Organization*. New York: Free Press, 1964.

Wollebæk, Dag, Per Selle, and Håkon Lorentzen. *Frivillig innsats*. Bergen: Fagbokforlaget, 2000.

Wollebæk, Dag, Per Selle, and Kristin Strømsnes. *Endringsprosesser i norsk frivillighet: En kunnskapsoversikt*. Rapport. Bergen: Senter for forskning på sivilsamfunn og frivillig sektor, 2008.

7

Reforming the Pastoral Managerial Structure
in Church of Norway

Exploring Whether and How the Managerial Role
of the Dean Has Been Strengthened

HARALD ASKELAND

Management and leadership have become an increasingly debated issue in
the Church of Norway over the past decade. First, there has been a growing awareness that management is an important issue if the church is to
develop its organization, its staff and its services. Secondly, when the Storting ("parliament") passed a new law on The Church of Norway in 1996,
they also established new lay managerial positions to serve the governing
bodies of the congregations. This sparked a new interest in management
in general, but also more particularly, in the role of clerical management.
Therefore, marked changes in the management structure and the organizing
of the clerical services in the Church of Norway have occurred during the
past decade. Clergy has traditionally been appointed to serve in a pastoral
service district consisting of one or several parishes, and has enjoyed an autonomous position regarding work and ministerial duties. The daily work of
each minister was traditionally regulated by the ordination liturgy, a common instruction and those services decreed by the bishop. This situation has
changed lately through the establishment of the deanery as a service district
and a new and more distinct management role for the dean. This transformation was organized as a reform of the clerical services. The Ministry of

Culture and Church Affairs initiated the reform and the bishops and the diocesan councils implemented it.

The purpose of this chapter is firstly to investigate the development of the dean's managerial role, and secondly how deans themselves and clergy perceive such a strengthened role. The chapter is based on material from a national evaluation of the reform conducted by a research team from Diakonhjemmet University College and KIFO/Institute for Church, Religion, and Worldview Research in Oslo.[1]

The main objectives of this reform has been to create better working conditions for clergy, to decrease rule-governing and enhance management by objectives and appraisal management of the clerical service in the Church of Norway. The second important objective was to establish a more active management of the clerical services. The research questions of this chapter are:

- How has the reform affected the organizing and management of pastoral services in the Church of Norway?

- To what extent has the role of the dean been strengthened and how might the managerial profile of deans be interpreted within a management theory framework?

UNDERSTANDING THE BACKGROUND OF THE REFORM

Initiative, Focus and Facilitation

The re-organization of clerical services was launched on July 1, 2004, and had as its primary objective to provide better working conditions for the individual minister. The basic prerequisites for achieving such an objective were deemed to be the establishment of larger service districts than the parish, and that a new and more active management of the clergy needed to be developed and enhanced. Based on these assumptions, the deanery was chosen as a new and common service district for clergy and the dean was entrusted to lead the clergy in the deanery. This, on one hand created a stronger managerial role for the dean, and on the other hand altered the traditional autonomy of parish ministers and the leading role of the senior minister of the parish district. One last important objective has been to contribute to a better relationship between the clergy and the local elected councils of the congregations. Such councils are elected in each parish and are established on two levels, each parish has a parish council and if several exist in a municipality a joint council of parishes is established. The law has also established a function of general manager, labeled churchwarden,

1. Stifoss-Hanssen et al., *Ny organisering av prestetjenesten.*

for the council(s) at the municipality level. These councils have a broad mandate and responsibility for the congregation and its spiritual life. The local congregational life and work (including expenses for church buildings, cemeteries and wage for local employees) are funded by statutory grants from the municipalities. The joint council of parishes employs a wide range of local congregational staff, while the clergy are appointed and employed by the diocesan council.

The reform has evolved over time and had been prepared by previous experimental change processes. Already in the 1990s changes were made in the dean's managerial role, which was facilitated by a revision of the service instruction for deans. Consequently, several projects had been conducted in which different models of organizing the clerical services were tested. Such projects included amassing experience with the deanery as a service district.

Already in the instructional paper for 2000 from the ministry to the diocesan councils, the allotment letter contained a prelude to the re-organization of the clerical services:

> The Ministry will also, in the annual governing dialogue for 2000, highlight the challenges concerning the organization and management of the clergy, . . . and a clarification of tasks between parish councils and the joint councils of parishes, including the minister's role in relation to these elected bodies.

It was further emphasized that ecclesial reforms (such as the new Church Act of 1996) were important for the clergy.[2] Alongside societal changes, legal reform of the organizing of parishes necessitated a need to rethink the organizational framework for the management of clerical services. The clergy was, on the one hand, expected to interact and cooperate with the elected councils in realizing the objectives set for the church and for congregational services. On the other hand, by being mandated and employed by state agencies, clerical services constituted an independent organizational part of the church and congregational services. The Ministry considered that further development in the Church of Norway should include focusing on the clerical services and a more objective-oriented management of this branch of service. The bishops were therefore requested, in partnership with the diocesan council, to:

> Establish experimental projects with alternative forms of organization and management of the clergy. In this context, it is of particular importance to gather experiences of alternative options when it comes to the size of clerical service districts. The deans will be key actors in setting up and implementing

2. *Kirkeloven.*

such projects. These projects should aim at establishing a clerical team in the order of five to ten ministers, while the basic
assumption that every parish should have its minister should
be safeguarded. Among the project objectives, the facilitation of
more orderly conditions in terms of working hours, and better
organization of various forms of leave and holidays should also
be included. *The experimental projects should also investigate
how specialized expertise can be leveraged across parish boundaries, and aim for a better interaction between parish* ministers and
specialized ministers who are working within the team's area of
responsibility.

In 2004, the service instructions for deans and clergy were revised. This
was reflected in the allotment letter from the Ministry, by increasing resources relating to the facilitating of the new responsibilities of the deans
and for the process of implementing the new service instruction for deans.
These resources were increased in 2005 and 2006. During the years of
implementation, the Ministry added and differentiated new objectives that
were incorporated into the reform. It was emphasized that the management
of the clergy should be based on the dual line of responsibilities, between
the clerical and the conciliar structure, and on interaction and cooperation
between clergy and other groups of church employees. Such a focus placed
special demands on management and the Ministry therefore emphasized
the development of the leading role of the deans in securing such coopera-
tive efforts among the clergy:

> Among other things, the necessity of cooperation, collaboration
> and coordination with the parish council and joint council of
> parishes is underlined in the service instructions. . . . It will also
> be natural to review the organizations of clerical services in each
> deanery. Important references for the impending change and fu-
> ture direction are the objectives and strategies that are adopted
> for the church and the different dioceses, which are binding for
> the clergy and the management of the clerical service.

The focus on changes in the geographical division of the clerical service
is amplified in the governing documents for 2005. The governing bodies
of the dioceses were expected to conduct a review of parochial units and
their division, aimed at the adaptations related to the provisions of the new
service instructions. This year it was also clearly addressed that the ongoing process actually implied reorganization. The main argument shifted
towards the necessity of strengthened management of the clerical service
involving stress put on division of labor and increased collaboration among

clergy. The reorganization was designed to allow for greater individual and on-site customization of the service.

Previous Research

The early changes in the service instructions for deans have been evaluated through an extensive quantitative survey conducted by KIFO, commissioned by the Ministry of Culture and Church Affairs.[3] The service instruction that had been introduced, was mainly considered expedient and with no reason for making drastic changes. It seemed to have been largely known, implemented and adhered to. The role of the dean appeared as intended: as an adjunct for the bishop. Most of these tasks replaced earlier clerical duties of the deans, and the leading and adjunct responsibilities took a larger part of their working hours. The working situation gave deans a long week with many working hours, clearly longer than parish ministers and chaplains. The management culture of the church featured many keywords, such as personal care and closeness; while many ministers expressed that, for them, the personal care was lacking. As a whole, the deans gave the general impression that they thrived in their positions, despite conflicting roles, limited resources and long working hours. Huse found that, as leaders, deans profiled their role differently, but they were also assessed differently by bishops and parish ministers. While the bishops emphasized the role of caregiver and supervisor, the parish ministers reported an increase in the administrative tasks of the dean, and the deans themselves emphasized the role of strategist. Based on his research findings, Huse developed a typology of managerial roles for deans:

- The *strategists* emphasized thinking strategy and gave high esteem to be supervisor on behalf of the bishop and to represent and participate in councils and committees, while they had less interest in performing ordinary clerical functions.

- The *independent* did not have any high profile in any specific area, but tended to have a low profile with respect to supervising tasks.

- The *clerical-deans* saw themselves primarily as ministers, while they were low-profiled on strategy, oversight and the encouragement of achievement.

- The *dutiful* had a high average rating in most areas: Being a minister, attending care, supervision, management and representation.[4]

---

3. Huse, *Prosten.*
4. Ibid., 141.

This typology appears to be a useful, albeit incomplete, categorization of deans as leaders. In creating a clearer and stronger managerial position for them, Huse's analysis indicated that too many deans profiled themselves in ways that contributed little to performing a dynamic managerial role. After Huse's evaluation, several studies have continued to investigate the development of the leading role of the dean.

The re-organization of service districts was evaluated through data from ten experimental projects, and several key insights were reported.[5]

- The experimental trial projects had been instructive, but also painful. However, nobody wanted to return to the previous situation.

- In most places the projects had created a climate of change.

- No apparent contradiction was perceived between abandoning the old service districts of ministers and retaining the minister's primary responsibility for a parish.

- The deanery would often be the most appropriate place for clerical work with many perceived advantages in having clergy employed and situated there.

- The strengthened position of the dean was considered positive. However, a stronger focus on the dean's managerial role was necessary.

- The establishment of a unitary organization for the clergy and the conciliar structure, including a unitary employer line for all church employees, was strongly recommended.

- Long distances hampered collaboration between ministers in the deanery.

AN INTEGRATED MODEL OF THE MANAGERIAL ROLE

Management research is a diverse field of study that consists of several traditions. In this chapter, I build on and extend research traditions, which have focused on empirically based studies of the work of leaders (or managers). The early research emphasized two general and broad categories of managerial behavior which have been labeled task-oriented or initiating structure, and relations-oriented or consideration.[6] These categories were documented as distinct dimensions of managerial work in the early Ohio State Leadership Studies[7] and the Michigan Studies.[8]

5 Huse and Hansen, "Nyorganisering i prestetjenesten."

6. Yukl et al., "Hierarchical Taxonomy," 15; Vie, "Shadowing Managers," 11.

7. Fleishman, "Description of Supervisory Behavior."

8. Likert, *New Patterns*.

While many scholars have focused on crucial singular management factors, others claim that management cannot be viewed as one singular factor: "Managing is not one of these things but all of them: it is controlling and doing and dealing and thinking and leading and deciding and more, not added up but blended together."[9] Such complexity points towards management being a contextually based practice, which might vary from organization to organization. In addition, managers execute tasks, which are not originally managerial but precisely because they are managers, their involvement is required in certain situations. A manager's status, contacts and knowledge are particularly useful in special circumstances.[10] Others have criticized the research for being too occupied with the variations and should rather seek to reveal the common patterns existing across studies enhancing theorizing.[11] This research interest has led to mostly descriptive analyses, and it has been argued that there is a need to turn to explaining the content of and contribution of management in and for organizations.[12] Several models have aimed at bridging the gap between the practice of management and the role or functions managers play in organizations. The models emerging from these efforts show considerable overlap, but also distinct differences. In developing models to capture the complexities of management, important dimensions seem to be common to different approaches. One such important, common, dimension is the relationship between an internal and an external orientation.[13] Another key dimension, utilized in several models, is related to the task or relationship orientation. This dimension is particularly evident in the work of Yukl, but also seems to underlie the recent model development of Mintzberg.

A way of combining these dimensions, relating closer to the classic dimensions of task- and relations-orientation has been applied in recent studies of relevant organizations within the voluntary sector. Schmid argues for a model based on these dimensions in his analysis of human and community service organizations.[14] In a recent work, Angell also argues that earlier models do not satisfactorily include faith-based welfare organizations. His main argument is that faith-based welfare organizations not only face demands on efficiency, but also equally meet demands of legitimacy. Their supplementary role, being faith-based in a predominantly public field,

9. Mintzberg, *Managing*, 44.

10. Ibid., 47.

11. Hales, "What Do Managers Do?"

12. Hales, "Why Do Managers Do What They Do?"; Martinko and Gardner, "Beyond Structured Observation."

13. Mintzberg, *Managing*; Hart and Quinn, "Roles Executives Play."

14. Schmid, "Organizational Change."

cannot be taken for granted.[15] While change and stability might be a better choice in studies of market-based organizations, where organizations and their functioning and long-term survival are focused, tasks and relations might be more suitable studying managerial practice at the micro-level. In the model of Schmid, these two dimensions form four quadrants labeled Task oriented-Internal, Task oriented-External, People oriented-Internal and People oriented-External,[16] while Angell has developed four roles labeled Administrator, Supplier, Integrator and Bridge-builder.[17] A model built on these dimensions will guide the analysis of data, and its applicability is discussed later in this chapter.

Of special interest to the study of management in religious organizations are the questions of identity and values on the one hand, and the relationship to the context on the other hand.[18] The question of values and identity has not enjoyed prominence in management research focusing on managerial practice. Some exceptions are Henry Mintzberg,[19] who underlines the task of strengthening culture as a part of leadership, and Hart and Quinn,[20] who underline values as an important part of both visions and relations to co-workers. Although Mintzberg highlights this task, it is not clearly elaborated. Attention is drawn to the work of Selznick on the task of leaders who work for institutional embodiment of the purpose of the organization, where the institutional leader is concerned with the promotion and protection of values.[21]

Most of the managerial theory-based models seem to rely on research which is especially relevant for market based business organizations. Even if they appear to be of relevance for public (and probably voluntary) organizations experiencing market exposure, Angell argues that an alternative would be to substitute the stability/change dimension with the task/relations dimension.[22] The main argument is connected to the institutional environment experienced by general and faith-based welfare organizations. In such environments, legitimacy should be emphasized as much as efficiency. To achieve legitimacy, the organization must appear and be recognized as relevant and aligned with societal values and standards. Such a position neces-

15. Angell, "Leiarar og leiarroller."

16. Schmid, "Organizational Change," 199.

17. Angell, "Leiarar og leiarroller," 20.

18. Askeland, "Diaconal Hospital Managers"; Skjørshammer et al., "Verdibasert virksomhetsledelse."

19. Mintzberg, Managing.

20. Hart and Quinn, "Roles Executives Play."

21. Selznick, Leadership in Administration, 27–28.

22. Angell, "Leiarar og leiarroller," 18.

sitates a broader understanding of the external orientation of organizational management. While Mintzberg has been explicitly criticized for omitting an understanding of the institutional aspects of environments,[23] Quinn might be criticized for a too narrow and strategic-instrumental understanding and definition of the external roles of leaders. I suggest that this line of arguing is relevant for understanding the kind of organizational management studied here. In addition, Schmid, reporting from community service organizations, underlines the critical relation of interacting with and mediating between the organization and the community. Such an orientation was also clearly articulated in the interview data of this study.

In this chapter, I propose a model, drawing on the mentioned work of Angell and Schmid but one further developed (see Figure 1). Before presenting the results from analyzing the interviews, I present the categories developed for analysis:

- The institutional leader represents the overarching responsibility for the performance and results of an organization or organizational unit. At the same time, this also represents the notion of "institutional leadership" in which the management of purpose and meaning and the promotion of values (or faith-base) are central.

- *The director* combines the functions of initiating structure, developing procedures and monitoring compliance as well as coordinating and planning work processes in order to achieve goals in an efficient manner. Thus, the role has a broader definition than the administrator-role as used by Angell.

- *The service-developer* combines the traditional functions of the producer and the innovator. The role is external in its orientation, focusing on how tasks are accomplished by developing strategic services and goals based on monitoring and adjusting to the external environment.

- *The integrator* is internally and relationally oriented, focusing on functions necessary to bind the system together as a functioning whole. Such functions are related to motivating employees, developing and empowering them as competent actors, consulting with them and guiding them into an integrated team.

- *The mediator* is externally oriented towards building, maintaining and developing external relations. The more instrumental, and efficiency oriented, aspect of the leader's responsibility is downplayed while provision of legitimacy is given priority. Mediator functions include forming of alliances and also balancing and buffering of external pressure.

23. Willmott, "Studying Managerial."

Figure 1 Alternative typology of organizational functions
and managerial roles

The model is for the time being more suggestive in nature, and will guide the interpretation of both the standardized and open questions of the questionnaire. The material is not expected to fit with clear role-profiles of the deans, but will hopefully contribute to showing some profiling of their conception of their main tasks.

METHODOLOGY: SELECTION OF INFORMANTS AND DATA-GATHERING

This chapter analyses material from an evaluation, commissioned by the Ministry of Government Administration, Reform and Church Affairs, of recent re-organizing of the clerical services. The focal point of the chapter is how the role of the dean has been developed, regarding both a strengthening of the role and the new profile of the role.

Data for the evaluation was gathered through a multi-methodological approach. The methodological design of the study has been:

- A web-based questionnaire was administered to all deans and clergy in the Church of Norway. Out of 1292 respondents invited to participate, a total number of 516 responded after two reminders. The items used were closely linked to the aim of the evaluation. In the questionnaire, the deans were asked to answer both closed and open-ended questions, and the analysis is based on both types of material.

- In three, strategically chosen, dioceses (Oslo, Møre and Sør-Håloga-land) several interviews were conducted. These interviews combined focus group interviews with three groups; the deans of, a sample of clergy from and other congregational employees in these actual dioceses.

- Interview with the bishops and personnel manager of the three dioceses.

- A document analysis of annual allotment papers from the Ministry and a review of prior research on the topic of deans and leadership.[24]

DEVELOPMENTS IN THE
MANAGERIAL ROLE OF THE DEAN

The Development of the Dean as Leader: Towards a More Distinct Managerial Role?

From the data, there are three roles or functions concerning the dean as leader, which especially emerge from the interviews. The first role is the role of spiritual leader, a second role concerns the personnel human resource management role and function of the deans and the third role is that of the administrative manager. There was a widespread perception, especially among the clergy, that the reform and other changes in the conditions for the exercise of clerical ministry, has weakened the dean's opportunities to be a spiritual leader. Fulfilling the function as administrative leader required a level of attention in the dean's practice to have been mostly at the expense of the spiritual managerial function. This was seen as a consequence of the reform. Not only was the clergy concerned and promoted this view but some of the deans interviewed expressed the same opinion. It was clear that a higher ratio of ministers interviewed had this perception, compared to the deans. In the interviews with deans, very different assessments were expressed:

> I think that it is very important to me as dean how I justify my provost service. . . . It is not so important who takes care of the clerical services, the important thing is that it is exercised. We need to ensure that the clergy is able to work with the important services: preaching of the Word, administering the Sacrament, and other services. My legitimacy as dean and minister is that I, through necessary administrative activities which are part of my ministry, might facilitate the work of the clergy in my deanery. . . . So I think it is important that the dean not only has

24. Stifoss-Hanssen et al., *Ny organisering av prestetjenesten.*

bureaucratic skills, but is an ordained minister who can really understand, assess and challenge the spiritual service that the clergy proclaim in their *ministry*.

Among the deans, there were those who experienced this balancing of duties as contradictory or at least challenging, while others did not have this experience. In addition, some of the bishops and directors at the diocese suggested that there could be satisfactory tensions attending to both these dimensions. Spiritual leadership seemed to be used to label those activities concerned with preaching and teaching. Such an understanding of spiritual leadership seemed to be common for those using that phrase in the interviews.

For the deans, administrative function meant being able to control resources and to use them in the best possible way that seemed expedient. This was seen as their mission and responsibility as leaders, even if it was not always seen as an easy task. Some expressed a lack of acceptance among clergy for this part of the job which concerns governing and controlling. Among the clergy interviewed, several admitted that in the present situation, clergy do not necessarily appreciate being governed; they like to govern themselves.

The third management function, the personnel function, is, as expected, very much about encouraging clergy, to "see" them and support them in their work. Not surprisingly, this was a special concern amongst the clergy. As one of them said:

> I think it should have been made even clearer for the deans, how incredibly important it is to keep up the spirits of their employees. I say this because the clerical service is a tough service. This holds true either we do things one way or another. It is incredibly important that managers are aware of precisely such a role; to mean something to their employees.

In this context, the analysis revealed that the recent developments may have contributed to creating new and greater expectations of the dean as leader, expectations that may be difficult for the dean to live up to. Such a difficulty was partly seen in relation to existing resources. For example, scarce personnel resources made it difficult for deans to utilize the competence and diversity among the clergy as was the intention of the reform. This concern emerged from interviews with both deans and clergy. For example, many deans had problems in getting the work schedule to add up. These problems were so time-consuming that there was not much time available to contribute to the professional development of clergy. Regarding the availability of human resources, there might be distinctions between being a dean in an urban or a rural area. Deans in cities might draw on more staff to allocate resources according to needs and skills. Thus, their role as leaders was the one issue that raised interest among deans in the interviews, and especially the balance between having a spiritual and having a more administrative management role.

How is the Dean's Profile as a Leader Perceived?

Among the bishops and the directors of the dioceses, many positive comments were expressed about leadership identity among the deans. At the same time, many contended that this was an issue that had not yet been fully realized. For example, several underlined that deans had become increasingly aware of the need for and responsibility to stay in contact with the local parishes and especially the parish councils in their deanery. They realized, however, that developing a clear leader identity among the deans was not done instantly or over-night. One of the interviewees put it this way:

> I do believe that the development of a clear leadership identity amongst deans is underway, but they live in tension between the many tasks of their position. . . . If I were to say something about the exercise of management, I would probably say I wish they were able to delegate more of the many technical tasks and spend more time preaching and teaching—a more distinctly spiritual leadership.

From the interviews with bishops and directors of the dioceses, the main conclusion was that the dean's role as leaders had become clearer. They also underlined that "deans have a different legitimacy than before." These developments helped in creating greater predictability for clergy, although there were dioceses where geography makes practical life somewhat difficult. They found a connection between the fact that their identity as leaders had become clearer and that deans had become more confident in their leadership role. In addition, the interview-material expressed a view that the deans appeared and performed with a clearer managerial identity and profile than previously:

> The dean is more like a leader today, not just a pastoral leader, but a leader of the clergy. . . . In addition, I see this more clearly in relation to the aims of the service instruction and to the enhanced collaboration and coordination between the local councils and the clerical service.

Deans themselves did not convey a similar clarity of their own identity as leaders. Among those interviewed, there were those who affirmed such an impression at the diocesan level, but there were also those who expressed questions and uncertainties about their role. Similarly nuanced responses we received from the clergy interviewed. The sense of a built-in ambiguity of the new role of the dean was evident. Such an ambiguity concerned the association of the dean with a local parish. In several interviews, the dean was leader of the deanery clergy while at the same time subordinated as parish minister to the senior minister of his or her own parish; this was raised as a controversial theme. It seems reasonable to expect that this does something to the identity of a leader, trying to combine what are incommensurable roles.

The interview material leaves the impression of a generation gap between "younger" and "older" deans. Younger deans had been employed more by qualifications for management, and had increasingly been aiming for such a job—and thus developed a leader identity. The older deans probably had to evolve into the role after entering the position, taking more time to develop a similar identity as a leader.

A Performative Perspective: Various Management Functions

An important aspect of the reform was to strengthen the dean's role as a leader. As the reform evolved, the organizing of clerical services, with increased attention on management by objectives, emphasis on supervision and securing leisure time for clergy, became more in focus. The service instruction for deans, adopted in 2004, emphasized the aim that deans should spend more time in fulfilling managerial tasks of the deanery. From 2004 to 2009, resources were allocated and earmarked to strengthen the ministry of the deans including grants for administrative support. In addition, a program aimed at enhancing the managerial competency of deans was conducted in this period.

Various questions in the survey were intended to target the evolution of the dean's managerial role. These questions referred to issues measuring different dimensions of the managerial role, and were specified as to time spent on different tasks as well as to assessments by the clergy of quality and priorities, cf. Table 1. Each question was scored on a scale from one to five, with one indicating small amount of time and five indicating large amount of time.

It is worth noting that for several questions there are relatively small differences between the self-assessment of the deans and the assessment provided by the clergy. Such areas are management by objectives and governance of the clerical services, organizing of their own pastoral work, economy and administration and cooperation with the conciliar structure and the churchwarden as administrative head of office. Other areas displayed marked differences in assessment, such as personnel management and pastoral and spiritual leadership. For both of these areas, the deans indicated higher scores on use of time than the assessment by the clergy. These differences in assessment are of interest, when compared to the qualitative material. Both in the interviews and in open-ended questions of the questionnaire there are interesting findings. Many respondents expressed a concern that the reform had led to an increased administrative orientation in the role of the dean, and that such a change had weakened the dean as a pastoral and spiritual leader. This result might also be seen in relation to how ministers assessed quality and optimal prioritization of tasks by the dean, cf. Table 2. The questions were scored on a scale from one (low quality/priority) to five (high quality/priority).

Table 1 Time spent on specific managerial tasks assessed by the deans themselves and ministers. (Mean. 1=small amount; 5 large amount of time)

Specific managerial tasks	Deans report on own time-use for managerial tasks	Ministers assessment of time-use on tasks by the dean
Professional management and development of competence	3.5	3.0
Management by objectives and governance	3.4	3.1
Human-resource management	3.5	4.1
Pastoral and spiritual leadership	3.6	2.8
Work-distribution among clergy and working schemes	4.2	3.5
Organizing of dean's own clerical service	3.1	2.9
Economic and administrative management	3.6	3.5
Cooperation with councils and church wardens	3.7	3.5
Coordination of dean's service with plans of councils	3.3	2.8

The managerial tasks (or functions) considered to be of the highest quality are those of financial and administrative management and those of cooperation with the church warden and parochial councils. Along with personnel

management and allocation of work between clergy, these were the tasks
or functions that got the highest scores on quality. The tasks or functions
concerned with management by objectives and governance or coordination
with plans of the conciliar structure were however assessed weaker with
regard to quality. This may indicate that those tasks which have the greatest
proximity to the every-day life of the clergy are viewed as being of higher
quality. An indication that the latter tasks or functions seems to be at a distance of every-day life might be inferred by a high proportion answering
they did not really know.

Table 2 Quality and optimal prioritizing of specific managerial tasks performed
by own dean, assessed by ministers. (Mean. 1=low priority/quality; 5=high
priority/quality).

Specific managerial tasks	Quality of tasks performed by own dean	Optimal prioritizing of tasks
Professional management and development of competence	3.4	3.8
Management by objectives and governance	3.3	3.6
Human-resource management	3.5	4.1
Pastoral and spiritual managerial	3.3	3.9
Work-distribution among clergy and working schemes	3.5	3.7
Organizing of dean's own clerical service	3.4	3.1
Financial and administrative management	3.6	3.2
Cooperation with councils and church wardens	3.6	3.6
Coordination of dean's service with plans of councils	3.2	3.4

In connection with the revision of the service instruction for deans, the pri-
or review indicated there had been an emphasis on collaboration with the
conciliar structure and those staff members employed by the councils and
representing other ministries. The deans were also expected to coordinate
the clerical services with plans made by the councils. Both these dimensions

have been seen in relation to the deans performing a more holistic role as church leaders. Such role-figures are important, not only because they serve on the councils but because they lead together with representatives from congregational employees and ministries. The material indicates that both with regard to the use of time and in assessed quality and priority, intra-organizational cooperation was regarded as important both by the deans and by the clergy. Less importance is put on such intra-organizational coordination, indicating that the clerical service might (or should) be seen as independent of the councils plans. However, this is not a uniform picture across the church; it seems to vary amongst different dioceses.[25] While in only three out of eleven dioceses did the clergy regard cooperation of less importance (Borg, Stavanger, and Bjørgvin), in six of them (Borg, Agder and Telemark, Stavanger, Nidaros and Nord-Hålogaland) coordination scored significantly lower. For almost all dioceses, clergy regarded coordination as of less importance than cooperation. The deans seem more inclined to prioritize cooperation than the clergy.

Developments in the Managerial Role of the Dean

This section will address two questions related to the development of the managerial role of the deans. *First*, whether the role has been strengthened through the reform. *Second*, in an open-ended question, the deans were asked if their roles had become more significant because of the reforms. In addition to being addressed in the interviews conducted, the deans were given an open-ended question as to whether their role had become more significant because of the reform. Sixty-five respondents answered this question, and the answers have been analyzed and divided into a few main categories.

Apparently, the question had been perceived in somewhat different directions. The majority of responses either simply confirmed or denied that the managerial role of the dean had become more significant and important because of the reform. A few specific examples of responses that are typical in this respect are:

> My managerial role as dean has in principle become more significant as a consequence of the reform.

and:

> Yes, I'm a dean.

25. Ibid., 53–54.

The category, which simply confirmed that the dean's role had been strengthened, contains twenty answers. In addition, a few made additional comments and specified why they conceived this as so. Five of the deans attached an increased importance to very specific elements or aspects of the managerial role. This increased importance was related to larger deaneries with districts of responsibility, to an enhanced possibility in contributing to congregational development or to the fact that they were given more authority and financial responsibility. A typical response in this group was:

> It has become more significant, because the dean now has the opportunity to make a difference. Among other things, we might contribute to cooperation and developing functioning plans within the deanery ensuring the need for leisure time. We might also promote cooperation among clergy across parish boundaries and to secure necessary work force in periods with much to do.

Another important category, which also emphasizes the strengthening of the managerial role, concerned the clarification of the dean's role and the added responsibilities. Such a profile was expressed in around twenty answers, or a third of the respondents. In part, it is argued that the managerial role has become clearer regarding expectations:

> It has become clearer—and the dean has in many ways taken over the role and functions of bishop and the diocesan administration. The bishop has become distant and the dean closer. The role as a leader has therefore become significantly more important.

Within this group, responses also made it clear that this was due to the distribution of responsibilities and to the new opportunities to exercise management. Elements in this clarification were enhanced room for maneuvering and an increased authorization to lead which increased the ability to achieve something. Some examples of answers in this category are:

> As a dean I have a significant impact on the everyday working life of the clergy, in order to facilitate and motivate their service.

and:

> Some increased leeway for maneuvering to create local development, and an increased possibility of leveling the workload.

Even if the main tendency points towards a strengthened role, there are nonetheless nuances in responses. One such nuance was that the role was

not always given the necessary authorization to achieve the aims of the reform. Others were concerned that the development meant a drift of purpose
and profile with which they were not fully comfortable:

> My managerial role as dean has become clearer and with a mod-
> ified service instruction plan for parish ministers I have *better
> tools. However, I am lacking clear delegation by the bishop on
> central issues.*

and:

> It has become more important as an administrator, but not as
> spiritual leader.

In addition, the clergy was given this open-ended question: What effect
would you say the reform has had on the dean's managerial role? Three
hundred and fifty one of the respondents answered this question and the
answers were formulated quite independently and with different emphases.
At the same time, the analysis fell into a few broad categories.

Essentially, the clergy wanted the dean's managerial role to be both
clarified and strengthened. In this category there were two main positive
reviews of the development: Leaders had become closer and things were
working well. More than 40 percent of the answers fell into this category.

A large group of just over 20 percent indicated that the role had been
strengthened but considered the development to have had a less positive or
directly negative effect. The majority in this group relate their skepticism
to the perception that the dean's role had become more bureaucratic. This
skepticism was partly related to concepts such as administrative or bureaucratic orientation, which they perceived as excessive auditing or micromanagement by regulation. This group of respondents seemed dissatisfied with
how the role had evolved. Instead of being strengthened in the direction of
professional and personnel management or as a pastoral or spiritual managerial role, it had on the contrary become administrative. Almost a third
of the respondents also thought that the role of the dean had become too
strong. This view was combined with a feeling that the role of the senior
parish minister had been weakened by loss of authority and by often being overruled by the dean. Several answers indicated the notion that clergy
had lost a spokesperson, and that the dean had become the extended arm
of the bishop. Less frequent, but important to note, were answers indicating
a lack of trust in the ability of the dean to lead constructively.

The second important question of this chapter concerns the development of the dean as a pastoral leader. As laid out in the previous tables,
both deans and clergy point to a weakened pastoral and spiritual leadership

role. This appraisal applied to both time used and quality of this particular aspect of management. While this concept seems important in the current discussion of clerical management in the Church of Norway, the concept itself suffers from lack of clarity. Such a responsibility was included in the new service instruction for both deans and clergy, but was not fully prepared conceptually. Neither was it elaborated in the supporting documents of the reform nor in the ecclesial discourse. In their responses to the questionnaire, clergy rated this function as one of the most prioritized next to personnel management and concern. The questionnaire included an open-ended question, in which the respondents were asked to complete the sentence: "For me, pastoral leadership involves. . . ." Among the deans sixty six responded to this item, and the material comprise many different and widely varying statements describing pastoral and spiritual leadership. Even if the material has not yet undergone any complete and thorough analysis, it has been subject to a preliminary analysis, which shows some rough categories.

Table 3 Categorization, including typical quotes, of theological and functional conceptualizations of pastoral leadership

Theological conceptualization	Functional conceptualization
Leading by the Word and Sacraments	Leading the clerical and worship services
Holistic responsibility for the life of the congregations based on ordination	Strategies, objectives and planning for congregational life
Building the congregation ("oikodoumene")	Cooperating with the councils to enhance holistic approaches
Teaching and leading for a life in faith	Relational: see, listen to and follow-up
Supervision of the spiritual condition of the congregation and co-workers	Contributing to consistency and stability

A first and main impression from the review is that the material basically fall into two rough categories, but also that there are intermediate forms. On the one hand, there are answers that predominantly seem to be conceived within a theological grounded language and theological founded terms. Around twenty, or almost a third of the responses, have been categorized in this group. On the other hand, there are responses that predominantly referred to being grounded in a more functional perspective, related to ecclesial organizational functions and management tasks. Around forty-five or just over two-thirds of the responses fell into this main category.

An initial and rough schematic overview of the main categories and some subcategories within each of these are shown in Table 3. The answers showed that the concept of pastoral leadership is far from being clear and consistent in content or common understanding. It seems a bit surprising that a functional conceptualization of the term was used by more than two-thirds of the respondents. An explanation for this might be the haste with which the term pastoral leadership was incorporated in the service instruction without providing the necessary elucidation or validation of the content. The material pointed out two main functions or tasks that form the core of the understanding of pastoral leadership: Central aspects such as leading the clerical ministry and services and collaborating with congregations and their representative bodies. Collaboration with the councils that contributes to a strategic and holistic approach was also underlined. In addition, tasks such as recognition and follow-up were mentioned frequently. In the above table, I have sought to juxtapose the differing theological and functional conceptualizations to show how they seem to correspond to each other. Whether the respondents use theological or organizational terms, they seem to correspond closely both in content and substance. Managerial responsibility is closely tied to the specific ministry of Word and Sacrament. It is also linked to a comprehensive and strategically oriented joint responsibility with the councils and is relational oriented in monitoring the employees' professional and individual needs.

This first rough sorting of the material in the evaluation report, displays some similarities with the main domains of the suggested management model (Figure 1) but does not totally overlap. The earlier analysis was more closely related to the concrete tasks of leaders, but this last section relates to the question of *pastoral leadership*. A first general impression is that phrases change and that the articulation of the content of this term is ambiguous. The answers are dominated by either a theological or an organizational language, indicating a lack of integration of such rationalities.

Relating the statements to the integrated model of management presented earlier (Figure 1), show that the terms usually connected with ministerial work and service, fit naturally into the core role of *institutional leader*. Whether theologically or organizationally framed, the core of pastoral leadership relates to leading the core functions of ministerial work. More precisely, the role is modeled on the role of assisting the bishop in overseeing the faith and life of ministers and congregations; leading by theology. This applies more to ministers, than to congregations. With regard to congregations, the pastoral institutional leadership role shows concern for a holistic approach to building the congregation as a community.

Table 4 Summarizing the content of statements regarding "pastoral leadership" related to the integrated management model (108 distinct statements of task or content was extracted from these answers).

Institutional leader			
Leading the ministry of the Word and sacraments, by overseeing faith and teaching, and stimulating theological work. Regarding congregations partaking in development of strategy and a holistic "building of congregation" are added.			
Internal-tasks	*Internal-relations*	*External-tasks*	*External-relations*
Director	Integrator	Service-developer	Mediator
Facilitating working conditions, distribution of services and frameworks for ministerial service.	"Seeing," supporting, inspiring and counseling ministerial subordinates. Empowering individuals and teams	Contributing to strategy and development, regarding focus on ministerial services and needs of congregations	Co-operating with parish councils, focusing on functioning in the local community

When it comes to the director profile, the earlier focus on administration is replaced with statements of more indirect content and more clearly organizationally termed. Most statements have to do with facilitating working conditions, distribution of services and facilitating frameworks for the ministerial service. Only two respondents mention administrating and managing. The integrator profile comprises the vast majority of statements: Most importantly, they want to "see," support, inspire and counsel their ministerial subordinates. In addition, tasks like empowering and helping to use the employee's particular gifts are mentioned. The service-developer profile consists mainly of formulations connecting their contribution to strategy and development, their focus on ministerial services and the needs of the congregations. Lastly, the mediator is the weakest developed profile. Only a few, actually less than a handful, mention tasks related to this profile. The functioning of the congregation in the local community and cooperation with the parish councils are the only aspects mentioned. In general, the picture given by the analysis shows a skewed profiling of "pastoral" leadership. The institutional profile is mentioned in nearly half (forty-seven) of the one hundred and eight statements extracted from the material. Close to that the profile of integrator was mentioned in nearly one-third (thirty-four) of the statements. The director and the service-developer had equal share of the statements (twelve), while the mediator was mentioned in only three answers.

CONCLUDING REMARKS

There is no doubt that the managerial role of the dean has been strengthened and considerable resources and attention have been used in enhancing and developing their skills as leaders. At the same time, not all respondents agree that the strengthening of the managerial role is necessarily a good thing. These disagreements may be related to the various components characterized with this managerial role. Deans and ministers alike agree that the administrative component has increased while pastoral leadership has been weakened. Most ministers do not approve of this development. This is partially because they dislike the consequences of a time allocation which leave the deans with less time to concentrate and attend to their subordinate ministers. Some ministers feel that the deans have become more powerful and directive, giving less leeway for their own traditional autonomy. It appears that the reform has strengthened the administrative leadership of the deans at the expense of pastoral leadership and personnel management.

The broad picture, naturally enough, looks different to the various actors. The emphasis and aims of personnel management and pastoral leadership by ministers seem based on their place and location in the ecclesial organization. On the other hand, some parish ministers feel that their own position is weakened and to some extent overrun. In addition, the new cooperation, and especially the coordination with the conciliar structure, received a lukewarm reception. The reform, therefore, is not just about the understanding of what constitutes good management, but also about changes in authority and traditions of autonomy amongst an important group of professionals.

Noticeable differences appear when the deans are asked about their own conception of "pastoral leadership." If this term is seen as, an "ideal-type" of management or leadership, parallel views or rationalities of management appear that are not yet integrated in their role-conception as leaders. They feel that the development of management functions enhances their leadership potential but simultaneously increases their administrative burden. These opinions, however, are only indirectly expressed in the "pastoral leadership" identity. The administrative and directive mandate facilitated by the reform is in these answers transformed to "facilitating working frames." Moreover, while the relationship to the local conciliar structure and the local churchwarden was given priority and time, this mediating role is almost totally absent from their conception of "pastoral leadership." Internal and relational focus, as mirrored in the integrator profile, dominated all the other functional profiles. This correlates to the task of personnel management of the earlier analysis, which was seen as one of the functions that had been downplayed because of the reform.

These seemingly parallel conceptions of pastoral leadership by the deans, points to important issues for further research. Firstly, it is important to address the parallel use of terms in describing and conceiving of the role and responsibilities of ministerial leaders. One way of approaching this issue is suggested by the integrated model of leadership used in this article, that is, by combining a more traditional functional perspective with the establishment of a core role of institutional leader. More refinement of the underlying assumptions and further empirical testing is necessary. A second way of further research would be to investigate the ways professional leaders integrate professional and organizational rationality, integrating these parallel rationalities into a new, hybrid leadership role. Such research could be inspired by studies of clinical managers in hospitals, who in combining professional and organizational competence and mandates are seen as being able to view management through a "two-ways-window."[26]

BIBLIOGRAPHY

Angell, Olav Helge. "Leiarar og leiarroller i Den Norske Kyrkja på lokalplan: Diakonen som leiar i ein norsk, luthersk tradisjon." *Nordiske Organisasjonsstudier.* Forthcoming.

Askeland, Harald. "What Do Diaconal Hospital Managers Really Do? Management at Diakonhjemmet Hospital: Context, Intention and Practice." *Diaconia: Journal for the Study of Christian Social Practice* 2.2 (2011) 145–69.

Fleishman, Edwin A. "The Description of Supervisory Behavior." *Journal of Applied Psychology* 37.1 (1953) 1.

Hales, Colin. "Why Do Managers Do What They Do? Reconciling Evidence and Theory in Accounts of Managerial Work." *British Journal of Management* 10.4 (1999) 335–50.

———. "What Do Managers Do? A Critical Review of the Evidence." *Journal of Management Studies* 23.1 (1986) 88–115.

Hart, Stuart L, and Robert E. Quinn. "Roles Executives Play: Ceos, Behavioral Complexity, and Firm Performance." *Human Relations* 46.5 (1993) 543–74.

26. Llewellyn, "Two-Way Windows," 593.

Huse, Morten. *Prosten. Ansvar, arbeidssituation og ledelse*. KIFO rapport nr. 10. Trondheim: Tapir akademisk forlag, 1998.

Huse, Morten, and Cathrine Hansen. *Nyorganisering i prestetjenesten. Evaluering av forsøkene*. KIFO Rapport. Trondheim: Tapir akademisk forlag, 2003.

Kirkeloven [Church Act]. *Lov 7. juni 1996 nr. 31 om Den norske kirke*. 1996.

Likert, Rensis. *New Patterns of Management*. New York: McGrave-Hill, 1961.

Llewellyn, Sue. "Two-Way Windows: Clinicians as Medical Managers." *Organization Studies* 22.4 (2001) 593–623.

Martinko, Mark J., and William L. Gardner. "Beyond Structured Observation: Methodological Issues and New Directions."*Academy of Management Review* 10.4 (1985) 676–95.

Mintzberg, Henry. *Managing*. San Fransisco: Berrett-Koehler, 2009.

Schmid, Hillel. "Organizational Change in Human Service Organizations." In *Human Services as Complex Organizations*, edited by Yeheskel Hasenfeld, 455–79. Thousand Oaks, CA.: Sage, 2010.

Selznick, Philip. *Leadership in Administration: A Sociological Interpretation*. Evanston, IL: Row Peterson, 1957.

Skjørshammer, Morten, et al., "Verdibasert virksomhetsledelse: Kan verdier og resultatstyring kombineres på en troverdig måte?" 109–30. Trondheim: Akademika, 2012.

Stifoss-Hanssen, Hans, et al., *Ny organisering av prestetjenesten ("Prostereformen")-- Evaluering*. Oslo: Diakonhjemmet Høgskole, 2013.

Vie, Ola Edvin. "Shadowing Managers Engaged in Care: Discovering the Emotional Managerial Work." PhD Thesis, NTNU Norwegian University of Science and Technology, 2009.

Willmott, Hugh. "Studying Managerial Work: A Critique and a Proposal." *Journal of Management Studies* 24.3 (1987) 249–70.

Yukl, Gary, Angela Gordon, and Tom Taber. "A Hierarchical Taxonomy of Leadership Behavior: Integrating a Half Century of Behavior Research." *Journal of Leadership & Organizational Studies* 9.1 (2002) 15–32.

8

Clergy Discipline Decisions in the Church of England and the Church of Sweden Compared

PER HANSSON

ECUMENICAL AGREEMENTS AND CLERGY DISCIPLINE

The Church of England and the Church of Sweden enjoy a longstanding relationship. Both were reformed in the sixteenth century and both maintained the historic episcopate and the apostolic succession. In the early twentieth century, contacts between the bishops of the two churches were undertaken, and in 1920 Anglican bishops first took part in a Swedish episcopal consecration. The ordinations of ministers and bishops were mutually recognized and clergy could be invited to preach and administer the sacraments in the two churches.[1] Even during the controversy on women ministers, Anglican bishops took part in Swedish episcopal consecrations in their mission churches.[2]

An even stronger relationship between the churches was established in the Porvoo Communion between the Anglican churches of the British Isles and the Lutheran churches in Scandinavia and the Baltic region in 1995. Among other points of cooperation, the agreement allows clergy to

---

1. Lyttkens, *Growth of Swedish-Anglican Intercommunion*; Österlin, *Churches of Northern Europe in Profile*; Brohed, *Sveriges kyrkohistoria 8.*

2. Hansson, *Svenska kyrkans primas.*

minister in the other churches of the communion.[3] The churches expect any applicants from the signatory churches to be "in good standing." However, definitions of this phrase may differ vastly from church to church, as each imposes different standards for the discipline of its clergy.

As the Church of England and the Church of Sweden have longstanding, close links and clergy interchangeability, it may be of interest to compare their respective understandings of what they expect of their clergy when it comes to conduct and ethical standards. This is revealed in decisions on clergy discipline. The aim of this chapter is to compare clergy discipline decisions in the Church of England and the Church of Sweden and to discuss the similarities and differences between the expectations imposed on the clergy. The comparison is carried out in two steps: 1) statistics on discipline decisions and 2) matching comparable discipline cases.

DISCIPLINARY SYSTEMS IN THE CHURCH OF ENGLAND AND THE CHURCH OF SWEDEN

The reader of this chapter may wish to recall the Church of England's disciplinary system[4] as well as the Swedish system.[5] Both systems have recently been changed: the Church of Sweden's discipline measures changed when the church was disestablished in 2000. A new system was adopted in 2003 by the Church of England, which has been in operation since 2006. Minor changes to the new systems have been carried out in both churches.[6] Both the Church of England and the Church of Sweden are episcopally led and synodically governed. Both churches acknowledge that the bishop has both *potestas ordinis* and *potestas iurisdictionis*.[7] Complaints about clergy must be presented to the bishop (England) or the chapter of the diocese (Sweden). After inquiry, decisions are made by the bishop (England) or the chapter (Sweden). Complaints may range from accusations of violating canon law to unbecoming behavior. Penalties include no action, criticism (rebuke), a period of probation, and prohibition. Both churches have systems for appeal. Although the systems of supervision are similar in many respects, some major differences do exist: decisions in the Church of England are generally made by the bishop in consent with the respondent, whereas the chapter in

---

3. *The Porvoo Common Statement*, § 58 b (v).

4. *Clergy Discipline Measure 2003*; Iles, "Clergy Discipline Measure 2003: A Canter"; Bursell, "More Turbulence?"

5. *Kyrkoordning* [Canon Law for the Church of Sweden]. Hansson, "Clerical Misconduct"; Hansson, "Clerical Ethos."

6. cf. Iles, "Clergy Discipline Measure 2003: A Progress Report."

7. Podmore, "Tale of Two Churches"; Huovinen, "How Can One Be."

the Church of Sweden acts more as a tribunal. Furthermore, the Swedish regulations are not as precisely outlined, and no support is provided for a minister under investigation.[8] Other differences are that the Church of England has a time limit of one year (with some exceptions) and only those with a proper interest are allowed to submit a complaint. The Church of Sweden has no time limit and anyone can file a complaint about any minister.

Ethical Guidelines for the Clergy

As mentioned above, many complaints in the Church of England are dealt with in relation to regulations in canon law on "conduct unbecoming or inappropriate to the office and work of a clerk in Holy Orders."[9] A similar regulation exists in the Church of Sweden Canon Law, namely that "he or she has damaged the esteem of ordained ministry to a great extent."[10]

In the Church of England, the current system was preceded by a report on clergy discipline.[11] The basic principles for disciplining the clergy are theological and are retrieved from Holy Scriptures, the Christian Tradition, and the historic formularies of the Church of England. The report quotes the canons of the Church of England, emphasizing "wholesome example" and suggesting that some "occupations, habits or recreations" are inimical to the calling to the ministry. The report concludes that those in holy orders, by their ordination, accept several responsibilities (institutional, teaching, representative, confidentiality). In addition to this, the report highlights the responsibility to be a good example: "Clergy are expected to live a sacrificial life of self-denial in such a way that both the Church and society are provided with a wholesome and attractive demonstration of godly living."[12] The conclusion is that, while clergy are recognized as inherently sinful along with all humanity, there are special requirements regarding how clergy conduct their lives.

The new system in the Church of Sweden was also preceded by an official report.[13] This report, however, deals only with the issues related to a new legal system and does not discuss any theological or ethical issues.

In order to define what is unbecoming or inappropriate, the two churches have outlined ethical guidelines for clergy conduct. This may be considered a sign that churches regard the ministry as a profession (in the

8. Hill, "Clergy Discipline."

9. *Clergy Discipline Measure 2003*, 8–1c.

10. *Kyrkoordning*, chapter 31 § 12.

11. *Under Authority.*

12. Ibid., 24.

13. *SKU 1998:5.*

sense the word is used in the social sciences), since a special set of ethics is considered one of the signs of a profession.[14] The Church of England has one document governing the entire church in this regard, stressing the necessity of developing a culture of professional ethics: "the cultivation of virtuous character based on theology, morality and spirituality."[15]

Some Swedish bishops have recently issued a "Codex ethicus" for the clergy in their respective dioceses.[16] These ethical guidelines have much in common across the dioceses: they are based on the rite of ordination and on the ordination vows. The Swedish guidelines give instructions on confidentiality (professional secrecy), financial transactions, and gifts to the clergy; they also provide special advice on daily prayer and worship, which are not obligations for the clergy in Swedish Canon Law. Furthermore, sexual relationships with parishioners and confidants are specified as problematic, and the codes emphasize that clergy are never allowed to use their position to gain sexual or financial benefits. A special section indicates that members of the clergy are never completely off duty: "the whole way of life is taken into account—there is no totally private life."[17] Holy matrimony, baptism of their own children, and worshiping are discussed in the context of credibility, not as responsibilities for those in the ministry.[18] The Swedish documents appear to be in line with the canon law: the esteem of the ministry is more important than acts, per se, being moral or immoral.

The Church of England's guidelines, on the other hand, are ordered according to the parts of the rite of ordination.[19] A new version is under way.[20] The hope is to inspire the clergy to "the highest possible standard of conduct throughout a lifetime of ministry."[21] There is an emphasis both on caring for the needy, the clergy, and their families, and on providing boundaries for clerical ministry. As in the Swedish documents, obedience to superiors is important, along with confidentiality, sexual relationships with parishioners are discussed, and it is indicated that the life of clergy should follow the pattern of the Good Shepherd.

14. Russel, *Clerical Profession;* Karle, *Der Pfarrberuf;* Hansson, "Clerical Ethos."

15. Bridger, "Theological Reflection," 20.

16. *Clergy Discipline Measure 2003; Codex ethicus. Diocese of Gothenburg; Codex ethicus. Diocese of Luleå; Codex ethicus. Diocese of Växjö;* Nordin, *Codex ethicus.*

17. Nordin, *Codex Ethicus 19.*

18. *Codex Ethicus. Diocese of Gothenburg;* Nordin, *Codex Ethicus.*

19. *Guidelines.*

20. *Guidelines Draft Edition.*

21. Ibid., 5.

The Swedish and English documents are similar to some extent, but there are also important differences. One difference is the point of departure being theology and Holy Scriptures in the English documents and the heavy stress placed on developing a virtuous character. Another difference is the focus on the clergy's prayer life in the Church of England's document.

These differences seem to be in line with the findings of Kleiven.[22] In a comparison between the Church of Norway and the Norwegian free churches regarding sexual harassment, he suggests that the Church of Norway deals with these issues based on legal references rather than theological ones, whereas the free churches tend to handle them in terms of ecclesiological ethics. The Church of Sweden here seems to resemble the Church of Norway, whereas the Church of England appears more like the Norwegian free churches.

FREQUENCY OF COMPLAINTS COMPARED

New Canon Law for the Church of Sweden was introduced in 2000, at the time of what is known as the church's disestablishment, what is often called its separation from the Swedish state. All cases of complaints against Swedish priests[23] during the first five years of the new legislation (2000–2004) were collected.[24] Such Swedish decisions are normally public documents. The Church of England's standard, in contrast, is that the bishop makes decisions by consent, and the documents normally remain secret. However, the Clergy Discipline Commission provides an overview of decisions that is made available to the entire church annually at the General Synod. I have used these reports here in order to compare the decisions taken in the two churches. Thus the first five years of the new regulations in both churches are compared although during different time periods: Church of Sweden 2000–2004 and Church of England 2006–2010.

Table 5 shows that the rate of complaints in relation to the number of clergy is higher in the Church of Sweden. One explanation for this might be that, in the Church of England, only cases with "sufficient substance in the complaint to justify proceeding"[25] are put forward for investigation. The bishops are urged to dismiss minor allegations which, if true, would not

22. Kleiven, "Intimitetsgrenser og tillitsmakt."

23. The Church of Sweden does not ordain "sacri ministerii" candidates to the diaconate as a step towards priesthood. The ministry of deacon in the Church of Sweden is permanent. There are approximately sixteen hundred deacons (not including those retired), and they have not been included in the Swedish material.

24. Hansson, "Clerical Misconduct."

25. *The Clergy Discipline Rules 2005*, 12(1)b.

merit a penalty.[26] Another explanation might be that only those with "proper interest" are allowed to file a complaint in the Church of England, whereas anyone can file a complaint in the Church of Sweden. Furthermore, there may be cultural differences regarding the tendency to make complaints. The distribution over dioceses is reasonably similar in the two churches: most dioceses have only a few cases in any given year.

Table 5 Formal complaints against priests in the Church of England and the Church of Sweden.[27]

	The Church of England, 2006–2010		The Church of Sweden, 2000–2004	
	Total	Percent	Total	Percent
All complaints over five years	327	1.8[28]	105	3.1[29]
Dioceses without complaints, less than one complaint per year	16	37	4	31
Dioceses with 1–5 complaints per year	25	58	8	69
Dioceses with more than 6 complaints per year	2	5	0	0

DEALING WITH COMPLAINTS

Table 6 shows that in both churches, approximately 40 percent of the complaints are rejected or not investigated further. In the Church of England, the relevant Bishop makes a decision on most remaining cases in consent with the respondent, and a small number are brought to formal investigation (to the Bishop's Tribunal). The Church of Sweden's approach is that all cases not rejected are brought to investigation. In most cases, the investigation is assigned to a member of the Chapter of the Diocese, normally one

26. Iles, "Clergy Discipline Measure 2003: A Progress Report."

27. Sources: Church of England General Synod Clergy Discipline Commission. Annual reports, 2007–2011. Records for all complaints against Swedish priests, 2000–2004.

28. The Church of England has approximately eighteen thousand priests and deacons; retirees are not included, *Church of England Licensed Ministries.*

29. The Church of Sweden has approximately three thousand four hundred priests; permanent deacons and retirees are not included.

of the judges. The Church of Sweden has not adopted the option of conciliation. However, it is not used very often in the Church of England and is
quite often unsuccessful.

Table 6 Formal complaints against clergy and how they were addressed.[30]

	The Church of England, 2006–2010		The Church of Sweden, 2000–2004	
	Total	Percent	Total	Percent
Rejected, no further investigation	135	41	41	39
Conditional deferment	11	3	Not an option	—
Resolved by conciliation[31]	6	2[32]	Not an option	—
Resolved by consent	65	20	Not an option	—
Formal investigation	45	14	62	59
Withdrawn	6	2		
Sum	268		103	
Balance brought forward	17	5	0	
Abstruse	42[33]	13	2	2
Total	327	100	105	100

COMPARISON OF PENALTIES

Table 7 shows penalties by consent and by bishop's tribunal in the Church
of England and all decisions in the Church of Sweden. As the legislation

30. Sources: Church of England General Synod Clergy Discipline Commission. Annual reports, 2007–2011. Records for all complaints against Swedish priests, 2000–2004.

31. Conciliation or an attempt at conciliation was made in 6 percent of the cases.

32. Fourteen unsuccessful attempts at conciliation were made.

33. The statistics for Church of England are somewhat ambiguous, and approximately 10 percent of the cases are not clearly accounted for. Cases referred to the
bishop's tribunal may be included here.

is different in the two churches, comparison is quite complicated; overall, however, the Church of England seems to exhibit a pattern of more rigid decisions. Two-thirds of the penalty decisions involve prohibition for a shorter or longer period and/or that the respondent loses his/her benefice (which also normally means loss of a place to live). To this it should be added that 11 percent are dismissed but not prohibited. The most severe penalties are thus applied in 77 percent of cases as compared to 21 percent of cases in the Church of Sweden. The most common penalty in Sweden is rebuke (before 2004, criticism), which is used in almost 75 percent of the cases. One initial finding of this study is thus that the Church of England is more rigid than the Church of Sweden; put another way, the Church of England deals with disruptive priests in a firmer manner.

Table 7 Penalties in the Church of England and the Church of Sweden.[34]

Decision	The Church of England, 2006–2010		The Church of Sweden, 2000–2004	
	Total	Percent	Total	Percent
Prohibition	13[35]	18	10	21
Limited prohibition	34	48	Not an option	
Dismissal	8	11		
Injunction	3	4	Not an option	
Period of probation	Not an option		3[36]	6
Rebuke, criticism	8	11	35	73
Rebuke and injunction	5	7	Not an option	
Sum	71	99	48	100

In addition, five cases in the Church of England were decided after a decree of divorce or an order of separation had been made against the respondent following a finding of adultery, behavior such that the petitioner

34. Sources: Church of England General Synod Clergy Discipline Commission. Annual reports, 2007–2011. Records for all complaints against Swedish priests, 2000–2004.

35. In addition to this, in five cases, a penalty of removal from office or prohibition was imposed following divorce decree or order for judicial separation.

36. The period of probation was introduced in 2004.

could not reasonably be expected to live with the respondent, or desertion.[37] It cannot be assumed that all clergy divorces were dealt with in this manner.[38] The two churches are very different when it comes to clergy discipline and divorce. Swedish law does not include adultery or "unreasonable behavior" as grounds for divorce, and divorce as grounds per se for church discipline is not found anywhere in the Swedish material. However, some cases of adultery appear among the evidence described below.

To sum up, the rate of prohibition for life is almost the same in both churches, 20 percent. In the Church of England, limited prohibition and dismissal are often used, with these harsher penalties totaling 77 percent of all cases. The Church of Sweden's rate for the same disciplinary measures is only 21 percent. It should be noted, however, that a prohibited Swedish priest may recover his or her license after some years with the consent of the bishop and the chapter. In addition, the Church of Sweden has a number of unrecorded cases, since the local church council may, with the permission of the chapter, use civil law to rebuke or dismiss clergy. However, this is not allowed if the chapter states that the behavior in question is in conflict with the ordination vows. If so, the chapter will make the decision. Also notable is that quite a few parishes have paid off (i.e., an agreement to quit combined with severance payment) their clergy (no statistics available).

Comparison of Matching Cases

As already mentioned, it is not possible to fully access the disciplinary proceedings in the Church of England, with the exception of cases brought to the bishop's tribunal, the Arches Court of Canterbury, or the Chancery Court of York. All cases in the Church of Sweden are public, though they are generally anonymous out of consideration for the people involved. Therefore, no names are published in the Swedish cases discussed below.

Only thirteen Church of England cases involving twelve priests are public and published on the Church of England's website. In the following sections, decisions in the Church of England are compared with some cases in the Church of Sweden, matching English cases with similar Swedish cases. It must be noted that there is no perfect match, but I argue that the cases are similar enough for comparison. The cases listed in Table 4 indicate that more than 75 percent of the Church of England cases are related to inappropriate intimate relationships. Other cases involve offenses against financial or administrative regulations. It is impossible to know whether these cases reflect all the cases in the Church of England. If so, there is an

37. *Clergy Discipline Measure 2003*, S30 1 b.
38. Iles, "Clergy Discipline Measure 2003: A Progress Report."

apparent difference between the two churches: in the Church of Sweden 45 percent of the complaints for the period 2000–2004 related to sexual behavior or addiction. Other cases involved financial irregularities (15 percent), offenses against regulations (7 percent), or lack of cooperation or leadership (15 percent).

In Table 4, all published Church of England cases are matched with similar Swedish cases. In order to gather more cases for comparison, those throughout 2013 are included. It was not possible to match cases 7, 10, 11, or 12 (Gilmore, Robinson, Tipp and Northern, and Landall) with any Swedish case. As the table shows, six cases in the Church of England relate to intimate relationships with parishioners (King, Gair, Okechi, Rea, Rowland, and Meier). In all these cases, the priest was dismissed and prohibited either for a period or for life. The Church of Sweden's similar cases reveal another pattern of penalty. In case 1 (adultery with a married man), the Swedish priest claimed that the relationship was conducted in her free time and that as a private matter it had no bearing on her ordination vows. The chapter rejected this, and the priest was criticized: the chapter stated that her conduct was injudicious and blameworthy, but she was not prohibited. This case is comparable to that of King in the Church of England, who was prohibited for four years and dismissed.

In case 2, Gair was prohibited for seven years and dismissed for a relationship with a parishioner seeking counsel. This case is comparable to that involving a Swedish priest's intimate relationship with a woman after a short acquaintance: the chapter expressed that priests must always presuppose that people address them as priests: "The relationship between a priest and his or her parishioners must never be obscured by the suspicion that kindness, care, or consideration in reality serve selfish purposes. A priest must refrain from entering into intimate relationships under circumstances giving the impression that the priest has made use of his or her position for personal advantage." The priest explained his behavior by stating that he "took the chance." He was prohibited and subsequently dismissed.

An intimate relationship with a person seeking counsel was also at the center of case 3. In the Swedish case, the woman became pregnant and the priest suggested an abortion. The pregnancy ended in miscarriage. The chapter decided on a rebuke. This is comparable to that of Okechi, who was prohibited from serving in the Church of England for ten years and dismissed after having sexual relations in a similar situation. Case 3 can also be compared to that of Meier (Case 13), who had an intimate relationship with a vulnerable young woman. Meier was prohibited for life from the Church of England.

Another Swedish priest established a sexual relationship with a woman during his third marriage (case 4); he pretended he was divorced. The chapter argued that matrimony involves fidelity, sincerity, and honesty and the priest was prohibited. In Table 8, this case is compared to that of Rea, who left his wife and moved into the house of a parishioner. Rea was prohibited for fifteen months.

In case 5, a Swedish priest admitted to alcohol abuse and to trying to have intercourse with one of his wife's friends. He was accused of rape by the woman, though the court rejected this claim. There were also suspicions that he had been driving while drunk. The chapter decided upon prohibition, but the priest was reinstated after a few years. This case is comparable to the case of Davies (alcohol abuse and "swinging"), who was prohibited for twelve years.

A Swedish priest in his late thirties had a sexual relationship with a fifteen-year-old girl who was not a parishioner (case 6). The relationship was legal. The chapter stated that the affair was "to some extent inconsistent with the ordination vows." The meaning of this statement is not clear. This is somewhat comparable to the case of Rowland, who had an affair with a parishioner. In this case, a marriage was damaged and the priest was dismissed and prohibited for ten years.

The above-mentioned five cases in the Church of England must be added to this list in which admitted adultery in a divorce court led to penalties (removal from office or prohibition) imposed by the Bishop. It must also be remembered that English clergy in these cases were generally prohibited, dismissed, and lost their place to live. No cases regarding divorce per se are found in the Swedish material.

To sum up, it is evident that the Church of England's penalties in cases including inappropriate intimate relationships are more severe than those imposed by the Church of Sweden. It is more common in the former than the latter for a priest to lose his or her benefice or face a long prohibition. The Church of Sweden does not treat extramarital intimate relationships as severely as the Church of England does. Furthermore, it may be noted that argumentation differs between the churches. The Church of Sweden Canon Law prescribes that the chapter may act against a priest if, for example, "he or she has damaged the esteem of ordained ministry to a great extent."[39] This regulation is related to the way the parish and society react to the priest's behavior, not to any specific theology of marriage, morals, or ethics. The line between accepted and unwanted priestly behavior therefore shifts when the public's views change. The ethical guidelines discuss these issues in

39. *Kyrkoordning*, chapter 31 § 12.

connection with the credibility of the church, not as theological or ethical/ moral responsibilities. The Church of England's decisions, in contrast, are based upon a restricted view of divorce and upon the understanding that it is the duty of the priest to "at all times be diligent to frame and fashion his life and that of his family according to the doctrine of Christ." [40] "Guidelines for the Professional Conduct of the Clergy" discusses "moral integrity" and "faithfulness in marriage." These different points of departure seem to have led the two churches to different views on priesthood, divorce, and extra-marital sexual activities.

Table 8 Matching decisions in Church of England and Church of Sweden.

		The Church of England, 2006–2013[41]		The Church of Sweden, 2000–2004	
	Case	Complaint	Decision	Complaint	Decision
1	King	Conduct unbecoming. Inappropriate relationship with married woman. Intercourse not proved.	Inappropriate for a priest. Prohibited for four years.	Adultery with married man. No pastoral relations. Priest's marriage survived, but the man's marriage did not.	Rebuke.
2	Gair	Intimate emotional relationship with parishioner seeking counsel for marital problems. Intercourse not proved.	Unprofessional behavior. No remorse. Seven years of prohibition.	Intimate relations with parishioner after short acquaintance.	Prohibition (leading to dismissal).

40. *Canons of the Church of England*, c26; Iles, *Clergy Discipline Measure 2003.*

41. Retrieved 2014-04-28 from http://www.churchofengland.org/aboutus/structure/churchlawlegis/clergydiscipline/tribunal-decisions.aspx.

		The Church of England, 2006–2013[41]		The Church of Sweden, 2000–2004	
	Case	Complaint	Decision	Complaint	Decision
3	Okechi	Sexual relations with parishioner seeking support.	Inappropriate with respect to the high standards required of the clergy. Removal from office and ten years of prohibition.	Intimate relations with person seeking counsel leading to pregnancy (miscarriage).	Rebuke.
4	Rea	Conduct unbecoming. While married (marriage under breakdown), left his wife and moved into the home of a parishioner, forming an intimate relationship.	Unprofessional behavior. Fifteen months of prohibition.	Intimate relationship with another woman during his third marriage.	Prohibition.
5	Davies	Drunk at services. Told colleagues that her marriage was an open relationship. "Swinging" during holiday.	Alcohol abuse and sexual misconduct. The priest should set an example of faithfulness in marriage. Twelve years of prohibition.	Drunk while driving. Making unwelcome sexual advances to women. Accused of rape; no crime proved.	Prohibition (later reinstated).
6	Rowland	Intimate relationship with parishioner employed by the parish.	Unprofessional behavior damaging marriage and the parish. No remorse. Dismissal and ten years of prohibition.	Intimate relationship with fifteen-year-old girl. Not a church member.	Statement.

7	Gilmore	Eager and unwelcome improper sexual advances.	Sexual molesting unbecoming a priest. Dismissal and two years of prohibition.	No matching case.	
8	Faulks	Lacking financial routines.	Administrative failings. No crime. Period of probation.	Priest asked parishioners to send money to his own bank account to cover costs related to confirmation class. Other minor financial offenses. Crime or financial gain not proved.	Rebuke. Paid off by parish.
9	Wray	Theft of money due to the diocese and the parish of approximately £21,000. Police investigation could not prove crime.	Dishonesty, inefficiency in the performance of duties of the office for at least fourteen years. Dismissal and prohibition for life.	Ordering catered meals for group gatherings at the expense of the parish (£50). No crime proved in police investigation.	Rebuke (dismissed by parish).
10	Robinson	Neglect or inefficiency in the performance of duties of the office.	Neglect in performance of duties of the office. Suspended for five years from making or sharing in making any appointment involving direct or indirect contact with children.	No matching case.	

	The Church of England, 2006–2013			The Church of Sweden, 2000–2004	
	Case	Complaint	Decision	Complaint	Decision
11	Tipp and Northern	Serving in the same parish. Moving in together while both were married to others, leaving their spouses, positions without notice.	Abandoned their pastoral responsibilities and spouses, forming an unbecoming relationship. Dismissal and prohibition for life and twelve years, respectively.	No matching case.	
12	Landall	Complaints by children. Placed permanently on the Children Barring list and the Adult Barring List— meaning he was prevented from exercising parish work. No details revealed.	Guilty of neglect in the performance of the duties of his office. Prohibition for life.	No matching case.	
13	Meier	Intimate relations with 18-year-old former parishioner staying as au pair in his house	Conduct unbecoming or inappropriate to the office and work of a clerk in Holy Orders. Prohibition for life.	See Case 3	

Two cases (8 and 9, Faulks and Wray) concern financial irregularities. Faulks (lacking financial routines) in the Church of England can be compared to a Swedish priest who requested that money be deposited into his personal bank account for costs related to confirmation class. No crimes were proved. Faulks received a period of probation, and his Swedish colleague was rebuked. However, the latter was paid off by the parish and had to move to another post.

The other case (9) relates to theft. In both the English and the Swedish cases, the police investigation did not prove any crime. Wray was suspected of withholding £21000, and the Swedish priest £50. Wray was dismissed and prohibited for life. The Swedish parish dismissed its priest, and the chapter decided upon a rebuke. Considering the difference in the sum of money in these cases, differences in penalty standards cannot be argued.

In these two cases, it cannot be noted that the different churches have different standards.

DISCUSSION

The systems for disciplining clergy in the two churches have both similarities and differences. One difference concerns publicity. Although the Church of England has a system of discretion, it has been possible to compare the two churches to some extent. Complaints against Swedish clergy appear to be more frequent, but in cases brought to investigation English clergy run a higher risk of prohibition and dismissal (75 percent compared to 21 percent). The cases matched in Table 4 indicate that the Church of England deals with problems of sexuality and inappropriate intimate relationships in a different, harsher manner than the Church of Sweden does.

It can be assumed that the different approaches to those issues involve both societal and theological elements. In the World Values studies, Sweden is something of an outlier as the most secular country with the highest scores concerning self-expression values. Britain, on the other hand, has more traditional values and somewhat lower scores on self-expression values.[42] Sexual-ethical permissiveness is generally higher in Sweden than in Great Britain.[43] In line with those findings, adherence to traditional values on marriage and sexuality may be more expected in England than in Sweden. Sexual-ethical permissiveness may lead to greater acceptance of non-traditional acts and relationships in the Church of Sweden. English law upholds marriage to a greater extent than Swedish law, for example, and the Church of Sweden permits marriage in the church after divorce with no restrictions, something that is also true for the clergy.

Theological standpoints regarding holy orders reveal that the Church of England, on theological grounds, expects its ministers to live faithfully in marriage, holding them to a higher standard than the Church of Sweden expects of its priests. The Church of England also imposes higher expectations

42. Inglehart, and Welzel, "Changing Mass Priorities."
43. Halman, and Luijkx, "Impact of Religion."

on its clergy than the Church of Sweden, especially when it comes to inappropriate intimate relationships, and reacts in a harsher manner when these expectations are not met. This might partly be explained by the different outcomes in the World Value studies, but also by the different points of departure for the ethical guidelines of the two churches (theological and the esteem of the ministry, respectively). It seems that, in these issues, the Church of Sweden, like the Church of Norway, applies a legalistic view rather than an ecclesiological one. In this respect, the Church of England seems to be more similar to the Norwegian free churches.

It thus appears that different values in the two countries, different points of departure for ethical guidelines and the tendency to view the church as a legal or ecclesiological entity contribute to different outcomes when these churches discipline their clergy.

We can assume that quite a few Swedish clergy, had they been disciplined according to the Church of England's standards, would have been prohibited and/or dismissed. In the Church of Sweden, however, these priests are considered clergy in good standing. A Church of England Bishop who accepts a Swedish priest should therefore perhaps consider that "in good standing" may mean something quite different in the two churches.

BIBLIOGRAPHY

Bridger, Francis. "A Theological Reflection." In *Guidelines for the Professional Conduct of the Clergy*, 13–22. London: Church House, 2003.

Brohed, Ingmar. *Sveriges kyrkohistoria 8. Religionsfrihetens och ekumenikens tid.* Stockholm: Verbum, 2005.

Bursell, Rupert. "More Turbulence? Clerical Misconduct Under the Clergy Discipline Measure 2003." *Ecclesiastical Law Journal* 11 (2009) 154–68.

Canons of the Church of England. Online: http://www.churchofengland.org/about-us/structure/churchlawlegis/canons/canons-7th-edition.aspx.

Church of England Licensed Ministries 2009. Online: http://www.churchofengland.org/media/1182125/church of england ministers 2009.pdf.

Clergy Discipline Measure 2003. Code of Practice. London: Church House, 2006.

The Clergy Discipline Rules 2005. Online: http://www.legislation.gov.uk/uksi/2005/2022/pdfs/uksi_20052022_en.pdf.

Codex ethicus. Etiska riktlinjer för diakon, präst och biskop i Göteborgs stift, antagna vid diakon- och prästmötesdagen i Göteborgs domkyrka den 1 juni 2005, efter överläggningar i kontrakten, vid prästsällskapets sammanträde den 10 september 2003 och vid diakondagen den 27 november 2003. Göteborg: Göteborgs stift, 2005.

Codex ethicus. För diakoner, präster och biskop i Växjö stift. Sine anno. Växjö: Växjö stift.

Codex ethicus. För präster och diakoner i Strängnäs stift. Strängnäs: Strängnäs stift, 2010.

Codex ethicus. Riktlinjer för tolkning av diakonens och prästens vigningslöften i Luleå stift. Framtagen av biskop och prostmöte i november 2006. Luleå: Luleå stift, 2006.

Guidelines for the Professional Conduct of the Clergy. London: Church House, 2003.

Guidelines for the Professional Conduct of the Clergy. Draft Edition. London: General Synod, 2014.

Halman, Loek, and Ruud Luijkx. "The Impact of Religion on Moral Orientations: Evidence from the European Values Study." In *Religion, Democratic Values and Political Conflict. Festschrift in Honor of Thorleif Pettersson*, edited by Yilmaz Esmer, et al., 23–44. Uppsala: Uppsala universitet, 2009.

Hansson, Klas. *Svenska kyrkans primas. Ärkebiskopsämbetet i förändring 1914–1990.* Uppsala: Uppsala universitet, 2014.

Hansson, Per. "Clerical Misconduct in the Church of Sweden 2000–2004." *Ecclesiastical Law Journal* 12.1 (2010) 17–32.

———. "The Clerical Ethos. The Church of Sweden Authorities and Clerical Ethical Standards." In *Church Work and Management in Change*, edited by Kati Niemelä, 76–100. Tampere: Church Research Institute, 2012.

Hill, Christopher. 2010. "Clergy Discipline and Pastoral Care: Bishop's Mitre or Judge's Wig?" *Theology* CXIII.874 (2010) 254–59.

Huovinen, Eero. "How Can One Be and Serve as a Bishop." *The Jurist* 66 (2006) 54–69.

Iles, Adrian. "The Clergy Discipline Measure 2003: A Canter Through its Provisions and Procedures." *Ecclesiastical Law Journal* 9.1 (2007) 10–23.

———. "The Clergy Discipline Measure 2003: A Progress Report." *Ecclesiastical Law Journal* 16.1 (2014) 3–17.

Inglehart, Ronald, and Christian Welzel. "Changing Mass Priorities: The Link Between Modernization and Democracy." *Perspectives on Politics* 8.2 (2010) 551–67.

Karle, Isolde. *Der Pfarrberuf als Profession. Eine Berufstheorie im Kontext der modernen Gesellschaft, Praktische Theologie und Kultur.* Gütersloh: Chr. Kaiser/Gütersloher Verlagshaus, 2001.

Kleiven, Tormod. "Intimitetsgrenser og tillitsmakt. Kirkesamfunnets bruk av retningslinjer i møte med seksuelle krenkelser sett i lys av et diakonifaglig perspektiv. " PhD diss. Oslo: Det teologiske menighetsfakultet, 2008.

Kyrkoordning med angränsande lagstiftning för Svenska kyrkan. Stockholm: Verbum, 2010.

Nordin, Hans-Erik. 2010. Codex ethicus. För präster och diakoner i Strängnäs stift. [Codex ethicus. The Diocese of Strängnäs]. Strängnäs: Strängnäs stift.

Lyttkens, Carl Henrik. *The Growth of Swedish-Anglican Intercommunion Between 1833 and 1922.* Bibliotheca theologiae practicae 24. Uppsala: Uppsala universitet, 1970.

Österlin, Lars. *Churches of Northern Europe in Profile: a Thousand Years of Anglo-Nordic Relations.* Norwich: Canterbury, 1995.

Podmore, Colin. "A Tale of Two Churches: The Ecclesiologies of The Episcopal Church and the Church of England Compared." *Ecclesiastical Law Journal* 20 (2008) 34–70.

The Porvoo Common Statement. Uppsala: Nordiska ekumeniska rådet, 1993.

Russel, Anthony. *The Clerical Profession.* London: SPCK, 1980.

SKU 1998:5. Personal, tillsyn, överklagande. Svenska kyrkans utredningar 1998:5. Uppsala: Svenska kyrkan, 1998.

Under Authority. The Report of the General Synod Working Party Reviewing Clergy Discipline and the Working of the Ecclesiastical Courts. London: The General Synod of the Church of England, 1996.

9

A Deliberate Action

Leaving the Evangelical Lutheran Church of Denmark

KAREN MARIE SØ LETH-NISSEN

MEMBERS LEAVING CHURCH: BACKGROUND

Over the past ten years, the Evangelical Lutheran Church of Denmark[1] has seen a steady decrease in the membership rate, falling from 83 percent in 2004 to 78 percent in 2014, a fall of 5 percentage points, and approximately 0.5 percentage points per year.[2]

One explanation for the falling rate is the fact that while the Danish population has increased from five point four 4 million in 2004 to five point six million in 2014, the share of non-Christian immigrants and their descendants has been growing even more.[3] The membership rate over the whole population is therefore declining as a result of this. A decline in membership rate is not the same as a decline in membership in numbers, so the actual membership numbers must be examined in order to see how things are evolving.[4] The number of members fell from four point five million in

---

1. English name taken from: Folketinget, *My Constitutional Act.*
2. Kirkeministeriet, *Kirkestatistik.*
3. Lüchau, *Seks teser*, 313.
4. Ibid., 312.

2004 to four point four million in 2014, a fall of one hundred and ten thousand in ten years, approximately eleven thousand per year.

From January 1, 2011 to January 1, 2012, the number of members fell by fourteen thousand six hundred, a decrease of 0.3 percent. The decline happens for two reasons:

1) Each year more members of the church die, than children being baptized into the church as new members. Of the deceased about 90 percent are members of the church, while only approximately 70 percent of infants are baptized.[5]

2) Each year sees a larger number of direct resignations than direct enrollments other than baptism. 2012 was an unusual year with a significantly higher number of resignations, namely twenty one thousand, with only six thousand six hundred enrollments. The year 2011 was more to the normal with thirteen thousand five hundred resignations and six thousand one hundred enrollments, as was 2013 with twelve thousand two hundred resignations and six thousand four hundred enrollments.[6]

The facts presented here represent a challenge to the Evangelical Lutheran Church of Denmark. There is a decline in membership rate as well as a significant number of direct resignations each year, and it calls for a closer examination of why the resignations take place. Denmark has not had a tradition of examining the qualitative basis why people choose to opt out of the church, and there are thus no Danish studies to rely on. The purpose of this study is to initiate hedging motives, thoughts and reflections in the processes that lead to resignations, as well as try to single out factors pushing people towards resignation.

THEORY

Membership in the church can be defined as a lifelong relationship between the church and the member, containing religious, jurisdictional and traditional aspects. The membership is inaugurated by baptism.[7] Previously, the membership by baptism marked the entering into both society and church,[8] but during the nineteenth century, baptism has increasingly been solely a matter of entering the church. It is now a choice that parents take on behalf of their children.[9] Membership in the church is a choice, but not a choice that is only taken once. You can argue that the membership is up for nego-

5. Kirkeministeriet, *Kirkestatistik.*

6. Ibid.

7. *Lov om medlemskab af folkekirken.*

8. Iversen, *Dåben som optagelse,* 72–86.

9. Ibid., 85.

tiation throughout life, at every contact the individual has with the church.[10] It is always possible to resign, with the consent of your parents before the age of eighteen.[11]

As Lüchau and Andersen have argued, the well-educated, well-earning younger men in the larger cities is the group of church members most likely to opt out of church, but for what reasons do they opt out? General considerations point to the secularization of society, the individualization process and the general loss of tradition[12] making resigning from church possible. Individuals are not as tied to the same life choices as family and friends as they were before. To Taylor, secularization as a concept is not designating the process of pushing out religion from society, but more as a change in the conditions under which religion is part of the society. Taylor describes the development as a shift from a society where faith in God stands unchallenged and unproblematic, and where not believing is unthinkable, to a society where faith is one possibility among many others.[13]

Being able to resign is thus a result of the development of the society over the last few decades, especially the *ethic of authenticity* of the 1960s. The focus on authenticity has put pressure on individuals to *find yourself.*[14] You have to make choices in life to be living life properly. Choosing becomes in itself an identity marker.

How is the choice of resigning from church made, then? This study focuses on the process leading to resignation from church, and has a specific focus on what could be described as *drivers* and *triggers* in the process of resignation.[15] *Drivers* can be described as the events, considerations and motives that led towards the resignation. The *trigger* is the catalyst for the resignation to finally take place. Since a trigger in practice acts as the straw that breaks the camel's back, triggers can in principle be anything, but the drivers are crucial for understanding the deeper layers of the process leading to resignation.

FORMER RESEARCH ON THE TOPIC

An older study of the area of leaving religion is Pål Repstads "Fra ilden i asken" ("From the fire to the ashes") from 1984. Repstad is focusing on

10. Lüchau, *Seks teser*, 316.

11. *Lov om medlemskab*, ch. 1, § 2 and 3.

12. Taylor, *Secular Age*.

13. Ibid., 15, 423.

14. Ibid., 475.

15. The distinction between drivers and triggers has been developed through discussions with Danish sociologist Peter Lüchau while working on the interviews.

religious pacification, a term describing the process an individual is going through when he or she stops being actively participating in religious activities. Repstad interviews twenty-one informants, all of whom have been active youths in a Christian association in the Church of Norway or a free church. He takes four main perspectives in his qualitative study, some of which may be present in each pacification process simultaneously:

- Perspective of meaning: the informant was pacified because religion no longer conveys meaning to the person's life experiences (using theories of Max Weber and Peter L. Berger). The increasing lack of meaning for some members may be due to education and new insights.[16]

- Social ties perspective: the informant was pacified because they no longer have close social ties to the religious group (using theories of Emile Durkheim).[17]

- Perspective of profit: based on a cost / benefit thinking that sees participation as a way to tangible rewards and prestige. When these rewards disappear, it is a contributing factor to the pacification.[18]

- Perspective of the occasion: the informant is pacified because he/she no longer has the opportunity to participate. It may be lack of time; moving away; becoming less mobile; no longer having children at home who could give occasions for going to church; using leisure time in a summer home or camping; women working instead of being at home and active in the religious community.[19]

Repstad's study gives meaningful explanations for pacification of the informants, who identify themselves with both the perspectives of meaning, social ties and occasions. Perspective of profit is harder to agree to for the informants.[20] Repstad's work can be used as a perspective on this Danish pilot study, particularly the perspectives of meaning, social ties and occasions.

In Sweden, the Church of Sweden in 2000 separated from the state, and then saw a wave of resignations. Jonas Bromander in 2002–2003 examined the reasons for members' resignations in his qualitative study.[21] Bromander's findings were that the resignations from the Church of Sweden were the product of a yearlong process, and characterized by a declining church loyalty. The direct cause was often the size of the church tax, perhaps

16. Repstad, *Fra ilden til asken*, 18–22.

17. Ibid., 24.

18. Ibid., 28.

19. Repstad, *Fra ilden til asken*, 29.

20. Ibid., 229–30.

21. Bromander, *Utträden*, 7.

because in Sweden the inability to pay the church tax is considered to be a legitimate reason for the resignation.[22] Other reasons for resigning were bishop K. G. Hammars partaking in public debates and the Church of Sweden's economic affairs.[23] Bromander declares the declining church loyalty as crucial to the resignation process, and looks at how people are alienated over time from the Church of Sweden. His informants expressed that they do not feel their beliefs are consistent with the church's faith. At the same time, they are not socialized to church during childhood, nor do they meet the church naturally in their everyday lives. Bromander concludes that when they do not meet the church and do not use the church, they become very easily alienated over time and thus more likely to opt out of the church.[24] His findings correlate with Repstad's insights on the perspectives of lack of meaning and occasion as a reason for religious pacification.

Kati Niemelä in 2003 studied why Finns withdrew from the Finnish Evangelical Lutheran Church. In the same year, a new law was passed which made it possible to resign from the church by letter. The church then saw a large increase in resignations.[25] Niemelä based her study on five hundred and thirty eight letters, both e-mails and handwritten that people had written to her with their reasons for leaving the church. She includes in her analysis both the content of the letters and results from two quantitative studies, "Urban Young Adults 2004" and "Gallup Ecclesiastica."[26]

Niemelä uses argumentative analysis as a method in which the reasons or arguments for resigning are the object of her analysis. Her results show that one hundred and sixty eight persons have resigned due to a conflict between the church and their attitude to religion and philosophy. A conflict with the church's general attitudes led one hundred and forty-two people to take the final decision. To one hundred and one people the resignation was the result of a personal disappointment with the church anchored in a particular situation. Only fifty-seven, below ten percent, stated that the resignation was for economic reasons. Fifty-five had what Niemelä characterizes as negative attitude towards the church, and the remaining eighteen had reasons that did not fit into the other categories.[27]

Niemelä furthermore concluded that there was a generation gap in the causes of withdrawal. The young (under thirty) leave the church mainly

22. Ibid., 62.
23. Ibid., 76.
24. Ibid., 75.
25. Niemelä, "Alienated," 195–96.
26. Ibid., 199.
27. Ibid., 200.

because they do not wholeheartedly endorse the church's message, and because the church does not make sense for them personally.[28] Older people tend to see membership as part of being a Finn and a good citizen.[29] The older are more likely to resign because they are disappointed with the church.[30] Niemelä's findings correspond with Repstad's perspectives of lack of meaning and partly lack of social ties as reasons for resignation.

Concerning the economic argument for withdrawal, the former Finnish studies found that economic factors played a key role among the factors that led to the resignation, particularly during the financial crisis in the 1990s. According to Niemelä's study, as of the turn of the millennium this has changed because it is not an important factor but is rather an unusual reason for resignation.[31]

A Finnish quantitative study by Lyytikäinen and Santavirta has looked into the connection between church tax and membership. It shows that the size of the church tax has only a small effect on the resignations, as the decision seems to be driven mainly by non-economic variables. The authors argue that a bigger factor than economy in the decision process may be the easy opting-out website established after a Finnish law reform in 2003.[32] However, you could argue that economy or the ease of opting-out is just the last step in the process of resignation. The actual decision could have been taken long before as will be shown in this Danish study.

As the Swedish and Finnish old national churches face the same challenges as the Danish Evangelical Lutheran Church[33] a comparison of reasons for leaving the church will be made in this study. Are the same reasons to be found in Denmark as in Sweden and Finland?

In Denmark there are, as mentioned above, no studies on qualitative basis. Peter Lüchau and Peter B. Andersen made in 2012 a quantitative analysis of data from Statistics Denmark, the central statistics bureau of Denmark, focusing on socioeconomic factors aiming to find out, who are at higher risk of opting out. It turned out that the group that is most likely to resign, consists of men aged eighteen to forty-five who live in the metropolitan area, have a higher education and a higher income than the average Dane. Lüchau and Andersen have also been comparing results with the Nordic studies' socio-economic data on the individuals who are most likely

28. Ibid., 211.
29. Ibid., 214.
30. Ibid., 211.
31. Ibid., 212.
32. Lyytikäinen and Santavirta, "Effect," 16–17.
33. Iversen, "Den danske folkekirke," 33.

to opt out of the church, and they conclude that there is a great similarity with the Danish data in the field.

HYPOTHESIS: WITHDRAWING FROM CHURCH IS A LONG PROCESS

The Evangelical Lutheran Church of Denmark, represented by the local ministers and church offices, are not asking systematically about the reasons for resignation, when members terminate their membership. There is no tradition for this, perhaps for reasons of discretion and respect for privacy. But ministers have the opportunity to ask the retired members why at the time of the resignation.[34]

In the Danish context, we thus have no data on members' motives or considerations related to the resignation from the church. Every year, when church statistics for the previous year are published, the media is filled with articles that explain the decision to resign from the church as if it was made due to economic reasons.[35]

Based on the Swedish study, the present study examines the motivations that come into play in the process of resignation. At the same time, it will be examined whether it can be supported, that the economy and the debate on same-sex marriages plays a crucial role in the resignations in Denmark. The Swedish and Finnish studies concluded, each in their way, that the economy is not the greatest factor, but rather acts as a trigger for the resignation.

The hypothesis of this study is that neither personal economic matters, the easy opting-out website nor gay marriages play a crucial role, but that the process of withdrawal is a thought through process, that spans several years and that the final decision is triggered by different catalysts. The study is preliminary and is based on in-depth interviews with four persons, all resigned from the Evangelical Lutheran Church in Denmark, all fall roughly within Lüchau and Andersen's definition of who is at greatest risk for withdrawal.

34. Kirkeministeriet [Ministry of Ecclesiastical Affairs], e-mail message to author, June 2013.

35. For the abnormal year 2012, the additional number of resignations is explained as occurring because of the Danish debate on same-sex marriages being allowed in the Evangelical Lutheran Church of Denmark. However, in 2012 it was made public in Denmark that you could opt out of the church by sending your local minister an e-mail. This could have triggered a wave of resignations from people ready to leave the church and could also be an explanation for the high level of resignations in 2012 (*Politiken*, September 10, 2012). This explanation is in line with the Finnish study on church tax (Lyytikäinen and Santavirta, "Effect").

METHOD

The purpose of the interviews in the study has been to get as close as possible to people's thoughts and reflections on resigning from the church, as well as identifying factors pushing towards resignations, and it was therefore decided to use qualitative, semi-structured interviews to collect data, as these open up to the informants' language and thoughts.[36] Since the hypothesis was that the resignation occurs as the culmination of a year-long process, it was interesting to look at the informants' relationship to the church throughout their life, and thus using life story interviews provides background.[37]

The relatively limited material does not allow a generalization of the results of the survey, but is only intended as an initial identification of a currently hidden area.

The use of life stories as data is inspired by both Pettersson, Bromander and Furseth, but the analysis using life stories is mainly based on Furseth, as sketched out here. Furseth's concept of life stories can cover entire life spans or only parts of them, and they can deal with all aspects or only one aspect of life. They have a synthesizing character, as it is "the attempt to describe or tell the totality of her or his life as a subjective synthesis that makes life stories unique."[38] A life story interview is a dialogue between the informant and the interviewer, but also a dialogue with oneself and one's past.[39]

Life stories as data can be analyzed in various ways as Furseth describes. This study has chosen the life course analysis, which studies life phases to uncover the underlying structures that form the individual's life, to single out specific conditions for different life courses, which make it possible to generalize. Focus is not on people's own interpretation of their own life or worldviews, but on what people do, or what they have done, and what socioeconomic and cultural factors shape and form their lives. This kind of analysis emphasizes transitions and events in the informants' lives. Important is life age and historical time, since all lives are shaped by the possibilities and events of a certain historical time. This method creates a dialectical perspective, because it connects social history and life history. Another important implication in the analysis of life stories is to remember that life stories cannot be taken "at face value," but are complex data, and at the same time historical and social facts and subjective representations of these. This study analyzes the life stories in a holistic approach, taking the

36. Kvale, *Interview*, 19.
37. Pettersson, *Kvalitet*, 189–90; Bromander, *Utträden*, 26f; Furseth, *From Quest*, 27.
38. Furseth, *From Quest*, 27.
39. Ibid., 34.

narrative as a whole, and taking out passages and analyzing them in the light of the whole narrative.[40] In this short presentation of four individuals' life stories, it is not possible to give more than a brief sketch of the transitions and events in their lives. A more thorough analysis would be able to connect the life stories to historical and socioeconomic factors that have shaped their lives.

The analysis of the data has been done through rewriting the life stories of the interviews into short narratives,[41] with the inclusion of direct quotations to support narratives. The informants have been found through the internet-based Facebook, using the network of the author to refer to relevant interview persons. This way, contacts were made with two people who agreed to join the study. The two others were found through Facebook interest groups with names like "Out of the church." One other person agreed to participate, but he had both resigned and re-entered the church. Since his statements may be colored by his later re-entering, it was decided to exclude his interview from the study. The four people were all men, aged between eighteen and forty-five at the time of resignation, living in Copenhagen or Aarhus (which has been chosen as equivalent to the metropolitan area). They hold master's degrees or have applied for admission to the university. The three highly trained have a higher income than the average of Danes.

The interviews were conducted in June 2013 as qualitative, semi-structured, retrospective interviews, life stories according to Furseth, using tools developed by Per Pettersson,[42] and based on a Danish adaptation of Bromander's Swedish interview guide.[43] During the interview, the participants were presented with a checklist (also an adaptation from the Swedish study)[44] and asked them to check when in their lives they had been in contact with the Evangelical Lutheran Church in Denmark. Interviews took place in the informants' homes. One person did not want the author to visit him at home, and this interview took place at a café. The four interviews each lasted about 1.5 hours and were transcribed and anonymized according to ethical standards by the author of the article.

40. Ibid., 33–38.

41. Kvale, *Interview*, 183.

42. Pettersson, *Kvalitet*, 189–95.

43. Bromander, *Utträden*, 28–31. Bromander has used Pettersson's tools in his study as well.

44. Ibid., 83–84.

RESULTS: ANALYSIS OF THE INTERVIEWS

Table 9 Informants

	Year of birth	Year of resignation from church	Marital status	Profession
Kjeld	1965	2012 (at age 47)	Divorced	Development engineer
Andreas	1966	2009 (at age 43)	Divorced	Development engineer Volunteer, working with youths in atheistic association Training for psychotherapist
Emil	1992	2012 (at age 20)	Single	Unskilled labourer Applicant for university studies
Kurt	1961	1984 (at age 23)	Single	Photographer University studies, natural sciences

Kjeld: From Family Man to Middle-aged Single

Kjeld is forty-eight years old. His parents grew up in Northern Jutland, but moved close to the Danish capital, Copenhagen, for jobs. He was baptised as an infant and raised according to traditional values. He has taken a long education as an engineer. He settled down north of Copenhagen with his wife and children, was married in a church and had the children baptized and confirmed. After the divorce, he resigned his membership in the Evangelical Lutheran Church in Denmark.

His process of reflecting on resigning spans fifteen years. As he answers, when asked about what it meant to him to be a member of the church:

"Yes, but gradually it didn't really matter."

In fact, his reflections about the membership began when he was at university, where he adopted what he himself calls a scientific worldview. Already then, he felt like an atheist, but still called himself a Christian human being with no belief in a God: "No, I have reached the conclusion that I am an atheist, and this is also part of the decision, but it's far from the only reason." And:

> . . . I believe myself to be, very much so, a Christian, because I live in and grew up in a Christian country . . . so all my values are based on Christian faith. It is a very important part of it to say, "Yes, there is no doubt that I am a Christian," though I do not have a belief in a God.

> I[Interviewer]: So you would actually call yourself both Christian and atheist?

> R[Respondent]: Yes, I will do that because my culture is Christian.

Marriage and baptism of the children took place in local churches, and he felt they were part of tradition, more than religious ceremonies. The baptism of the oldest child is described as his most important contact with the church besides his own confirmation. The family used the church on family occasions, and at almost no other times. In his years as a family father, he has continued reflecting on his membership in the church, and uses the metaphor that he felt it as if weights were moving from one side of the scale to the other until the tipping point came, and he resigned.

The important drivers in his process towards resigning were his education and the divorce, which has disillusioned him. After the divorce, he decided to resign from the church in order to better his finances and then be able to keep the house as the framework of his life with his children.

> Yes . . . and then this came along, the divorce, and you start to look at what with the economy, because there is some money in it, after all. In fact quite some money in it. It's a pretty expensive membership when you just look at it as a membership."

> I: Now it's maybe ten to fifteen years ago, you first considered opting out of the church. Is it something you've thought about many times since?

> R: No, not really, it's just been like, lying in the back of the head, and then it may have been a little more prominent in some periods. It is not something that has been intrusive. It has been a slow process. You could say the last straw was . . . it in connection with the divorce, where you just take a step back, and then

it comes up again with all the things about being married in a church and the promise you make there. And as I said, it is also the economy, it has also had its share of it, but far from the main part of it.

The divorce has given Kjeld the opportunity to reconsider his entire life, and he looks back to when he and his now ex-wife were married in church and vowed to stay together until death separated them. That promise did not last, and Kjeld is clearly influenced by the feeling of having broken his promise. Resigning his membership was a very hard decision, since church is still perceived as a very valuable part of the society to him, but he can't justify his membership to himself anymore.

I: So you could say, well, your reasons to resign, they . . . have they changed over time?

R: No, it . . . I really don't think so. Well, I would almost say that. . . . well, that I have stayed in church, because there are some basic things there that I also still think I favor. I just might say that their import have decreased, compared to some other things that I have valued.

Would Kjeld join again if the church tax was lowered?

I: Would you sign up again if church tax was lower?

R: I have not thought about it. It could be an element, but again, I also believe that it would be a process in which several things had to mature, coincide, or how you could put it. I . . . as I said before I don't totally reject the idea that it could happen . . . Right now I just think that it's the right thing, not being a member. . . . But I can imagine that it could happen. Because I also believe that if I had a need for a religious affiliation, it would be the church, I cannot really see any of the other things really appealing to me.

A reason for resignation is by no means the last year's debate on the marriage of homosexuals: "But it's nothing that I . . . of course they should be allowed to." Education and the accompanying change in worldview, as well as the divorce have been critical drivers for Kjeld's process towards a withdrawal from the church. The final straw, the trigger, was the bank's review of his budget in relation to his wish to keep the house after the divorce. Economy has this way played a role as a trigger, but not as a driver. The debate on same-sex marriages in the church has had no weight.

With Repstad's line of thought you can say that Kjeld's process has been affected by the perspectives of firstly lack of meaning, when he had his education and was estranged from the thoughts of the church. You can never say that Kjeld had social ties to the church, but he certainly had occasions for coming. Now his youngest has confirmed his baptism, there is no more similar occasions coming up to tie Kjeld to the church, which means that the perspective of occasion is very important in the case of Kjeld.

Andreas: From Family Man to Spiritual Explorer

Andreas is forty-seven years old, an engineer and divorced five years ago. He grew up in Western Jutland, where his mother's family was part of the conservative Christian movement, Inner Mission, and was close to the Evangelical Lutheran Church in Denmark. His upbringing was based on traditional values. He settled in Copenhagen, and trained as an engineer. He and his wife were wed by a retired minister on a little island, and had their child baptized. After the divorce, he has explored new and more spiritual sides of life, and resigned his membership from the Evangelical Lutheran Church of Denmark four years ago. He is now taking an education as a psychotherapist.

Andreas' process of resigning had a duration of approximately ten years. During his adult life, Andreas has not been using the church for more than family occasions. The first driver in Andreas' process of resigning has been his education, since he adopted a scientific worldview during his training years. "Previously, I was probably more like a rational engineer, where everything had to be so . . . all this with religion and church. . . . I put it down in some boxes, right, and then I said, it's not for me, this. And then we close the lid."

Later in life he encountered the thoughts of atheist and scientist Richard Dawkins, which drove Andreas into a reflective process of whether to resign from church or not. It was very important to Andreas not just to say no to the church, he wanted to put another community instead of the church, and to find another way of supporting social work as well. He joined an atheistic movement, where he still works as a volunteer with youths, but doesn't see himself as an atheist. He calls himself spiritual and has in recent years begun exploring the Buddhist environment in Copenhagen. His way into the Buddhist environment was to go through a course in mindfulness.

> I: Are there any events in your life that have been particularly important to your philosophy of life? Has something happened that made you, for example, more interested in a spiritual way of life?

> R: Yes, that's probably a consequence of the crisis I came in when
> I got divorced. . . . I think it goes back to that. It was certainly
> then I began to be more seeking. . . . Before that, it was probably
> more of an anti-church attitude that I lived with, you might say.
> . . . But after that I just had a need for something different, so I
> started to look back in some way.

> I: Yes? So the divorce, it pulled like the rug from under your
> feet?

> R: No, that would be to say too much, but, no, I was probably
> just getting other interests. Well, and then I also needed. . . . I
> also went into therapy. So it has been a great. . . . I also began
> to engage in something like volunteer work, and . . . I got many
> new interests, that is, and is actually starting to educate myself as
> a psychotherapist now. Because well . . . because of the interest I
> have in what I have seen over the last three or four years. With
> . . . being close to people, the relationships, that is.

Andreas sees the church's offer of preparation for confirmation as very irrelevant to young people. Andreas' process of resignation was characterized
by the desire to find an alternative community. He sought it in an atheistic organization, but found a lack of spirituality. He went on a course in
mindfulness, and searched from there and found a spiritual community in
the Buddhist community of Copenhagen. However, he was still not ready
to withdraw from the national church because he wanted an alternative to
the support he gave to social projects through his church. When he got the
idea, that he could support an African sponsor child for the same amount
as he paid in church tax, he resigned, because now he could legitimize the
decision to himself. Sponsoring an African child gives meaning to him, and
it made the hard decision easier, but it still took courage for him to resign:

> R: I thought it took courage. I have a mother who still has her
> childhood faith intact, and she still cannot really understand
> this. . . . It was a showdown there, there was a conflict with her, I
> had to take, too, just as it not only was . . . it was not just sending
> the papers away, like. . . . There was something at stake, too.

> I: So you've told it to your family?

> R: Yes, yes.

> I: Yes. So it was not an easy decision?

> R: Yes.

Leaving the Church was not easy for Andreas. It was a process spanning many years, where he moved from being very atheistic and critical towards religion into being more spiritually seeking, ending up with a sponsor child as an alternative to his membership in the church. So using Repstad, it can be concluded that Andreas did not want to resign from church before he had found meaning elsewhere, which he eventually found in the Buddhist environment. As Andreas grew up with close social ties to the church, he also wanted to find social ties elsewhere before he could resign, and he found that in the Atheistic movement. One could argue that the perspective of profit is relevant there also as Andreas wanted to be able to give support to a needy child before he could resign. Giving support can be seen in the perspective of profit as it gives you the status of a helper and therefore strengthens your identity. Bromander has an informant, too, who speaks hypothetically about converting his church tax into supporting the NGO Save the Children.[45] You could argue that you see the perspective of profit here as well.

Drivers in the resignation process of Andreas were his scientific education, his meeting the atheistic thoughts of Dawkins, the divorce and all the new insights the period after the divorce have given him.

Economy has never been a driver or a trigger to Andreas, as he sees it as a very important thing to support social work. He would not re-enter if the church tax was lowered.

The debate on same-sex marriages has made Andreas angry with the church. He thinks it should just be implemented. Likewise for the ongoing debate on women ministers. Both he sees as an expression of an outdated fundamentalism.

Emil: From a Family in Crisis to an Existentialist Identity

Emil is twenty-one years old, works as an unskilled worker in a bank, and applied for university studies in the year the interview took place (2013). He grew up in a suburb of the city of Aarhus in Eastern Jutland. His family had no relationship with the church but the baptism of the children as infants. He was brought up on more modern values. One of his siblings had a serious disease when Emil was twelve years old. The disease affected the life of the whole family. He confirmed his baptism as fourteen years old. The parents divorced three years ago. He resigned from the church when he was twenty.

Emil describes his relationship to the Evangelical Lutheran Church in Denmark as "unbelievably passive", and the membership has had almost no

45. Bromander, *Utträden*, 64.

meaning to him: "I: What did it mean to you to be a member of the church? R: Well, I think, like to so many others, it didn't really matter."

Emil's process of resignation spanned three years, but took off in the preparation for confirmation, which was experienced as a rather marginal affair of very little importance. He says about the teachings of the local minister:

> R: Well, I'm not sure that there was anything wrong there, maybe it was because of the general attitude among my peers. It was that it was just bullshit, most of it.

> I: Also when you went to preparation classes?

> R: Also this, about the faith in God, as . . . as a physical phenomenon. That it really wasn't laid out that you can distinguish between the two, at least not in way for me to understand it. . . . On the other hand I do not think that you can understand it.

> I: But you saw that it was not presented as an option?

> R: Yes, because I said. . . . No, it was probably more my father who said, well, then, you really just take it as you yourself want it.

> I: Your father said that?

> R: Yes, pick the things you want . . .

And about his relationship to confirmation and baptism, he says:

> R: Well, weddings, I feel fine about. But such a thing as baptism and confirmation, it . . . especially baptism, I think it's kind of an abuse of the child. And I really think that confirmation, it is a major abuse. Because the fact is that you really lure young people with such materialistic things, and they do not even know what they are saying yes to. You are not formed at that point in your life. This is the time where you are most confused in your entire life.

Church has not been part of his life at all; he never attended a service with his parents. The only use of the church has been in connection with funerals in the family. These are described as very meaningful.

His mother resigned membership some years back, she has explained to Emil that she felt church too full of guilt and shame. His own identity is described as intellectual and he hopes to become a researcher at university. Apart from the possible influence from the crises in his family, he sees his decision of resignation as part of forming his identity, and has put a great deal of reflection into the decision: "Well, I also feel that way, you damn have to consider these many things, and it's also good just to take a break . . . one should not be too emotionally affected when you make a decision. One should not take decisions in rage, when in dissatisfaction or . . ."

Before resigning, he spent time researching on Christianity, in order to be aware of the consequences of his choice. He explains that his resignation was not so much a rejection of the church as an institution, as it was a break with Christianity as such:

> But it has also been kind of a showdown with . . . with Christianity. Determinism and that . . . morals and stuff. It was also a very, very big part of . . . well, it was not at all about something specific . . . not so much on the concrete level, the church as a great institution.

> I: Yes. It is just as much because you needed to make a statement to yourself that you condemn Christianity?

> R: No, I do not condemn Christianity. I consider myself . . . just more like being universally religious.

The trigger to the actual resignation was when he read the news that now you could resign your membership by e-mail.

> R: I had gone with the thoughts for a long time. Then I saw in the news that now it was crazy easy. No one knew that it was easy to opt out. . . . So I thought: "I'm writing an email immediately."

> I: So its been on your mind for a long time?

> R: Yes, I had made the decision. . . . But I should . . . pull myself together . . .

> I: . . . and then you saw it in the news?

> R: Yes.

> I: Was it an easy or difficult decision?

> R : Well, I do not really, no, it is pretty much a complex decision. There were many things to be considered, and it is not easy to join again, because . . . then you have to go through a lot of processes.

> I: You would at least need to talk to the minister to re-enter.

> R: Yes. . . . And, well, it was probably a tough decision. . . . But, but I still feel that it was the right decision. Well, you can't go and undo things you have done in just six months, then I think you break down as a person.

He did so at once, and was very disappointed at the insignificant reaction he got in a standard letter.

The drivers for Emil's resignation could be his sister's disease, as well as his parents' divorce. His growing identity as a coming college student and his existentialist views are important drivers, too. The trigger was the easy access to the resignation.

In Repstad's sense of perspectives, you can in Emil's case talk about a total lack of meaning in relation to the church. He has had no social ties at all, so there has only been the perspective of occasions to keep him in church. After his confirmation, the frequency of occasions has been too low to keep him from resigning.

Economy was no motif at all to Emil. Emil would not join again if the church tax was lowered. The debate over same-sex marriages was not a motive for the withdrawal. On the contrary, Emil is very happy that same-sex marriage was introduced as an option for church members.

Kurt: From Shy Youngster to Disillusioned and Reflective World Traveler

Kurt is fifty-two years old, works as a freelance photographer and is single. He was baptized as an infant, and grew up in the city of Aarhus in Eastern Jutland. The family used the church for family occasions, and his parents wished him to confirm his baptism when he was fourteen, which he did. Kurt travelled the world for three years in his early twenties. He resigned his membership in the Evangelical Lutheran Church in Denmark as twenty-three years old. He holds a master's in natural sciences.

Kurt's process of resigning lasted nine years, and began when he was preparing for confirmation. He actually felt that the minister preparing him

for confirmation was driving him out of the church, because it made it too
easy for Kurt to think, "You are just making it all up."

> I: How long did it . . . so when did you first think of opting out?

> R: I actually think it was when I was confirmed: "Was this really
> quite right?" . . . And I can actually remember a very specific
> event. . . . We sit for confirmation preparation class, and . . . I
> probably did not put it like that, but I was in a setting where
> someone told something about what the Bible was . . . well, I
> thought it sounded really very true. And then our minister tells
> us a story about a man. . . . And so should we relate to the story.
> And we all agreed, well, that story is nonsense, . . . it's just a
> show, and so he uses it to tell us that miracles in fact happen.
> Up in the sky . . . he uses it in some way . . . but I just remember
> that I thought, "Well, the whole thing is just a construction." It
> dropped the penny actually for me . . . when it should really have
> been, I think, been used to tell something about that anything
> is possible when . . . with God's help, but then I said "No." Ex-
> cuse me: "Hell, no. It is not possible." Well, it was a fanciful tale
> that had nothing to do with reality, and that was where I started
> doubting a little.

He finished school and travelled the world for several years, experiencing
peoples' lives everywhere. He says that he realized that everybody seems to
need religion, but that religion basically is the same everywhere. Coming
home he finally decided that there was nothing in religion for him, and left
the church, in what he describes as an easy decision. It is now thirty years
ago.

> I: At the time you resigned, was there a particular incident that
> caused you to make the decision?

> R: No, it was a . . . a grand tour of that I was thinking about
> things and I thought it became more and more absurd . . . be-
> ing a member of the organization. . . . And then at one point I
> thought, well, I should pull myself together, and then I resigned
> . . . it was probably maybe one or two years after this [his world
> travel], so let's say 1984, though I am not quite sure.

> I: Yes. But that means, that being out traveling the world, it was
> . . . how to say . . . it helped to mature your decision?

R: Yes, that's it. Well, I'm simply out and see people live their lives with another religion. And I see that it is absolutely very meaningful to them, and certainly I think that is fantastic. I stayed for a month in Kathmandu, among other things, at a time . . . and I got up before the sun rose, many mornings, and sat down in the local temple, such an enclosed courtyard where people come in, completely sleepy and then they have to hurry to pray to a number of gods. Because the gods represent differ-ent things. For example, if you have a sick child, it's one particu-lar God, you sacrifice to, and pray, and you can see that they are completely . . . tears flowing down their faces. . . . But if you have the Christian conviction, then you say: "What a pity that they do these things, because it doesn't . . . there is no god there, the god does not exist. Because there is only one true God, forever and ever. And this guy, it's just a social–cultural construction, but to them . . . to them it makes sense of course. But he does not really exist. Our God exists in reality." And those two things makes me just absolutely convinced that people create gods.

He has worked actively for the atheistic movement in Denmark, and his father resigned his membership after the mother's death a few years ago.

The drivers in Kurt's process can be seen as both the irrelevant meet-ing with church as a youth, and the formative journey he undertook. The economy has not affected Kurt's decision: ". . . I have not resigned because of money. It's . . . the fundamental things." Kurt would not join again if the church tax was lowered.

The trigger in Kurt's case is not so easy to grasp. This could be related to the fact that the resignation took place many years ago. The perspective in Repstad's sense that gives sense in Kurt's process is the lack of meaning, which is very dominant with Kurt. In fact, it is so dominant that still, after all these years, he is trying to convince others to resign from the church, too.

Kurt resigned many years before the debate on same-sex marriages was current, and the debate therefore has not affected his decision.

DRIVERS AND TRIGGERS IN RESIGNING
FROM THE CHURCH

How do the results of the analysis fit with the hypothesis? The interview analysis shows that these four men have been through a lengthy resignation process, spanning from three to fifteen years, and that several different driv-ers have been involved in the process. Each of them indicates different trig-gers when they finally resign: bad economy, finding a good alternative, and easy access to resigning. As mentioned earlier, the triggers are not especially important in understanding the process. Triggers are just catalysts and not causes.

The drivers on the other hand are crucial. The main drivers in this study are: higher education bringing on a scientific view of the world and its origin; the confirmation preparation seemed irrelevant; that there have been life crises such as illness in the family or a divorce; and a long educational journey that gave insight or disillusionment.

Economy's role as a driver is non-existent. It has not been important to them to save the church tax. All were asked if they would join again if the church tax was lowered, and the answer was in every case, "No." Kjeld had the economy as a partial trigger, and he answers to the question of re-entering that there would have to be many more things that had to change than just the economical side of it.

The debate over same-sex marriages in church has apparently not meant anything in relation to the resignations. Two of the informants have resigned before the debate took off in 2012, and the topic has not affected them much in the withdrawal process.

Repstad described in his study the mechanisms behind leaving a religious community, from being active to being passive, before finally leaving the community. The perspectives of meaning, social ties and occasion were very useful to bring into this study, and maybe also the perspective of profit. To all four informants, the church's way of interpreting the meaning of life did not give meaning to their lives. None of them had any social ties in a religious community. One, Andreas, was raised in a religious community in Western Jutland and therefore had social ties as a child, but had lost them because of moving away to get his education. To Andreas it was very important to find a substitute for the support to the needy that he was giving through his church tax, and you could argue that his finding a sponsor child as an alternative and is relevant under the perspective of support. Two of the informants, the family fathers Andreas and Kjeld, had through their children and wives had occasions to attend church during the years, but with the aging of the children and the divorces, these occasions were no longer there, and the pacification from the church was complete. As Repstad says, it is the lack of meaning, lack of social ties, lack of profit and lack of occasions that sum up to the process of religious pacification and, in the case of this study, resignation from church.

When the results are compared with the Swedish study, from which it takes its design, it is clear that there are similarities in relation to the lengthy and complex process. Many factors have to come together to get to the point of resignation. One difference is that the economy in Sweden more often acts as the trigger. Bromander states that the frequency of the economy as a trigger may be due to poor economy being a socially legitimate reason to resign for Swedes. The question is whether there are differences in this matter to Danish conditions. Are Danes not so keen to tell you that there is something they can't afford? The question cannot be answered from this study.

A comparison with the Finnish study is harder, but common to Finnish and Danish conditions is that the economy does not play any role in the withdrawal process. Niemelä demonstrates that especially younger people resign as a manifestation of honesty when they do not see a connection between the church's faith and their own faith. Such a relationship cannot be seen out of this first Danish study.

PERSPECTIVES CONCERNING CHURCH LEADERSHIP

The informants of the study had four reasons, four main drivers, in their process to leave the church: Irrelevant confirmation preparation, acquired scientific worldview, church membership as an identity marker and life crises that led to existential reflections.

In relation to church leadership, this points to four things the church could reflect on: Can preparation for confirmation be made more relevant for the youths attending it?[46]

Is a scientific worldview really in opposition to being a believer and member of the church? The church could consider focusing on this debate in both mass media communication and adult education in the parishes.

Could life crises acting as the trigger of existential reflections be an open door to the church instead of a closing one, as this study hints? Many churches in Denmark establish community groups for grieving together after the loss of near relations. One could argue that going through a divorce, as was the case for two of the informants, is a grieving process, too. Are community groups for divorcees a possibility for the church? Would groups be a way to reach out to these men and women instead of letting them go?

Church membership as an identity marker is the hardest one to act on, as this concerns major developments in society.[47]

46. Schweitzer et al., *Confirmation*.
47. Taylor, *Secular Age*.

BIBLIOGRAPHY

Andersen, Peter B., and Peter Lüchau. "Individualisering og aftraditionalisering af danskernes religiøse værdier." In Små og store forandringer, edited by Peter Gundelach, 76–96. København: Hans Reitzel, 2011.

Bromander, Jonas. Utträden som utmanar: Analys av de processer som leder till utträde ur Svenska Kyrkan. Uppsala: Svenska kyrkan, 2003.

————. Medlem i Svenska kyrkan: en studie kring samtid och framtid. Stockholm: Verbum, 2005.

Folketinget [the Folketing]. My Constitutional Act with Explanations, 2013. Online: http://www.thedanishparliament.dk/Publications/~/media/PDF/publikationer/English/My%20Constitutional%20Act_omslag_version12_samlet_web.pdf.ashx.

Furseth, Inger. From Quest for Truth to Being Oneself: Religious Change in Life Stories. Frankfurt am Main, New York: Peter Lang, 2006.

Iversen, Hans Raun. "Dåben som optagelse i kirken og/eller samfundet." In Dåb og medlemskab i folkekirken, edited by Hans Raun Iversen, 72–86. København: Forlaget Anis, 2000.

————. "Den danske folkekirke i nordisk belysning." In Fremtidens danske religionsmodel, edited by Lisbeth Christoffersen, et al., 23–39. Frederiksberg: Forlaget Anis, 2012.

Kirkeministeriet [Ministry of Ecclesiastical Affairs]. Kirkestatistik. Online: http://km.dk/folkekirken/kirkestatistik/folkekirkens-medlemstal/.

Kvale, Steinar. Interview: en introduktion til det kvalitative forskningsinterview. København: Hans Reitzel, 1997.

Lov om medlemskab af folkekirken. Bekendtgørelse af lov om medlemskab af folkekirken, kirkelig betjening og sognebåndsløsning. Lovbekendtgørelse nr. 622 af 19. June 2012. Online: https://www.retsinformation.dk/Forms/R0710.aspx?id=142350/.

Lüchau, Peter. "Seks teser om danskernes medlemskab af folkekirken." In Fremtidens danske religionsmodel, edited by Lisbeth Christoffersen, et al., 311–28. Frederiksberg: Forlaget Anis, 2012.

Lüchau, Peter, and Peter Birkelund Andersen. "Socio-Economic Factors behind Disaffiliation From the Danish National Church." Nordic Journal of Religion and Society 25 (2012) 27–45.

Lyytikäinen, Teemu, and Torsten Santavirta. "The Effect of Church Tax on Church Membership." Journal of Population Economics 26 (2013) 1175–93.

Niemelä, Kati. "Alienated or Disappointed? Reasons for Leaving the Church in Finland." Nordic Journal of Religion and Society. 20 (2007) 195–216.

Pettersson, Per. Kvalitet i livslånga tjänsterelationer: Svenska kyrkan ur tjänsteteoretiskt och religionssociologiskt perspektiv. Stockholm: Verbum, 2000.

Repstad, Pål. Fra ilden til asken: en studie i religiøs passivisering. Oslo: Universitetsforlaget, 1984.

Schweitzer, Friedrich, Wolfgang Ilg, and Henrik Simojoki. Confirmation Work in Europe. Gütersloh: Gütersloher Verlagshaus, 2010.

Taylor, Charles. A Secular Age. Cambridge, Mass.: Belknap Press of Harvard University Press, 2007.

10

From "Who Is in Charge?"
to "How Are We in Charge?"

Is It Time for a Shift in the Leadership Paradigm?

HEGE STEINSLAND

DUAL STRUCTURE AS A FRAMEWORK FOR LEADERSHIP

The Church of Norway is a complex entity. Every attempt to draw an organizational map makes this very clear. There is an ongoing effort to analyze and work on possible improvements in accordance with organizational and leadership structures.[1] Two distinguishing features of the Church of Norway are its double structure, soon to be further explained, and number of leadership positions. In the local parish, employed leaders are from both lines in the structure, and at least a couple of elected leaders are from the boards. The focus of this article is mainly on the employed leaders who, together, have responsibilities toward the local church.

Because the scope of this chapter does not allow for a full description of the structure of the Church of Norway, only a short review is provided as a framework. Like other national churches, the Church of Norway has a territorial division. The congregations, which are located within a municipality,

---

1. Askeland, "Hva betyr det om kirken forstås som organisasjon?"; Hauken, "Todelt ledelse"; Henriksen, "Makt og avmakt blant ledere"; Huse, *Prosten*; Krogh, "Det som ikke skjer lokalt"; Nødland et al., *Samstyring i ubalanse*; Skårberg, "Der linjene møtes."

are autonomous. There are two democratically elected governing boards locally within the municipality that operate on behalf of the congregation. One of these boards is the parish council, which is responsible for taking care of everything that can be done to awaken and nourish Christian life in the parish, such as preaching the Word, serving sick and dying people, baptizing and teaching children and young people, and so forth.[2] The other board, the joint council of parishes (*Fellesrådet*) is responsible for the following: financing and managing buildings and churchyards, employing individuals to work at the buildings and churchyards, and maintaining contact with the municipality. An administration led by an administrative leader, the church warden, discharges these responsibilities on a daily basis, and this is a common service for all the congregations within a municipality. The church warden serves as employer and manager for all employees, with the exception of the ministers.[3]

The clergy, however, are employed by the state, not the parish. The ministers work locally in their respective congregations, but their superior is the dean who serves as their employer in the deanery. The dean in turn is under the leadership of the bishop. The leadership exercised by the dean and the bishop involves both supervisory aspects and other aspects of the role of employer.

These two lines within the Church of Norway are grounded in different legislation. The lay structure is rooted in church law, which is decided in the Storting. The clergy are rooted in service instructions for ministers, deans, and bishops, which are decided in the Government ministry. This leads to a double structure for financing, with the ministers being financed by the state and the local parish being financed mainly by the municipality.

Hence, the Church of Norway consists of two parallel structures, each with its own leadership structure. A significant lay leadership needs cooperation and communication with a significant clergy. One of the ways in which to make this happen is through cooperation in the dual leadership embodied by the dean and the churchwarden.

During my ten years of service as a churchwarden, I encountered challenges in making this dual leadership work. That experience inspired me to conduct a study on this particular (and strategically important) dual leadership involving the churchwarden and the dean.[4] In this article, I endeavor to address the following two questions: How does the dual leadership of the Church of Norway affect the relationship between leaders and the

2. *Kirkeloven*, § 9.

3. Ibid., § 14.

4. Steinsland, "Men jeg ønsket å være."

performance of leadership? And how might alternative conceptualizations of leadership offer insights into coping with the challenges of a dual leadership structure?

Before I delve deeper into this topic, I must first clarify the distinction between *dual leadership* and *shared leadership*. Dual leadership is a description of a leadership structure involving two leader positions, unlike a unitary leadership with one leader at the top of the organization. Shared leadership is an approach to leadership practice that focuses on, and takes advantage of, the capacity for leadership within organization.

IS THE LINK MISSING OR JUST MISTY? PREVIOUS RESEARCH ON DUAL LEADERSHIP

Since the 1996 Church of Norway Act came into effect, research has been conducted on this area, with a particular focus on leadership qualities, leadership roles, and structural aspects.[5] Lately, owing to changes in the relationship between the Church of Norway and the state, studies have been carried out so as to build a good knowledge base from which to make decisions regarding the future development of the Church of Norway.[6] However, in my opinion, little attention has been paid to the relational aspects of leadership cooperation in a complex structure with multiple leadership positions; thus, many leaders are simply expected to work things out together.

In 2013, I conducted a study involving two of the leadership groups that together represent the formal leadership in a local church.[7] I asked five informants (two deans and three churchwardens) how the existing dual leadership structure affected the relationship between the dean and the churchwarden, and the leadership as such, in their specific experience. According to my findings, none of my informants experienced what scholars would describe as a robust and interdependent relationship.[8] Nor did I find examples of mutual experience of leading together toward the achievement of common goals among my informants, even in those situations where the climate and the intention were positive.[9]

5. Askeland, "Hva betyr det om kirken forstås som organisasjon?"; Christensen, "Som hånd i hanske"; Hauken, "Todelt ledelse"; Huse, *Prosten*.

6. Den norske, *Ledelse i folkekirken*; KA Kirkens Arbeidsgiver- og interesseorganisasjon, *Framtidig organisering*; Nødland et al., *Samstyring i ubalanse*; Arbeidsgruppe, *Kjent inventar*.

7. Steinsland, "Men jeg ønsket å være en som kunne løftet ham."

8. Kvalsund and Meyer, *Gruppeveiledning*, 20.

9. Steinsland, "Men jeg ønsket å være en som kunne løftet ham," 29.

A different experience involving the dual leader relationship of the dean and the churchwarden is shared in an unpublished report written by the dean of Namdal.[10] This "inside view" was written in common understanding with the churchwarden. In my opinion, this account is a valuable contribution worth mentioning because it describes a case that is quite unique and represents a different experience from my material. For approximately ten years, the dean and the churchwarden worked together on a pilot project, endeavoring to set up a dual leadership in a new local church organization that had been formed by the merger of several smaller units. Torset described how they, from day one, focused on the differences between them and in what way these differences would be a challenge and a resource. The dean and the churchwarden spent a lot of time working together, with respect and, not the least of which, loyalty existing between them. At the beginning of this pilot project, they were well aware of the obvious question that hung in the air between them: Who is the real boss here? This was a challenge, and they decided to confront it together. They made certain changes to clarify that they both shared a concern and a responsibility for the whole. One such change involved taking turns in leading the team meetings. While conversing with Inge Torset, the dean commented that they grounded their way of thinking about their leadership in values from a shared horizontal leadership. At the same time, they experienced the need for vertical leadership while building a new culture and set new acceptability standards. In these challenging situations, they considered themselves fortunate to be able to work together and support each other.[11]

A report that had been ordered by the Ministry of Culture to evaluate the management of the local church was delivered in 2014 by International Research Institute of Stavanger (IRIS).[12] The authors of the report examined the relationship between the two counsels that operate on behalf of the congregation. They described their findings as "unbalanced governance" and pointed to the challenges experienced in achieving a holistic leadership and long-term strategies. One of the findings in this recent IRIS report was that the local church, or the parish, struggles with limited access to resources, a lack of holistic leadership, and a weak emphasis on spiritual and strategic work.[13]

Taken together, this material shows that there are challenges to overcome to be able to lead adequately within this complex structure.

10. Torset, "Forsøk med interkommunalt kirkelig fellesråd i Midtre Namdal."

11. Ibid.

12. Nødland et al., *Samstyring i ubalanse.*

13. Ibid., 108.

Overcoming challenges seems possible when they are acknowledged and the time and energy to work on them are prioritized.

Dual Leadership: Research from Other Fields

In her 2010 doctoral dissertation, Hilde Fjellvær examined different leadership models in pluralistic organizations.[14] A pluralistic organization is characterized by competing logics and by ambiguity owing to these competing logics. Some examples of logics are mission, profession, resource, bureaucratic, and business logics. The types of pluralistic organizations examined in her work were hospitals, newspapers, universities, and cultural institutions.[15]

Fjellvær defined a dual leadership as two fairly equally mandated leaders dividing the executive leadership roles and functions between them.[16] Dual leadership is described as an alternative to the more common unitary leader structure. To manage the challenges involved in leading pluralistic organizations, some choose to integrate them all in a unitary leadership, whereas others choose to separate them by using a dual leadership in which the tasks are divided into different departments. The departments are usually sorted under administrative tasks and professional tasks.

In a unitary leadership, everyone (professional staff and administrative staff) reports to the same leader. In a pure dual leadership, there are two equally mandated executives, one for the administrative department and one for the professional department. The administrative staff members report to the administrative executive, and the professional staff members report to the professional executive. However, Fjellvær found that several organizations chose a combination of the structures; that is, both leaders had responsibilities in both fields, and the reporting lines could go from professionals to the administrative executive, and vice versa. This type of structure is referred to as a hybrid leadership structure.[17]

A very interesting contribution of relevance to this article is the work done by Wendy Reid and Rekha Karambayya in Canada, who pointed out that dual executive leadership in creative organizations has been understudied. They claimed that studying the conflict dynamics of this relationship could provide greater insight into managing organizations with a similarly structured leadership.

14. Fjellvær, "Dual and Unitary Leadership."
15. Ibid., v.
16. Ibid., 12.
17. Ibid.

Conflict Within the Dual Leader Relationship

Reid and Karambayya focused on how dual executive leaders in creative organizations work with conflict in their relationship and what impact the conflict dynamics in the dual leadership has on the rest of the organization.[18] They recognized that there are several aspects that provide some understanding of how conflict is likely to arise in these relationships. One aspect is that the two leaders were hired independently of each other. A second challenging aspect they recognized is that the two leaders usually had different backgrounds in terms of education and experience and often brought different perspectives and logics into the debate on how to manage the organization. At the same time, there was an emphasis on interdependency between the leaders. The artistic leader depended on the administrative leader to handle the finances, and the administrative leader depended on the artistic leader to create a program that appealed to both sponsors and audiences. A third challenging aspect is that considerable differences existed among the staff members. On the one hand, the creative staff members (artists) tended to be unionized and often worked late mornings, evenings, weekends, and double shifts. On the other hand, the administrative staff members were rarely unionized and usually worked from nine o'clock to four o'clock.[19]

Reid and Karambayya inquired about how executive leaders managed conflict and what influence the conflict dynamic had on the work within the organization. The analysis suggested two responses: The dual leaders either retained conflict between them or disseminated it through the organization. They discovered four types of previously unreported conflict behavior in this dual leadership structure[20]: Advice seeking involves attempts to consult other organizational members and gather information regarding the issue of conflict. Mediation happens when either a board member or a staff member enables communication between the two leaders. Alliance seeking involves behavior by one leader to leverage power through alliances with other organizational members so as to create opposition to the other leader. Abdication of decision making occurs when the two leaders are unable to make a decision and they send the issue up to the board or down to the middle managers for resolution.

Reid and Karambayya took their study one step further and investigated the impact that the relationship's conflict dynamics had on the rest of the organization and the ability of the members of the organization to

18. Reid and Karambayya, "Impact of Dual Executive Leadership," 1074.

19. Ibid., 1080.

20. Ibid., 1085.

realize their responsibilities. This approach, which had not been previously taken, provided some very interesting insights. The impact on the organization was measured with regard to three organizational elements that were internal to the organization. In short, a high correlation was found between how the dual leadership worked with conflicts in their relationship and the effectiveness of the organizational processes. One example of conflict handling had a positive effect on all three processes: Task-oriented conflicts occurring within the dual leadership seemed to make the operational functions more effective, the leader attribution process stronger, and the morale higher. By contrast, emotion-oriented conflict—disseminated through alliance seeking, mediation, or abdication—made the operational functions less effective, the leader attribution process weaker, and the morale lower. These findings underline the importance of advanced skills in dialogue and conflict resolution within the dual leadership.

Contributions from Shared Leadership

Over the past few decades, a shift in thinking has occurred regarding the notion of leadership. Research has increased on (and much has been written about) alternative approaches to leadership, with labels such as shared leadership,[21] leaderful leadership,[22] and extraordinary leadership[23] being applied. What they all have in common is a shift from the notion of one leader leading from the front, often referred to as a "heroic leadership" approach, to leadership as an ability and a capacity for leadership within the organization, often referred to as a "post-heroic leadership" approach. Conger and Pearce defined shared leadership as a dynamic, interactive process of influence among the individuals in a group, with the purpose of leading each other so as to achieve the goals for the group and the organization.[24]

Lately, the notion of post-heroic leadership has been increasingly developed and practiced. Kotter described the importance of adopting this approach as follows:

> The key to create and sustain a successful twenty-first-century organization is leadership. But not only at the top of the hierarchy, with a capital L, but also in a more modest sense (l) throughout the enterprise. This means that over the next few decades we will see both a new form of organization emerge to

21. Conger and Pearce, *Shared Leadership*; Fletcher and Käufer, "Shared Leadership."
22. Raelin, *Creating Leaderful Organizations*.
23. Williams, *Genuine Contact Way*.
24. Conger and Pearce, *Shared Leadership*.

cope with faster-moving and more competitive environments and a new kind of employee, at least in the successful firms.[25]

This approach offers a type of leadership where the formal leader includes others in the leadership, trusting that the wisdom and experience of all individuals in the organization make them much more fit to handle complexity in a fast-changing environment than do the wisdom and experience of just one individual. This approach usually springs from a unitary leadership as the way in which the top leader chooses to execute his or her leadership.[26]

Many scholars and management practitioners have argued that dual and shared leadership cannot function effectively.[27] By contrast, a number of leadership scholars have found that when leadership is shared and distributed, work groups are more effective,[28] schools are more democratic and accessible,[29] and organizations are more coordinated and responsive to the environment.[30] An important distinction, however, is that the mentioned leadership studies have a self-chosen and emergent nature.[31]

Research within this approach tends to point to certain behaviors and skills. Fletcher and Käufer pointed out that shared leadership works only when those involved have relatively strong skills in dialogue.[32] As mentioned previously, Reid and Karambayya showed the importance of managing conflicts within the dual leadership.[33] It is likely that insights from studies on shared leadership are transferable to dual leadership, especially with regard to the skills required to make a dual leadership work effectively, both within the dual leadership itself and throughout the organization.

Michael Wood studied top management teams in churches with three or more ministers within specific churches in the United States.[34] His research contributed to the theoretical implications of shared leadership by showing that the behavior experienced within the team was more significant in determining the practice of shared leadership than the presence of

25. Kotter, *Leading Change*, 183.

26. Conger and Pearce, *Shared Leadership*; Fletcher and Käufer, "Shared Leadership"; Joiner and Josephs, *Leadership Agility*.

27. Alvarez and Svejenova, *Sharing Executive Power*; Locke, "Leadership."

28. Bang and Midelfart, *Effektive ledergrupper*; Reid and Karambayya, "Impact of Dual Executive Leadership."

29. Gronn, "Distributed Leadership."

30. Heenan and Bennis, "Co-Leaders."

31. Reid and Karambayya, "Impact of Dual Executive Leadership."

32. Fletcher and Käufer, "Shared Leadership."

33. Reid and Karambayya, "Impact of Dual Executive Leadership."

34. Wood, "Determinants of Shared Leadership."

a specific organizational structure. He also reported that a horizontal team structure had little or no influence on team members' engagement in the practice of shared leadership. For members who engaged in shared leadership, Wood found that their perception of being empowered to function as a leader within the team organizational structure was of great importance.[35] In addition, Wood revealed four distinct dimensions in shared leadership: joint responsibility for competition of tasks, mutual skill development, decentralized interaction among personnel, and emotional support.

METHODICAL ISSUES: AWARENESS THROUGH DESCRIPTION

The purpose of my study from 2013 was to gain insight from individuals holding a leadership position in the dual leadership structure and to reveal how they experienced its effect on the relationship and the leadership.[36] I searched for specific and subjective experiences. To fulfill this purpose, I chose a phenomenological approach, using interviews as a method for gathering data.[37]

The dual leadership involving the dean and the churchwarden is manifested in multiple ways owing to differences in geographical frameworks, culture, and individuals holding the positions. My intention was not to gain a quantitative overview but rather to attain insights in a few cases by speaking with key individuals. I chose to speak with five informants who, together, represent three types of leader relationships between a dean and a churchwarden in the Church of Norway. In two of the cases, I interviewed both parties in an actual dual leadership. I talked to them individually, using an interview guide to direct the conversations so that the same topics were covered in each interview. In these two cases, the dean and the churchwarden were at the seat of the deanery, and they worked quite closely together. They shared an office at the same venue and met face-to-face on a regular basis. In the third case, I interviewed only the churchwarden in the dual leadership. The churchwarden was one of several churchwardens within a deanery and was stationed in a different municipality than the dean. This arrangement, which was common for most churchwardens, presented some challenges for the churchwardens and the dean to meet and stay in touch on a daily basis. I believed that interviewing churchwardens in different work arrangements would provide greater insights. The two deans I interviewed had experience in relating to several churchwardens. Each of

35. Ibid., 76.

36. Steinsland, "Men jeg ønsket å være en som kunne løftet ham."

37. Moustakas, *Phenomenological Research Methods*; Postholm, *Kvalitativ metode*.

the two churchwardens in the dual leadership (dean and churchwarden) related to one dean, an individual they met on a daily basis. I also wanted to learn more about how this dual leadership structure was experienced by a churchwarden working at a distance from the dean.

When I decided to interview two pairs of informants in a dual leadership comprising a dean and a churchwarden who interacted with one another on a daily basis and worked within the same environment, and one informant (a churchwarden) who worked at a geographic distance from the other member (a dean) in a dual leadership, I selected the informants based on availability.[38] I considered each experience to be unique and was not looking for anything specific from my informants. The informants included both men and women who ranged in age from their mid-thirties to their mid-sixties. One pair had worked together for more than a decade, whereas the other pair had worked together for only a couple of years.

The process of gathering material was similar in these three cases. I conducted the five interviews, transcribed them, and sorted and analyzed the material, looking for differences and similarities. I searched for messages to emerge from both different categories and phenomena and for a pattern or a common message to emerge from the material.

FINDINGS: DIVERSITY OF EXPERIENCES AND A UNIFYING DESIRE

Relationship and Leadership

The three cases showed a spectrum of experiences: The churchwarden who worked at a geographic distance from the dean described the relationship with the dean as a "non-relationship," meaning that contact between them was very minimal and rare. They had a few formal meetings during the year but no close and interdependent cooperation. This informant did not have a feeling of shared leadership with anyone else. When beginning the job, he anticipated that it would entail leading toward common goals and fulfilling goals together with the rest of the team. The churchwarden was, as he expressed it, a "boss of paper and money" in reality, meaning that he did not have direct influence on the work that was carried out in the congregation, nor the time necessary to engage in this work. In his experience, the local ministers preferred not to be involved in team cooperation. In short, a relationship did not exist between the churchwarden and the dean who worked

38. Thagaard, *Systematikk og innlevelse.*

at a geographic distance from each other; nor did a shared leadership exist between the churchwarden and the local ministers.[39]

One pair of informants had been working together for nearly a decade. They gave very similar accounts of their relationship, describing it as difficult, and they had resigned in order to make it better. The battle for power was explicitly acknowledged by both of them. On the one hand, the churchwarden had a good feeling about how things worked in his area within the church. People seemed happy, and they managed to work together as a whole toward the achievement of certain goals, thereby building a constructive culture. On the other hand, the dean struggled to find his place in connection with the democratic structure. He could anchor his leadership in the clergy but not in a democratic board, and he struggled with that situation. The dean was confident in his pastoral work, but he had a really hard time finding his place alongside the churchwarden. Both the churchwarden and the dean regretted that this unwanted situation had arisen and admitted that they had envisioned something else for this relationship. Although they had pointed out the difficulties to one another, they never managed to do anything about them. This type of troublesome relationship resulted in parallel work being conducted rather than cooperation and shared leadership.

The other pair of informants had been working together for a much shorter period of time. They saw each other as a resource and were concerned about how to make this relationship work. Both of them included each other in the leadership, but they had different views regarding who else was included. Their descriptions of their relationship also differed. On the one hand, the dean had a very positive description of the relationship. As he expressed it, their relationship allowed them to share experiences and discuss how to handle difficult cases together. On the other hand, the churchwarden was more insecure about the relationship with the dean. He was uncertain about what to discuss with the dean and to what extent, as well as how to handle disagreements. If the churchwarden experienced a conflict involving one of the ministers in the deanery, he was unsure about how the dean would perceive this conflict and if he could count on support and cooperation to handle the conflict. The main problem in this relationship appeared to be finding time to talk things through in a secure and calm atmosphere. They were both very busy, constantly running to different meetings and carrying out tasks, and spent very little time together. There was no sense that their relationship was built on mutual trust. Business was carried out with a vague awareness of shared purposes, goals, and strategies.

---

39. Steinsland, "Men jeg ønsket å være en som kunne løftet ham."

A common purpose seemed more like an assumption than something that was expressed explicitly and embodied in a strategy.[40]

Among the relationships I studied, I did not find any robust and interdependent relationships.[41] Instead, I found one "non-relationship," one difficult relationship leading to parallel work but no cooperation, and one positive but not well-developed relationship. One of the dual leadership pairs seemed to lack the skills and support necessary to work together through the difficult times toward a more robust relationship. The other pair seemed to lack the time and willingness necessary to prioritize working on the relationship.

In addition to the insight gained in the two main categories, directly investigated in the interviews, several subcategories emerged from the material. I will comment on two of them here because they are of particular relevance to this article. One of the subcategories that emerged quite clearly was about objectives. I identified this subcategory as having several different features. One feature was the feeling of confusion about not being able to work together toward the achievement of goals. A second feature was a sense of having the same goals but not being able to name them. A third feature was an assumption that although goals were shared, tension in the relationship created a situation where the leaders could not work together to achieve them or to support each other along the way. None of my informants had a profound experience of working together toward explicitly stated common goals.[42]

Another subcategory worth elaborating on in relation to the notion of shared leadership involved the leadership and governance of a significant group of employees. Highly skilled individuals with a specialization in core competencies within the church, such as catechists, deacons, and organists, obviously fell somewhere under the dual leadership. In my study, I found that this group served under a "hazy" leadership. One churchwarden considered these employees to be leaders in their respective fields and, for this reason, more suited to lead themselves than to be led by him. A second churchwarden said that he did not have the time or capacity to lead them and just had to hope and trust that they did a good job. A third churchwarden considered his responsibility to restrict itself to formalities due to employment. One dean expressed a desire to work with this group and the ministers together, but he was uncertain about his mandate to do so. The other dean felt mandated to do so, but he had a tendency to forget

40. Ibid.
41. Fletcher and Käufer, "Shared Leadership"; Kvalsund and Meyer, *Gruppeveiledning*.
42. Steinsland, "Men jeg ønsket å være en som kunne løftet ham."

this group, focusing instead on the ministers and their work, for whom he was formally and more directly responsible. This group of staff members therefore tended to serve somewhere in between the two leaders, not really benefiting from the leadership of either of them.[43]

Although I did not discover similarities in my material that were specifically connected to the leadership structure in the Church of Norway, I found something of more general interest. While searching for commonalities within this material, I gradually recognized that all my informants did have something in common: In different ways, they all struggled with the gap between their vision and the experienced reality. They all wanted something more or something else for the relationship and for the ability to lead. In "Theory U: Learning from the Future as It Emerges," Otto Scharmer pointed to this as a very important realization when the individuals constituting a system discover this situation together and recognize that they are also able to do something about the situation. This realization (of really wanting and expecting something else and something new from the future) opens up many possibilities. The key, according to Scharmer, is to be empowered together to do something about the situation.[44]

DUAL LEADERSHIP: VIABLE RESOURCE RATHER THAN UNMANAGEABLE PROBLEM?

Thus far in this chapter, I have presented findings to address the first research question: How does the dual leadership in the Church of Norway affect the relationship between leaders and the performance of leadership? From my own research, I have discerned three different experiences: One churchwarden working at a distance from the dean mentioned challenges arising from geographic distance and lack of interaction. The churchwarden described being in a non-relationship within the dual leadership and having no experience of actually leading together. One pair of informants (a churchwarden and a dean), who met on a daily basis, provided quite similar accounts of their relationship, describing it as difficult. They both acknowledged the battle for power between them and admitted that, despite working together for a decade and mentioning the problem several times to each other over the years, they had not managed to do anything about it. They regretted this, but they had resigned themselves to the fact that their relationship was difficult. Because their relationship was so difficult, they conducted their work in parallel and were even tempted to put obstacles in the way of the other rather than offer support. A second pair of informants,

43. Ibid.
44. Scharmer, *Theory U.*

who also met on a daily basis, had a very positive description of each other and an expectation of being a mutual support and resource. However, they differed in their description of how secure they felt in the relationship. The dean seemed to think everything was fine, but the churchwarden felt unsure of how open he could be and to what extent he could count on support in a concrete conflict situation. Their intentions to lead and face challenges together were clear, but they spent far too little time together to fulfill their intentions in reality. They were so busy with their own work that they failed to prioritize working on their relationship and fulfilling their intention of sharing leadership.[45]

In their study on cultural institutions organized in a dual leadership, Reid and Karambayya also pointed out several aspects that can challenge this relationship.[46] One challenging aspect is the fact that the leaders in a dual leadership are hired independently of each other. A second challenging aspect is that the leaders in a dual leadership often have very different backgrounds in terms of their education and experience. A third challenging aspect is connected to differences in the staff (e.g., different tasks and work hours). These aspects seem to be transferable to the context of the dual leadership in the Church of Norway to some extent.

In addition, Hilde Fjellvær showed how a dual leadership is often a deliberate choice in pluralistic organizations as a way in which to handle complexity and several different logics within the same entity. In many cases, the decision to divide the tasks of the dual leadership into departments, usually administrative and professional departments, seems like a good idea.[47]

The rationale behind the dual leadership in the Church of Norway is of a different kind than that explored in the research by Fjellvær. The dual leadership in the Church of Norway is a result of the existence of two lines, one of clergy leadership and one of laity leadership, usually referred to as the ordained ministerial and conciliar line. A common denominator for the dual leadership presented in the research by Fjellvær and in the structure in the Church of Norway is that there are good reasons for it—namely, it can distribute power and take care of diverse tasks. However, as my research shows, there may be a risk that the leaders within the dual leadership are pulled in different directions from each other. With this backdrop, I will now turn to my second research question: *How might alternative conceptualizations of leadership offer insights into coping with the challenges of a dual leadership structure?* To address this question, I want to delve deeper into

45. Steinsland, "Men jeg ønsket å være en som kunne løftet ham."
46. Reid and Karambayya, "Impact of Dual Executive Leadership."
47. Fjellvær, "Dual and Unitary Leadership."

the concept of shared leadership. Whereas dual leadership is a structure, shared leadership is an approach. I find it interesting to consider shared leadership as an ideal for how the leaders within a dual leadership build their practice.

In my research, I found that a large group of employees in the Church of Norway served under a "hazy" leadership. Within the dual leadership structure, these employees served under the churchwarden, but they were quite self-ruled in reality. This group of catechists, deacons, and organists has service instructions that empower the members of this group to be leaders within their own respective fields. Hence, it does not seem appropriate to put them under more direct management control. However, in a vertical leadership approach, there might be an outspoken or hidden assumption that someone else (i.e., someone in charge) is responsible for the whole. The trap here seems to be a situation with a lot of leaders. A lack of coordination among these leaders may explain the absence of common goals and strategies that has been previously reported.[48] In accordance with the notion of shared leadership, this group would be included in a common leadership; this type of leadership is defined as a dynamic, interactive process of influence among the individuals in a group, whose purpose is to lead each other so as to achieve the goals for the group and the organization.[49]

A common leadership might be difficult to envision when the separation of administrative and professional tasks is considered. Therefore, I find Raelin's definition of leadership to be useful.[50] According to Raelin, leadership consists of four core dimensions: the clarification of purpose, the actualization of goals, the sustainment of commitment, and the response to change. These dimensions are better taken care of within the organization than by one or two individuals occupying a certain position because the scope extends beyond the departmental level.

Coping with the challenges posed by a structure with many leaders and a hazy leadership by introducing even more leaders and making no one in particular in charge might seem to be a contradictory approach. This type of organizational structure is known as a flat structure. However, a flat structure can lead to confusion and to the pulverization of responsibility. This is a very relevant critique, and there is also research to support it. Michael Wood, studying self-organized teams of ministers, found that the flat structure in itself had a negative effect on the relationship. Wood attributed

---

48. Nødland et al., *Samstyring i ubalanse*; Steinsland, "Men jeg ønsket å være en som kunne løftet ham."

49. Conger and Pearce, *Shared Leadership*.

50. Raelin, *Creating Leaderful Organizations*, 7.

the success of shared leadership not to the flat organizational structure in itself but rather to the empowerment of all team members to take responsibility within the team structure. In addition, Wood found that some specific behaviors were crucial in making shared leadership work effectively. These behaviors involved exhibiting joint responsibility for the competition of tasks, participating in mutual skill development, decentralizing interaction among personnel, and offering emotional support.[51]

Envisioning a new paradigm of leadership entails a change in focus on what tasks it involves and what skills it requires. Previously in this article, I highlighted some aspects of this. Fletcher and Käufer emphasized the need for advanced dialogue skills in a shared leadership.[52] Reid and Karambayya pointed out the importance of being able to handle conflicts adequately within a dual leadership.[53] The dean of Namdal described, based on his own experience in a dual leadership, how it is possible to build a robust relationship characterized by loyalty and joint responsibility, but doing so takes time and a prioritization of efforts to build this relationship—it does not simply happen overnight.[54]

Based on this information, I can see the contours of new leadership roles for the churchwarden and the dean in a dual leadership. In light of the concept of shared leadership, they will help empower local teams to take on a leadership role together. In addition, they will help facilitate the training and development of skills and insights in how to execute this horizontal approach to leadership.

The most powerful dual leadership of all would comprise leaders who serve as role models by practicing shared leadership themselves and developing skills in dialogue, adequate conflict resolution, and joint support and responsibility for the whole. Doing so would qualify them to be credible mentors for the development of leadership in the Church of Norway.

Even though structure is an important prerequisite for a healthy organization, it can never in itself imbue it with life and spirit. Only the individuals who constitute an organization can do so. An organization built and operated by individuals with strong dialogue and relational skills will be able to develop and fulfill its purpose in changing environments and conditions. In a pluralistic organization and a fast-changing world, no one should have to lead alone. Therefore, I argue that a dual leadership can be a resource if the system directs the dyad toward each other, supports them with tools

51. Wood, "Determinants of Shared Leadership."

52. Fletcher and Käufer, "Shared Leadership."

53. Reid and Karambayya, "Impact of Dual Executive Leadership."

54. Torset, "Forsøk med interkommunalt fellesråd i Midtre Namdal."

to handle the challenges that are inherent, and accepts and anticipates that time is needed to develop the relationship and the leadership. The aim is not to have a dual leadership who can handle everything by themselves and lead in a heroic manner but rather to have a dual leadership who can develop and spread leadership skills throughout the organization and plant the seeds of leadership in the community. To achieve this aim, it might make more sense to attempt to answer the question of "How are we in charge?" instead of the vertical leadership-based question of "Who is in charge?"

CONCLUSION AND FURTHER RESEARCH: REFRAMING THE VIEW OF DUAL LEADERSHIP

In this chapter, I described three different challenges experienced by leaders within the dual leadership in the Church of Norway. Reid and Karambayya provided insights into dual leadership in cultural organizations, with a transferability to other fields. One of the main findings in their research was that how the leaders within the dual leadership handle their relationship and manage to resolve conflicts has a measurable effect throughout the organization. Even though dual leadership is challenging, Hilde Fjellvær pointed out that many pluralistic organizations purposely choose this type of leadership structure as a way in which to deal with some of the complexity by allowing different departments to carry out certain tasks. Although the reason for dual leadership in the Church of Norway is different, it can still provide valuable insights. One example of a successful dual leadership is also mentioned in the present article. This experience showed that it takes time and a prioritization of efforts to build this relationship and, ultimately, make this type of leadership structure work effectively.

As an alternative conceptualization of leadership that is designed to cope with the challenges of everyday operations and changing environments and conditions, I explored the notion of shared leadership. A study by Michael Wood revealed that behavior plays a more important role than structure in determining the effectiveness of shared leadership. In the Discussion section, I argue that shared leadership might be a beneficial change in mindset to cope with the complex structure of the Church of Norway and that it might offer a better way of empowering skilled employees in the church to take care of and pull together their resources and to focus better on common goals and strategies.

Further research is needed to determine the effects of adopting this kind of leadership approach as a way in which to cope with the challenges arising from the Church of Norway's complex structure and from fast-changing conditions. Gaining insights into the effects of a deliberate practice of shared leadership—involving the dual leadership of the churchwarden and the dean, as well as the members of the local church staff—would be of value. Learning more about the effect of emphasizing the development of skills would also be beneficial, in addition to the ongoing work to improve and develop the structural framework of the Church of Norway in the future.

BIBLIOGRAPHY

Alvarez, José Luis, and Silviya Svejenova. *Sharing Executive Power: Roles and Relationships at the Top*. Cambridge: Cambridge University Press, 2005.

Arbeidsgruppe. *Kjent inventar i nytt hus. Kirkens ordning etter endringene i Grunnlovens §§2,4,12,16,21,22 og 27*. Utredning av arbeidsgruppe oppnevnt av kirkerådets direktør. Oslo: Kirkerådet 2011.

Askeland, Harald. "Hva betyr det om kirken forstås som organisasjon?" In *Ledelse i kirken*, edited by Harald Askeland et al., 23–42. Oslo: Kirkens arbeidsgiverorganisasjon, 2003.

Bang, Henning, and Thomas Nesset Midelfart. *Effektive ledergrupper*. Oslo: Gyldendal akademisk, 2012.

Christensen, Agnes Ellinor. "Som hånd i hanske . . . ? Om konflikt og konflikthåndtering i Den norske kirke sett i lys av den todelte ledelsesstrukturen." Master thesis, Diakonhjemmet Høgskole, 2014.

Conger, Jay A., and Craig L. Pearce. *Shared Leadership: Reframing the Hows and Whys of Leadership*. London: Sage, 2003.

Den norske kirkes presteforening. *Ledelse i folkekirken. Perspektiver på ledelse og framtidig organisering av Den norske kirke*. Den norske kirkes presteforenings studiebibliotek nr. 49. Oslo: Den norske kirkes presteforening, 2011.

Fjellvær, Hilde. "Dual and Unitary Leadership: Managing Ambiguity in Pluralistic Organizations." PhD Thesis, Norwegian School of Economics and Business Administration, 2010.

Fletcher, Joyce K., and Katrin Käufer. "Shared Leadership: Paradox and Possibillity." In *Shared Leadership: Reframing the Hows and Whys of Leadership*, edited by Craig L. Pearce and Jay A. Conger, 21–47. London: Sage, 2003.

Gronn, Peter. "Distributed leadership as a unit of analysis." *The Leadership Quarterly* 13.4 (2002) 423–51.

Hauken, Øyvind. "Todelt ledelse i den lokale kirke. Hvordan fungerer i dag det todelte lederskapet mellom sokneprest og kirkeverge i tre utkantsmenigheter i Den norske kirke?" Master thesis, Diakonhjemmet høgskole, 2007.

Heenan, David A., and Warren Bennis. *Co-Leaders: The Power of Great Partnership*. New York: John Wiley och Sons, 1999.

Henriksen, Jan-Olav. "Makt og avmakt blant ledere i Den norske kirke." In *Religiøse ledere. Makt og avmakt i norske trossamfunn*, edited by Berit Thorbjørnsrud and Cora Alexa Døving, 200–15. Oslo: Universitetsforlaget, 2012.

Huse, Morten. *Prosten. Ansvar, arbeidssituation og ledelse*. KIFO rapport nr. 10. Trondheim: Tapir akademisk forlag, 1998.

Joiner, Bill, and Stephen Josephs. *Leadership Agility: Five Levels of Mastery for Anticipating and Initiating Change*. San Francisco: Jossey-Bass, 2007.

KA Kirkens arbeidsgiver- og Interesseorganisasjon. *Framtidig organisering av arbeidsgiveransvaret i Den norske kirke.* 2008.

Kirkeloven [Church Act]. *Lov 7. juni 1996 nr. 31 om Den norske kirke.* 1996.

Kotter, John P. *Leading Change.* Boston: Harvard Business Review, 2012.

Krogh, Astrid Holmsen. "Det som ikke skjer lokalt, skjer ikke: om ledelse og lederroller på lokalplanet i Den norske kirke." Master thesis, Diakonhjemmet høgskole. Oslo: Astrid Holmsen Krogh, 2010.

Kvalsund, Ragnvald, and Kristin Meyer. *Gruppeveiledning, læring og ressursutvikling.* Trondheim: Tapir akademisk forlag, 2005.

Locke, Edwin A. "Leadership: Starting at the Top." In *Shared Leadership: Reframing the Hows and Whys of Leadership*, edited by Craig L. Pearce and Jay A. Conger, 271–84. London: Sage, 2003.

Moustakas, Clark. *Phenomenological Research Methods.* London: Sage, 1994.

Nødland, Svein Ingve, et al. *Samstyring i ubalanse. Evaluering av den lokale kirkes ordning.* Stavanger: Rapport IRIS—2014/054, Stavanger: IRIS, 2014.

Postholm, May Britt. *Kvalitativ metode: en innføring med fokus på fenomenologi, etnografi og kasusstudier.* Oslo: Universitetsforlaget, 2010.

Raelin, Joseph A. *Creating Leaderful Organizations: How to Bring out Leadership in Everyone.* San Francisco: Berrett-Koehler, 2003.

Reid, Wendy, and Rekha Karambayya. "Impact of Dual Executive Leadership Dynamics in Creative Organizations." *Human Relations* 62 (2009) 1073–112.

Scharmer, C. Otto. *Theory U: Learning from the Future as it Emerges.* San Francisco: Berrett-Koehler, 2009.

Skårberg, Bente. "Der linjene møtes. Prost og kirkeverge om enhetlig ledelse i den lokale kirke." Master thesis, Diakonhjemmet høgskole, 2007.

Steinsland, Hege. "'Men jeg ønsket å være en som kunne løfte han.' Om relasjon og lederskap i en todelt lederstruktur." Master thesis, NTNU, 2013.

Thagaard, Tove. *Systematikk og innlevelse: en innføring i kvalitativ metode.* Bergen: Fagbokforlaget, 2003.

Torset, Inge. "Forsøk med interkommunalt kirkelig fellesråd i Midtre Namdal. En prosessbeskrivelse og erfaringsdeling 2003–2011." 2012.

Williams, Birgit. *The Genuine Contact Way. Nourishing a Culture of Leadership.* Raleigh, NC: Dalar International Consultancy, 2014.

Wood, Michael. "Determinants of Shared Leadership in Managements Teams." *International Journal of Leadership Studies* 1.1 (2005) 64–85.

11

Change and Development for the Future

Entrepreneurship in the Church of Sweden

MARIA ÅKERSTRÖM

ENTREPRENEURSHIP: A NEW PERSPECTIVE ON WORKING WITH CHANGE IN CHURCHES?

This chapter focuses on entrepreneurship and other key points related to the organization and the people who work in it. Entrepreneurs and entrepreneurship are not only present in industry or business, but can be found everywhere. This means that every social context contains opportunities for entrepreneurship in the sense of new combinations.[1] The statement that entrepreneurship can be found everywhere is the point of departure for investigating the presence and condition of entrepreneurship in the Church of Sweden. Entrepreneurship has not been the subject of research within the context of the Church of Sweden. A few articles have explored entrepreneurship in faith communities in the United States. In his book from 1990 on implementing change in the Church of Sweden, which partly touches on the same area as entrepreneurship, Per Hansson wrote that there is no inclination within the church to implement change, but that the building

---

1. Schumpeter. "Theory of Economic Development," 1–3.

of relations is important.[2] The present study may lead to another result, as twenty years later there might be a greater willingness to change.

This chapter addresses entrepreneurial changes as well as social entrepreneurship in the Church of Sweden. Both aspects shed light on entrepreneurship within an ideological organization. The Church of Sweden is a special organization, sharing features with public and civil society and non-profit organizations. The focus here is on the grass-roots level in the local congregations, where the aim is to examine the presence of entrepreneurship as a phenomenon in the operation and leadership of local congregations in the Church of Sweden, and to investigate the conditions for entrepreneurship in this context. It is based on established theories on entrepreneurship in economics, education and the sociology of science. I start by looking for the presence entrepreneurship and then continue by analyzing which forms of entrepreneurship can be found.

METHOD, DESIGN, AND DATA

Basically, entrepreneurship can be defined as combining already existing products or ideas in new ways, or devising an innovation and putting it into action.[3] To ascertain whether and how entrepreneurship is present in the Church of Sweden, this study explores interviews, documents, and literature on the subject. Indicators of entrepreneurship are different behavioral attributes that are developed on a theoretical basis, with the aim of neither excluding nor including irrelevant cases. Not every case of change can reasonably be identified as a case of entrepreneurship, but, on the other hand, real cases of entrepreneurship and entrepreneurs should not go unnoticed. The behavioral attributes of entrepreneurship are listed in Table 11, while the behavioral indicators are found in the literature I refer to. It is important to use this theoretical underpinning to avoid designating every example of change as entrepreneurship. The attributes are used as a tool to analyze an empirical data set for identifying possible situations and cases of entrepreneurship. The empirical data material consists of documents and interviews with key personnel, conducted in five congregations, each one serving as a separate case. The point in using case studies[4] is to gain greater insights into the deeper nuances, dynamics, and interconnections of a given phenomenon, rather than exploring it in terms of a few characteristics shared between a large numbers of instances. Case studies can thus be used to describe how a phenomenon occurs.

2. Hansson. "Styrning och kultur."
3. Schumpeter, "Theory of Economic Development," 1–3.
4. Descombes, *Forskningshandboken*, 41–54.

A general objection to qualitative methods, such as case studies, is that they are vulnerable to the preconceived ideas and biases of the researchers, and will tend towards confirming already held beliefs.[5] But this is in no way an insurmountable problem, nor is it necessarily any greater a problem for qualitative case studies than for other methodologies. On the contrary, it has been argued that case studies have the advantage of stimulating alternative interpretations of a given phenomenon and challenging the researcher's preconceived ideas.[6]

To realize this potential in the present study it is necessary to be aware of the potential effect of the fact that the organization and the people are well known to me. This gives me both advantages and disadvantages. Whereas I have tried to relate critically to the information, I can never be completely neutral, something which is also difficult to achieve in the social sciences.[7] To avoid being biased, I compare the results of the empirical study with theory, seeking to discover blind spots or neglected items. This has been done through a combination of deductive and inductive methodology. The combination of these methods results in abduction where the methods work in tandem.[8]

Furthermore, the potential for generalization in case studies is typically connected to their ability to manifest patterns of processes, connections, and dynamics which, provided that the cases are carefully selected, will be generalizable in relation to the phenomenon in question.

In the analysis of the data material I intend to uncover expressions of entrepreneurship as they are shown in the different congregations. My purpose is not to analyze the quantity or the quality of entrepreneurship, only its presence, as determined by the theoretical model given below.

Semi-structured interviews are used to find these expressions of entrepreneurship, but also to study processes of change present in the stories told by the informants. The data material from the investigation is not collected from a "before" and "now" perspective. It comes from the present moment when the informant chooses an activity he or she wants tell me about.

The Choice of Congregations

The selection of the five congregations is based on the following criteria: Each congregation belongs to a single-congregation parish, meaning that the parish council is the governing body. The congregations are in the same

5. Gustavsson, "Kunskapande mångfald," 8.
6. Flyvberg, "Five Misunderstandings."
7. Gilje and Grimen, *Samhällsvetenskapens förutsättningar*, 266–76.
8. Stensmo, *Vetenskapsteori och metod*, 16–17.

region of Sweden which is a similarity factor. The differences are in the geographical structure and size of each congregation. They are known neither for their innovation nor for being reactionary. The congregations studied, ranging in size from small to large, have been given the following names in this study: "Lakeside," "Route Village," "Grove City," "Small Village," and "East Town." Two informants were interviewed in each congregation: the chairman of the parish council and the minister, who, as key personnel, have an overarching view of the organization. They respond to the questions in the interviews from their point of view, according to activities and organization. I also read and analyzed the strategy plans for each congregation.

Table 10 Case congregations

Congregation	Members	# Of employees
Lakeside	Approx. 22,000	Approx. 40
Grove City	Approx. 9300	Approx. 20
Small Village	Approx. 2100	Approx. 5
Route Village	Approx. 4000	Approx. 30
East Town	Approx. 23,000	Approx. 60

As a starting point for the investigation of the presence of entrepreneurship in these congregations I will begin by presenting theories of entrepreneurship.

ENTREPRENEURSHIP AS A PROCESS AND ENTREPRENEURIAL LEADERSHIP

Historically, the term entrepreneurship has existed since the 1500s[9] in the sense of a complex phenomenon that includes both individuals and the context of the individuals.[10] An entrepreneur is a person who practices a new combination in a company. This is the difference between an ordinary leader in a business and an entrepreneur.[11] During the late twentieth century the study of entrepreneurship was common in behavioral science, sociology, and psychology, but has since become popular in economic science disciplines.[12] This is associated with the fact that it is common to see the entrepreneur as a business leader. But an entrepreneur is also a creative

---

9. Leffler, "Företagssamma elever," 44.

10. Gartner. "Who Is an Entrepreneur?" 64.

11. Schumpeter, "Theory of Economic Development," 1–2.

12. Lundblad and Vejbrink, *I huvudet på en skapare*, 19–21.

person.[13] The financial aspect is only present when the creative results are brought out into the market. The entrepreneur is interacting with a number of actors in an organization and this cooperation develops the ideas and the emergent new ideas yield creative results.[14] In this process, built in a flow where the entrepreneur is not afraid to test new and unusual ways of doing things,[15] a variety of activities are seen from a new perspective.[16] These new ideas need to be communicated to advance the process,[17] and this requires a great effort on the part of the entrepreneur.[18]

Entrepreneurship can also be found within organizations and when it is this is called "intrapreneurship," a term coined by Pinchot.[19] Sundin[20] and Pinchot[21] define an intrapreneur as someone who acts within an organization and see it is a form of entrepreneurship. The expressions and functions of intrapreneurship are very similar to entrepreneurship but an intrapreneur sees solutions in well-known knowledge and is an employee of the organization in question. An intrapreneur is an entrepreneur with all his features, but does not run his own business organization and therefore does not act entrepreneurially. Many conditions, such as teamwork and commitment, are the same and the idea of the prime mover[22] is found in both an entrepreneur and an intrapreneur. The conditions for leadership are in many ways the same for an intrapreneur and an entrepreneur, and the expressions are the same. The difference is that the intrapreneur has his team in the organization.[23] Another expression for the intrapreneur is entrepreneurs who act within an institution. They initiate new ideas and processes in an institutional organization,[24] which is an important arena for entrepreneurship because it has the networks and the strong team feeling that is important for entrepreneurship.[25]

13. Morris and Jones, "Entrepreneurship in Established Organizations," 75.

14. Lundblad and Vejbrink, *I huvudet på en skapare*, 18; Bakka et al., *Organisation Struktur*, 224; Gartner, "Who Is an Entrepreneur?" 57.

15. Pinchot and Pellman, *Intrapreneuring in Action*, 13.

16. Andersson, "Intraprenörskap."

17. Nordlund, *Att leda storföretag*, 372; Skaug, *En förstudie om entreprenörskap*, 27.

18. Ibid., 101.

19. Pinchot III, *Intraprenörerna*, 65, 78–79.

20. Sundin, "Slutkapitel," 24.

21. Pinchot III, *Intraprenörerna*, 20–25, 65.

22. Philips, "Eldsjälar," 7.

23. Pinchot III, *Intraprenörerna*, 207–10.

24. Sundin and Tillmar, *Nurse and a Civil Servant*, 5–6.

25. Lundblad and Wejbrink, *I huvudet på en skapare*, 43–44; Selznik, *Modern organisationsteori*, 15.

An entrepreneurial leader does not only need to see changes at an early time, he has to develop and commit all the resources in the organization to achieve the goals and tasks.[26] One way of doing that is to focus on teamwork and a commitment[27] to fulfilling the visions[28] that he has. To do this, the leader has to encourage people to join him and then he needs to be socially competent in assuming natural power and gaining respect.[29]

The classical theories on entrepreneurship find new applications when they are combined with the social context.[30] The main reason for this is that there are new demands in the community and the change process then occurs in what is called a social entrepreneurship.

SOCIAL ENTREPRENEURSHIP

Entrepreneurship oriented towards the needs of people and whose main resource is human capital is what we call social entrepreneurship. Social entrepreneurship often addresses the needs of a group or a need based on an identified group.[31] Its aim is to raise the quality of life for individuals and link citizens together,[32] rather than to promote personal profit.[33] The aim, in other words, is rather to introduce social change[34] and to see the social benefits of the activities that take place between citizens.[35]

This social capital, based on relations between individuals,[36] is an example of a value that differs from the typical definition of capital. The rewards from this social capital are not primarily economic but rather a human value that cannot be measured in dollar and cents. Volunteerism can be connected to this, and to point out what is meant here, volunteerism is given a different dimension than an economic value. By making the goals of the voluntary work meaningful it is possible to show what social capital can be. Social entrepreneurship[37] is when someone creates entrepreneur-

26. Skaug, "Affärsstrategiskt ledarskap," 25.

27. Pinchot III, *Intraprenörerna*, 207–15.

28. Ahltorp, *Ledarskap ur ett ledningsstilsperspektiv*, 122.

29. Nordlund, *Att leda storföretag*, 29, 32; Skaug, "Affärsstrategiskt ledarskap," 103, 105.

30. Nicholls, "Social Enterprise."

31. Fayolle and Matlay, "Social Entrepreneurship," 1–2.

32. Hjort, "Medborgare är konsumenter?" 260–262.

33. Myers and Nelson, "Considering Social Capital," 275–77.

34. Montin, *Moderna Kommuner*, 115–16, 123.

35. Palmås, "Socialt entreprenörskap," 246.

36. Myers and Nelson, "Considering Social Capital," 273.

37. Andersson, "Intraprenörskap," 115–16.

ial opportunities locally but not for one's own profit or any profit goals at all. The impetus and rewards come from the improvement of one's own community.[38] This type of activity is often a process that runs over a considerable period of time with many different types of activities involved.[39]

To avoid seeing everything as entrepreneurship I have put together forms and expressions of entrepreneurship, intrapreneurship and social entrepreneurship in the table below for my further analysis. There are small differences between entrepreneurship and intrapreneurship as expressed in social entrepreneurship.

Table 11 Combination of behavioral attributes for entrepreneurship

	Behavioral attributes:
Entrepreneurship and intrapreneurship	Creativity, has a driving force, develops activities in new ways, sees new perspectives, tests new and unusual ways, is proactive, is an enthusiastic advocate, communicates, makes a great effort himself, acts in processes in a forward-thinking way, develops and involves resources, in step with the outside world, develops a vision, socially competent, has timing.
Social entrepreneurship	Uses human capital, sees to the needs of people, sees social capital, volunteerism, raises quality of life for individuals, improves their own community, non-profit purpose, sees the social process over time, actions have social benefit.
Differences between entrepreneurship and intrapreneurship	Entrepreneur: Business leader Intrapreneur: Acts within the organization, is employed

These behavioral attributes exist in an organization and the expressions are influenced by the structure and tradition in the specific organization, here the Church of Sweden.

THE CHURCH OF SWEDEN

The Church of Sweden is a non-profit organization but operates in an arena that is not unaffected by the market economy, where mechanisms of supply and demand govern the enterprise. The underpinning of the organization

38. Dorado and Shaffer, "Governance Among Confounding Logics," 36–37.
39. Shockley and Frank, "Schumpeter, Kirzner," 11–12.

is ideological and especially in this case, the theological perspective is important because it is the basic ideology on which the organization rests. The basic structure of the church order is territorial, but its operations are run by three groups: members, ordained clergy and deacons, and elected representatives.[40] The structure of the organization is a hybrid institutional organization having both the nature of the voluntary and the public organization, and based on a clear ideology.[41] The uniqueness of the Church of Sweden as an organization is that it is located at the intersection between ideology, tradition, and the community. There is an ideological basis in the theology, a tradition of values and structures based on biblical stories and a character of the public organization, as the Church of Sweden was previously part of the Swedish state and its political system.[42]

The congregation of the Church of Sweden is the team where the minister is the one who leads. It could as well have been the chairman of the parish church council leading the group. Strategy plans serving as documentation of main objectives and goals contribute to transformation and innovation in the organization.[43]

THEORETICAL MODEL

The entrepreneurial process in an organization can take place according to it structure and culture, which are phenomena that affect each other and what happens in an organization and can be used in a way that will have positive effects. To show the process and flow between culture, structure, and context, the theories of Fayolle,[44] Sahlman[45] and Austin, Stevenson and Wei-Skillern[46] are combined in Figure 2. The implication of the flow pattern and the letters P & R, C, D, O, are as follows: P & R stand for the people and resources available while C, D, and O stand for context, deal, and opportunity. There is a dynamic relationship and interaction between them as they are in the organization or in its vicinity. When P & R interact with O and C, it means that it is possible to make connections between them and the opportunities are given. This will create opportunities for new business ideas through the given times and contexts. These are dependent on D, that is, the agreements (programs) that are available and control the business. Together

40. Stålhammar, *Kyrkoherdens ledningsvillkor*, 49.

41. Bills, "Towards a Theory," 46–65.

42. Wijkström, *Svenska organisationsliv*, 55.

43. *Kyrkoordningen* 2014, 2 kap §6, 4 kap §2, § 11 and 5 kap §1.

44. Fayolle, "Research and Researchers," 46.

45. Sahlman, "Some Thoughts," 140–43.

46. Austin et al., "Social and Commercial Entrepreneurship," 5–15.

they form the process of entrepreneurship. The process of entrepreneurship shifts emphasis between the various components of the model, but there is always interaction and collaboration.[47]

Figure 2 Sahlman—the flow diagram

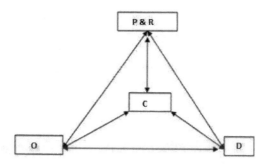

The starting points in Figure 2 lead to the following summary: Entrepreneurial situations can be found in many forms and systems that are manifested in the context. But the organizational forms and systems also set limits for the entrepreneur and the entrepreneurial process; the process depends on programs and agreements that exist in the organization. Even so, an entrepreneur sees opportunities in both people and resources and uses them for entrepreneurial purposes. All this together makes a flow in the process depending on the entrepreneur and the opportunities in the organization in question.

ANALYSIS OF ENTREPRENEURSHIP IN FIVE CONGREGATIONS

The empirical material is analyzed according to categories established from the research findings: the entrepreneur, social entrepreneurship, and process. The point is to show how entrepreneurship is present in these situations and tasks.

Presence of Entrepreneurship in the Congregations

The first example of entrepreneurship is provided by the chairman of the parish church council in Lakeside. She mentions how important it is to be an ambassador and to be seen outside the context of the church: "We must

47. Sahlman, "Some Thoughts," 140–43, 174.

be seen much more. We are all ambassadors even if we don't always see it that way. I think that all of us are ambassadors who confess our faith." A result of this ambassadorship is that "you'll get in touch with different contexts." In "regular activities" ". . . it's more important to be an ambassador," the chairman of the parish church council in Route Village believes. When new activities are introduced there is a possibility for new ideas and this requires new thinking where "being an ambassador" will also assist in communicating these new ideas.

An example of new ideas is when you consider using the church for many different purposes. There has been a long process of developing new ideas, and the rector at East Town thinks that "we have moved on (from the traditional use of the church building).[48] There are not too many barriers left." The chairman of the parish church council points out that just a short time ago it was impossible to have confirmation teaching in the church because it was reserved for services. Today he has heard from one of the employees that confirmation teaching in the church "was the best thing that has happened." The new way of using the church, not only for services, is an example of new solutions and it has given new opportunities for the churches in the town, the chairman of the parish church council in East Town thinks. He adds that in a town that has many churches close to each other they could "have different roles and tasks" in their activities. An example is to use different speech and style and in one of the churches where only "modern and colloquial speech is used." This has led in part to "changes in the church handbook."

The rector at East Town says that it is important that the congregation serves as a meeting place. When you meet each other in the church, the church "will be a meeting point in another way," the chairman of the parish church council at East Town says. When it comes to activities, "you can't be satisfied." You have to "push other people so things will happen," and he repeats this when he discusses this question with his colleagues in the parish church council. He looks to the future as well, and thinks that the Church of Sweden has to invest in youth. A "congregation without young people, then there is not much left." Children and young people must be recruited and cultivated, otherwise there will be no congregation left in thirty or forty years. This attitude shows how new ideas can develop the activities for the future and put the focus on the activities taking place today, and then yielding results in the future.

Discussions on priorities may be difficult, as they were in both Grove City and Route Village, but this is a way to set priorities for the future. One

48. Author's remark.

important aspect that influences the priorities is the changes taking place in rural areas. The chairman of the parish council in Grove City thinks "we are the last outpost that is struggling to run the business."

The chairman of the parish council in Grove City says that it is important "to show that we exist." They cannot sit in the churches waiting for the local people "to come to the service. We must be a part of society, we must be visible in a basic way. That's very important, I think," he says. One way to not sit and wait is to act through an ongoing entrepreneurial process.

The Entrepreneurial Process in the Congregations

One type of entrepreneurial process is when the rector at East Town thinks that the reason for the church being a meeting place is its central location in the town. The congregation has deliberately "promoted this meeting activity to bring children and young people to the church." The new approach to using the church in many different ways has been addressed through a long process and the rector thinks that "we moved on from it (the old way). There are not so many barriers left" (to the way the church building can be used)."[49] The process of change has to be long-term to satisfy the aim of the idea.

The activity in the service groups that prepare the services involves "teamwork" says the rector at Grove City. They all participate and "anyone can be a part of the group." There are similarities with the volunteers in Route Village. It is written in the strategy document that there must be "more volunteers. It is important to expand our own leadership," says the chairman in Route Village. Volunteers are in different fields and "we have tested some different models." It has been "an important question the last three or four years" and "the reason for that is to push the process forward." This is in contrast to the "professionalism in the 1970s and we must remember what happened then and look forward." One mission for Route Village, the chairman of the parish council thinks, is to be in touch with the people who want to "take care of their own church" and "the team that is built around the church." The organization of the employees has been revised because there are a lot of teams and places of work in the congregation. Everyone should be able to work in every place even if this does not occur in practice. This again is thinking in new ways and at the same time taking care of the resources that can be found among the employees. This has happened through "some kind of process of ideas" and has historical connections to when the church was part of the state, he believes.

49. Author's remarks.

The challenge, the chairman of the parish council at Small Village says, is "to give the best possible conditions for the parish to pursue its tasks" and give resources to the prioritized youth activities. There is motivation for this as before the priorities were finally decided there had been "very hard discussions." The fact that there were hard discussions behind every decision to set priorities shows the creative process that was involved in forming the new ways of planning the activities.

The chairman of the parish council at Grove City thinks that the priority given to funding of youth has turned out well. He also thinks that there are processes that govern the activity. When a congregation is put together with others it affects the allocation of money. Now the finances "are allocated for the whole congregation and if the small congregation had had its own finances there would have been nothing left to use."

The process of using volunteers has been under discussion in Route Village. They merged two parishes with "two different cultures." One of the parishes had many volunteers and the other had more employees," states the chairman of the Route Village parish council, and he thinks that the importance of volunteers must be a model for future church activities, and in this context different ways of being active have been tested.

Small Village has cooperated with other organizations in the work with asylum seekers. This was done through a process that is described by the Small Village rector as follows: "we, the Church of Sweden, the Mission church and the Red Cross, talked together and said here we need to do something and then we set up a meeting, once a week, and it has been very meaningful on a personal level." The activity in Grove City "must reach the people" says the chairman of the parish council. In the future, the rector believes that confirmation studies and activities targeting youths will be important: "we need to do this for the future."

The assembly instructions in Small Village establish that the congregation shall cooperate on diaconal matters with other actors in society. They also have a preschool, which is an example of cooperation. Preschools and working with asylum seekers are examples of entrepreneurial processes and the activities emerging from social entrepreneurship.

Social Entrepreneurship in the Congregations

The keen focus on activities for children and young people at Lakeside has led to a preschool and day-care center. Due to a political decision, the municipal day-care center had to close down and then the church decided to step in and start a day-care center. The vicar says: "all activity at the school was suddenly closed due to a decision by the government and then we started a day-care center, and in a few weeks we had many children join, and this has then developed into three preschools in the congregation."

The extensive activity with preschools and a day-care center has strengthened contact between generations. The children and their families "have very close contact to the church, so they come back," the rector finds. Economically, the activities in the preschool and youth center are breaking even due to grants given to Lakeside, and they are considering starting other activities in the city.

The rector at Route Village says that "in other places in society, perhaps preschools, day-care centers or workplaces, schools or homes for the elderly there are groups of people whom we show a tendency to forget and with whom we ought to have close contact. We always have a mission to go out to these people . . ." As formulated in the strategy document, diaconal work means: "giving a voice to the weak." It is also written in Small Village's strategy document that the congregation should cooperate with other actors in carrying out its diaconal work. Small Village runs a preschool and this is referred to in the strategy document as diaconal work.

Another example of diaconal work from the Small Village strategy plan is the idea of cooperating in existing societal activities. The "friendly turn" is an example of this. (The "friendly turn" is an activity performed by volunteers to help the elderly and the poor).[50] In Grove City, the church functions as a meeting place because of the preschool. "We have a preschool here which is very important. On Mondays there are open activities for infants and their parents who come here. Then we have groups of immigrants here who also use the rooms. And that is important. This is the way it has been in recent years." Small Village is planning to start a parish housing association where cooperation between the local authority and the church is seen as important. There is a long tradition of cooperation in Route Village since the 1960s. The Church of Sweden took part in "the construction of the Swedish model. We worked together with the local authority earlier . . . and were in the same building and that made cooperation easier." There are plans "for a meeting with the local authority to see how we can cooperate in the future," says the rector at Route Village.

The chairman of the East Town parish council describes a project where the youth activities will be expanded to "get hold of" young people who are out late at night. He describes the plans for a city project, where the diaconal activity is moved out into the city, to be available for people in a new way. Another diaconal action is that the churches are open in the day time. Now this is such a given that it is registered in the strategy document.

50. Author's remark.

It is a kind of social entrepreneurship that has emerged from an entrepreneurial process.

At the parish council in East Town, the head of the council highlights the activities for the elderly as a contrast to youth activities and believes that investment in young people is an obvious step to take. It will pay off in the future. The elderly in the congregation should be able to fend for themselves, but this statement is not too popular which contradicts the positive relationship between people,[51] and which is based on the work of the Church of Sweden. Here the relationship becomes a competitive situation that is dealt with entrepreneurially by the head of the parish council, who sees that there is potential for change now. The groups of the elderly are very present-oriented while the head of the parish council wants to change and build for a long-term future. One of the conclusions is that an entrepreneur has the ability to anticipate situations that may arise in the future and be prepared for this. Discussions about priorities may be difficult, as was the case in both Grove City and Route Village, but it is a way of setting priorities for the future. An important aspect that is influencing the choice of priorities is the changes taking place in the rural areas. The chairman of the Grove City parish council thinks "we are the last outpost that is struggling to run the business."

It is possible to discern three particular lines in the empirical data and research: reaching out to more people, cooperating with other organizations and investing in children and young people. All the interview subjects and strategy documents accentuate the importance of finding new ways and expressions for the church, in services, diaconal work, teaching and mission work. These lines have been analyzed together with the theoretical models in Figure 2 and the attributes in Table 11.

DISCUSSION OF THE FINDINGS

Entrepreneurship can be found in various activities in the Church of Sweden and its presence is discussed according to the data material and relevant theory. The justification for this approach is the attitude to entrepreneurship as described by several authors:[52] The entrepreneur is in a process together with a number of actors in an organization. The process is made up of both individual and collective actions and in this process the entrepreneur sees opportunities to develop and lead the church activities in new ways. In the following, the conditions and prevalence of entrepreneurship will be elu-

51. Modéus, *Mänsklig gudstjänst*, 156.
52. Lundblad and Vejbrink, *I huvudet på en skapare*, 18; Bakka et al., *Organisation Struktur Kultur Processer*, 224; Gartner, "Who Is an Entrepreneur?" 57.

cidated from a number of perspectives in categories based on the picture[53] of the entrepreneurial flow, where the main focus is on the expression of the entrepreneurial process. The process comprises situations, people and resources, processes, opportunities, programs, systems, contexts, forms and agreements. The specific aspect of entrepreneurial activities is the combination of individual and collective activities. When these categories are combined, they reveal the presence of entrepreneurship in a number of activities.

Entrepreneurial Process

An entrepreneurial process[54] is both individual and organizational. It is about constantly using a new perspective on a variety of activities. The image brings together the flow and the process involved in personal characteristics, organizational theory, and external influences.

An example of flow is when somebody is active and persistent. To start an entrepreneurial process the entrepreneur has to be a prime mover.[55] A chairwoman points out that she and several others have to be ambassadors for the ideology and theology that the Church of Sweden stands for. We need to be ambassadors to reach the people we want to come into contact with in different contexts, she says. She is persistent on this theme and does not give up on the idea. This is also an example of the entrepreneurial characteristic of communicating one's ideas and building on existing relationships within the ideological foundation of the Church of Sweden. Here is where we encounter entrepreneurial people, situations, and resources.

The entrepreneurial process is, in other words, a flow.[56] In this flow the entrepreneur is not afraid of testing new and unusual ways to accomplish particular aims. An example of this is when the local authorities discontinued a preschool and day-care center. The rector steps in and says that the Church of Sweden is ready to assume this task. In that case, special effort was required of the congregation in a particular context, and they ended up establishing and running a new preschool and day-care center. This situation revealed the ability to combine existing resources because people were willing to step in and take over the work when no other solution presented itself. The rector saw the opportunity to start a new activity. This is not the

53. Fayolle, "Research and Researchers," 46; Sahlman, "Some Thoughts," 140–43; Austin et al., "Social and Commercial Entrepreneurship," 5–15.

54. Andersson, "Intraprenörskap," 108–9.

55. Ahltorp, *Ledarskap ur ett ledningsstilsperspektiv*, 133.

56. Pinchot and Pellman, *Intrapreneuring in Action*, 13.

primary function of a religious organization but its ideology[57] and common values were the driving force that led to a solution. This reveals the
significance of entrepreneurship in various social activities and in many
areas, and is an example of an action taken by a hybrid organization. This
type of organization has activities in many areas that are not usually their
core activity. The Church of Sweden's core activity is defined as covering
four areas: teaching, mission, service and diaconal work. The example of the
entrepreneurial preschool initiative shows that the Church of Sweden is a
hybrid organization[58] because a preschool is not part of its core activity. The
hybrid organization is open to entrepreneurial actions and opportunities,
which is a way of seeing opportunities in context.

An important condition for the entrepreneurial process is the people
who act as entrepreneurs.[59] The findings have revealed both ministers and
parish council heads, in all the congregations, acting as entrepreneurs by
being proactive and enthusiastic advocates of the processes.[60] They see what
needs to be done at specific times and allocate both human and financial
resources to pursue a creative process, as was the case in Grove City. It was
also shown that the leadership can be given free rein to govern, thus foster-
ing the conditions for entrepreneurship through the freedom and creativity the opportunities provide. In these processes, collective and individual
entrepreneurship are combined, as was the case in the process of recruiting
volunteers in Route Village. A process for combining different traditions of
recruiting volunteers was in place, but an entrepreneurial driving force has
kept this process going.

Communication and ideas from the entrepreneur on how to work
with the project could be found on all levels of the organization.[61] Communication makes it easier in the institutional organization because there
are good networks. This does not prevent different opinions and ideas from
being heard through various expressions of the forward-looking process.
One specific responsibility that the parish council head talks about was an
essential component in this process, the idea of seeing what was needed and
solving the issue with flexible solutions. Part of the anchoring process is that
the entrepreneur himself shows deep commitment and is willing to make
a great effort himself.[62] The entrepreneurial process also means taking the

57. Rochester and Torry, "Faith-Based Organizations," 117–19.
58. Bills, "Towards a Theory," 53–56.
59. Pinchot and Pellman, *Intrapreneuring in Action*, 17.
60. Skaug, "Affärsstrategiskt ledarskap," 83.
61. Nordlund, *Att leda storföretag*, 372; Skaug, *En förstudie om entreprenörskap*, 27.
62. Skaug, "Affärsstrategiskt ledarskap," 101.

time necessary and not losing the passion for the process. The chairman of the East Town parish council talks about changing the activities in the church. There is no guaranteed way to change minds and ideas but he was persistent and allowed the process to take its course, and through resistance in the context he saw the opportunity to do something new. This is an example of leadership in an entrepreneurial process and an entrepreneurial form of leadership is an excellent basis for the activities.

Entrepreneurial Leadership

Entrepreneurial leadership focuses on teamwork and commitment, and the organization needs to give the entrepreneurial leader the opportunity to practice this. Legitimacy[63] is given to the leader who can develop visions and lead in a target-oriented way, and who can get every employee to feel involved. This is confirmed by the fact[64] that the entrepreneur should be socially competent but is in part contradicted because the entrepreneur in many cases[65] is a person around whom all power is concentrated.

A change-oriented leadership[66] is reflected in entrepreneurial leadership. What is special about entrepreneurial leadership is that the leader sees the process taking place in a specific moment and then cultivates the opportunity. This is a way of being in step with the surrounding world. An entrepreneurial leader may also be dominant in his forward-looking leadership when he wants to carry out the changes that are necessary to achieve the goals. This can be affected by the minister's dual role in his leadership role.[67] He also appears in the control function and can lead processes both as a leader and as a participant in the control function. The issue of united parishes and congregations is a question for the parish council which means that building for the future is when the rector and the elected representatives can act entrepreneurially by both governing and leading. Together they use the programs that have been established to reach goals which can be characterized as entrepreneurial.

In the following example, the entrepreneurial leadership experiences resistance, where the entrepreneur wants to change something too fast. But this is still an example of an entrepreneurial opportunity.

63. Ahltorp, *Ledarskap ur ett ledningsstilsperspektiv*, 122.
64. Nordlund, *Att leda storföretag*, 29, 32.
65. Skaug, "Affärsstrategiskt ledarskap," 103, 105.
66. Ahltorp, *Ledarskap ur ett ledningsstilsperspektiv*, 33, 88.
67. Hansson, "Synen på prästen," 64.

Conclusions about context and systems can also be illuminated by seeing change at an early stage.[68] Seeing a context today that will bear fruit in the future means that leadership resources are being focused on young people rather than the elderly, as has been the case in some congregations. There has been criticism of the head of the East Town parish council, who is responsible for the allocation of resources, but he has maintained the priorities and therefore has become an entrepreneur who sees the need for change at an early stage. This can be linked to the tradition of shared experiences[69] found in the church. Programs and traditions that prevailed in the past created congregations, but over time changes took place and the church developed in new ways. Developing and improving a phenomenon within the organization[70] is characteristic of an intrapreneur.

Social Entrepreneurship

Social entrepreneurship is a sign[71] of the demands that a changing world imposes on society, where the meaning of entrepreneurship spreads to activities that were previously only intended for the public sector. Social enterprises provide an opportunity to raise the quality of life for individuals where there is a social dimension that links the citizens of a community together.

Social entrepreneurship takes responsibility for both citizens and organizations[72] where the purpose is not mainly economic benefit, but rather to find a business that satisfies a need and thus can change the world. The driving force is the wish to improve the local community. Examples of this are when youth activities are highlighted as important and when young people are given a place in the church, as the chairman of the East Town parish council puts it. The chairman of the Grove City parish council also claims that they could not just sit and wait, they had to do something. These are examples of what is called a "driving force."[73] The same term[74] is used about actors in organizations. Establishing local non-profit aims[75] is a matter of bringing together local organizations and businesses and believing that intrapreneurship is more involved than traditional entrepreneurship.

68. Handy, *Empty Raincoat*, 51.
69. Stålhammar, *Kyrkoherdens ledningsvillkor*, 62–63.
70. Petersson, *Statsbyggnad*, 8.
71. Hjort, "Medborgare är konsumenter?" 260–62.
72. Dorado and Shaffer, "Governance Among Confounding Logics," 36–37.
73. Gawell, Johannisson, and Lundqvist, "Vi behöver fler samhällsentreprenörer," 9.
74. Philips, "Eldsjälar," 7.
75. Andersson, "Intraprenörskap," 117.

This also involves a process where the needs are adapted to the situations that arise. An example of this is when it comes to receiving and building relations with refugees, where associations and organizations collaborate to achieve their non-profit aims, as was the case in Small Village.

The entrepreneurship of a social entrepreneur is not an isolated moment,[76] but a process over time, while specific situations may arise in these processes. The rector in Lakeside says that the children they meet in the preschool and the day-care center come back, and then the church has established contact between generations. The activity in the social sector generates relations and activities related to the work in the congregations. This is an example of entrepreneurship that enriches the main task of the Church of Sweden. The idea of starting more social activities for asylum seekers is another example of the process, which is ongoing at Route Village, and which resulted from a discussion between several voluntary organizations in the village.

Some conclusions about social entrepreneurship are that when non-profit and public organizations operate in an entrepreneurial manner, not primarily for personal profit but to make a social contribution, characteristic modes of expression arise.[77] The cultural and process perspectives, combined with social entrepreneurship, and where the starting point is both the values associated with culture and the process, here deal with the concrete action. An example of a concrete action is what took place at Route Village. The tradition there is to cooperate with the local authority in various social projects. The entrepreneur combines tradition and the local conditions and finds new ways of taking part in social activities.

The history of the Church of Sweden as a state church[78] means that in an obvious way it is seen as an integral part of the community, not least by the common external structures within common geographic boundaries. This is a condition which opens opportunities for contacts with such community activities as school, family centers, and social services. There are examples of this in the empirical data. Representatives from both Lakeside and Small Village talk about their involvement in pre-schools and day-care centers.

Being a part of the community as a voluntary organization is unique,[79] and according to tradition, the Church of Sweden has been a part of the community. This can be an advantage for the Church of Sweden as the

76. Shockley and Frank, "Schumpeter, Kirzner," 11–12.

77. Myers and Nelson, "Considering Social Capital," 275–77.

78. Ekström, *Svenska kyrkans historia*, 43.

79. Ibid., 43.

population in rural areas drops and resources are reduced. The Church of Sweden is still present in the rural areas, with the church as a central element in the community so it is a symbol of the presence and activities that nevertheless remain when many other things disappear. This is an opportunity to let the former programs and the tradition constitute the basis for entrepreneurship.

The chairman of the parish council in Grove City speaks of the congregation as the last outpost when everything else has disappeared. When it is a question of establishing social enterprises, the Church of Sweden and its historic connection to the society can provide reasonably good conditions for social entrepreneurship. Entrepreneurship is favored as the method for finding new ways to enhance the quality of people's lives. An example of this is the "friendly turn" in Lakeside. Being a voice for the down-and-out and the oppressed is a basis for a social enterprise, and thus a condition for entrepreneurship. In the same way, the various forms of collaboration with the local authority are a condition that promotes entrepreneurship in the Church of Sweden. The good relationships that are important in this collaboration could benefit from the fact that the Church of Sweden has a long tradition of presence in the area and has been able to establish trust and a network that can provide the basis for conducting social entrepreneurship, a typical institutional example.[80] The diaconal work in Small Village has at least two examples of this: The first is their intention to be a voice for the less fortunate members of Small Village and their mission to help both young people and the elderly. This is done to take advantage of the value-creating power of the social context, which can give rise to new forms of activity through entrepreneurship.

An example of social entrepreneurship in social change[81] is when the parish council president mentions the rural exodus, seeing then that the church activities create an important gathering place, as has been the case in Grove City. What is important for social entrepreneurs is that their new activities have a social benefit.[82] One example of this is the need for a preschool in Small Village, a small village, and plans are underway for this. Another example is the way in which the Church of Sweden represents continuity in depopulated areas. The context needed a preschool and the church had the opportunity to organize such a solution. In this case the social entrepreneurship affects the entire social system through value

80. Lundblad and Wejbrink, *I huvudet på en skapare*, 43–44; Selznik, *Modern organisationsteori*, 15.

81. Montin, *Moderna Kommuner*, 115–16, 123.

82. Palmås, "Socialt entreprenörskap," 246.

creation, which leads to the view of individuals and society as a resource in entrepreneurship.

The structure and the culture combined with programs are conditions for the entrepreneurial process when they are combined in the following example: In the policy documents it is stated that the congregation's church charity work should be a voice for victims and the oppressed. Social entrepreneurship takes a responsibility for both citizens and organizations where the aim is something other than large economic gain. In some congregations it is important to find partners in the local government so that the congregation does not have to do everything itself. One example of this is the "friendly turn," where the entrepreneurship market is controlled by both the private and public sectors.

This is an example where the entrepreneurial process is created through an action originated by the locals. In a larger town the governing documents point out that it is important to have open forums as much as possible, day and night. The need for such forums has led to concrete action, the open church, now also mentioned as an objective in church policy. This is not charity in the traditional sense,[83] but rather business with the same content that charity normally has. It is really a matter of taking advantage of a new type of capital that differs from the capital of traditional entrepreneurship, i.e. social capital. An example of this is that business is about the interaction between those who work as employees and those who are elected representatives.

The interaction between different expressions of entrepreneurship becomes clear in the conclusions based on the research questions about the presence and form of entrepreneurship. The following conclusion can be drawn about entrepreneurship by looking at the attributes in Table 2. The conclusions are made according to their presence in the congregations.

What Kind of Entrepreneurship is Found in the Congregations?

Entrepreneurship is present in different ways with reference to the behavioral attributes in Table 11. Six lines of entrepreneurship can be seen in the attributes. These are: Creativity, being a team leader through communication, being proactive, being visionary, seeing different capital and seeing different results in the activities. It is important to check if the entrepreneurial process is strongly connected to one person. If that person should leave, the whole idea could fail and be lost. Therefore, the team is important as a guarantee for the ongoing process.

83. Ibid.

To be active in the entrepreneurial process the entrepreneur needs to see new perspectives in the activities and combine it with all other resources in the organizations. One example is the day-care and pre-school solution. This is a new activity, not one of the usual activities in a church but the rector sees the needs and combines the resources in a creative way. This is another attribute of an entrepreneur who listens to the outside world and takes hold of the opportunities that are given. This leads to social entrepreneurship that raises the social quality of the people involved.

To combine resources and do new things in a specific moment the entrepreneur needs to have a team and to be a good team leader. He needs to communicate, treat people well and be a prime mover. Nurturing the driving force in others helps the entrepreneur to be proactive. This is about seeing the situation in a long-term process and acting now while waiting to see the result in the future. Being proactive means involving and looking after young people, arranging activities for them and allocating financial resources that will "pay off" in the future.

Being proactive is also having the courage to stand by the ideas that will have results in the future. When entrepreneurship is proactive it is also a visionary entrepreneurship. The ambassadors that speak well about the activities of the church are promoting the Church of Sweden. Enthusiasm is required to start new activities and allocate resources that will only begin to show results at a later point in time.

Resources are not only about money. They are also about social capital that gives the entrepreneur opportunities to practice entrepreneurship. Many activities require volunteers and the result is not primarily economically beneficial. It makes social change for people an active part of social work, for example when working with asylum seekers. The good relationship to the communities facilitates this work so the entrepreneur cultivates these relations and the connection to the outside world. All the various forms of entrepreneurship have an effect on the form it takes.

How Does Entrepreneurship Appear?

The entrepreneurship connected to the attributes in Table 11 shows that entrepreneurship appears both inside the organizations and is directed out to the community. Inside the organizations it is called intrapreneurship, but the form is the same.

When an opportunity arises the entrepreneur takes hold of and develops it. An example is using the church in new ways. The rector sees the need and is the prime mover in convincing others about the scheme so that in the end the new method is successfully introduced. Another example is to become involved in social work, for example the different day-care center and pre-school solutions, and also working with asylum seekers and introducing the "friendly turn."

Entrepreneurship arises in the processes of being proactive and having a vision for the future. It means investing early in activities for young people and allocating money for projects that will not have an economic result in the next year, but may produce results twenty years down the road. This attitude risks the relationship that is an important building block in the Church of Sweden. But the rectors and chairmen are convinced that they are doing the right thing and are proactive and persistent in their efforts.

Being observant of the world around you means reflecting on the situation in the rural districts where the locals are losing more and more services. In this situation the church can be an actor that makes use of local resources and human capital to the benefit of the local citizens.

CONCLUSION

The presence and form of entrepreneurship are found both individually and collectively. When the leader can have a dialogue and lead a team in a creative process, entrepreneurship takes place. The individual can also use the group as a network for conducting entrepreneurship in context. This leads to entrepreneurial processes and entrepreneurial leadership and activities in social entrepreneurship that takes place in different ways in the Church of Sweden's activities, both normal and social-sector activities.

The development of entrepreneurship can be utilized in the Church of Sweden when there is a basic structure of growth relationships. Discussing new ways of thinking is a part of this growth and the process of change that is important for entrepreneurship. While relationships can promote entrepreneurship they also build on the institutional perception of values, which often means being friendly and accommodating. This is not always possible when it comes to promoting a new idea. An example of this is when the entrepreneur sees the need for change at an early stage and wants to implement it. There may be obstacles to the change where not all parties agree to it. Then it is up to the entrepreneur to be able to combine tradition and innovation in such a way that the change can be implemented. One obstacle may be the tradition that everyone should be treated equally in an organization that has a public character. But when making change it is not possible to consider everyone's opinion equally. What is important is that everyone is allowed to speak as the organization of the Church of Sweden is based on a voluntary and ideological commitment to each individual.

In ongoing processes it turns out that both the leaders and people under the leaders are entrepreneurs and start the various activities that allow the Church of Sweden to change its activities and focus. This means that many people are involved in the process and can make it last longer which will then impede entrepreneurship, whereas the entrepreneur wants rapid action. On the other hand, letting everyone be heard and involved may produce more good ideas and turn the Church of Sweden more and more into a learning organization. Process-oriented leadership is a prerequisite for entrepreneurship when the leader can see and take advantage of the human and economic resources. A leadership that can combine this with the needs that become evident in the world is using a clear entrepreneurial approach. The fact that an entrepreneur sees the need for a process early on makes it easy to start the change before the need becomes apparent to everyone else. A prescient leader who can see change and is able to root his ideas in both the employees and leadership team will be a catalyst for entrepreneurship opportunities in the future Church of Sweden.

BIBLIOGRAPHY

Ahltorp, Birgitta. *Ledarskap ur ett ledningsstilsperspektiv: teambyggare, innovatörer, nätverkare och dirigenter.* PhD diss., University of Lund, 2003.

Andersson, Lena. "Intraprenörskap—Ett FöretagsNära entreprenörskap i det offentligas regi." In *Perspektiv på förnyelse och entreprenörskap i offentlig verksamhet,* edited by Anders Lundström and Elisabeth Sundin, 9–16. FSF 200:1. Örebro: Forum för småföretagarforskning, 2008.

Austin, James, Howard Stevenson, and Jane Wei-Skillern. "Social and Commercial Entrepreneurship: Same, Different, or Both?" *Entrepreneurship: Theory & Practice* 30 (2006) 1–22.

Bakka, Jörgen F., Egil Fivelsdal, and Lars Lindkvist. *Organisation Struktur Kultur Processer.* Liber: Malmö, 2006.

Bills, David. "Towards a Theory of Hybrid Organizations." In *Hybrid Organizations and the Third Sector,* edited by David Bills, 46–69. New York: Palgrave Macmillan, 2010.

Descombes, Martyn. *Forskningshandboken—för småskaliga forskningsprojekt inom samhällsvetenskapen.* Lund: Studentlitteratur, 2000.

Dorado, Silvia, and Dave Shaffer. "Governance Among Confounding Logics: The Case of De Paul Industries." *Journal of Social Entrepreneurship* 2 (2011) 27–52.

Ekström, Sören. *Svenska kyrkans historia, identitet, verksamhet och organisation.* Stockholm: Verbum, 2004.

Fayolle, Allain. "Research and Researchers at the Heart of Entrepreneurial Situations." In *New Movements in Entrepreneurship,* edited by Chris Steyaert and David Hjorth, 35–50. Edward Elgar: Northampton, 2003.

Fayolle, Allain, and Harry Matlay. "Social Entrepreneurship: A Multicultural and Multidimensional Perspective." In *Handbook of Research on Social*

Entrepreneurship, edited by Allain Fayolle and Harry Matlay, 1–11. Cheltenham: Edward Elgar, 2010.

Flyvberg, Bengt. "Five Misunderstandings about Case-Study Research." *Qualitative Inquiry* 12 (2006) 219–42.

Gartner, William B, ""Who Is an Entrepreneur?" Is the Wrong Question." *Entrepreneurship Theory and Practice* (1989) 47–68.

Gawell, Malin, Bengt Johannisson, and Mats Lundqvist. "Vi behöver fler samhällsentreprenörer." In *Samhällets entreprenörer En forskarantologi om samhällsentreprenörer*, edited by Malin Gawell et al., 7–13. Stockholm: KK-stiftelsen, 2009.

Gilje, Nils, and Harald Grimen. *Samhällsvetenskapens förutsättningar.* Göteborg: Daidalos, 2007.

Gustavsson, Bengt. "Kunskapande mångfald—från enhet till fragment." In *Kunskapande metoder inom samhällsvetenskapen*, edited by Bengt Gustavsson, 7–20. Lund: Studentlitteratur, 2004.

Handy, Charles. *The Empty Raincoat. Making Sense of the Future.* London: Arrow Business, 1994.

Hansson, Per. "Styrning och kultur: En studie om förändringsbetingelser i kyrklig församlingsverksamhet." PhD diss., Uppsala University, 1990

———. *Svenska kyrkans organisationskultur.* Stockholm: Verbum, 2001.

———. "Synen på prästen i Svenska kyrkan under 100 år." In *Mellom embetsmyndighet og demokrati. Presttjenesten i Skandinavia siden 1905*, edited by Hans Arne Akerø, 55–67, Oslo: Den norske kirkes presteforening, 2006.

Hjort, Daniel. "Medborgare är konsumenter? Om entreprenörialiseringen av det offentliga." In *Perspektiv på förnyelse och entreprenörskap i offentlig verksamhet*, edited by Anders Lundström and Elisabeth Sundin, 259–274. FSF 200:1. Örebro: Forum för småföretagarforskning, 2008.

Höög, Jonas, and Olof Johansson. "Struktur, kultur, ledarskap—ett projekt och dess resultat." In *Struktur, kultur, ledarskap—förutsättningar för framgångsrika skolor*, edited by Jonas Höög and Olof Johansson, 15–24. Lund: Studentlitteratur, 2011.

Kyrkoordningen med angränsande lagstiftning för Svenska kyrkan. Stockholm: Verbum, 2014.

Leffler, Eva. "Företagssamma elever: Diskurser kring entreprenörskap och företagsamhet i skolan." PhD Diss., University of Umeå, 2006.

Lundblad, Niklas, and Kristina Vejbrink. *I huvudet på en skapare: på spaning efter entreprenörskapets kärna.* IPF-rapport nr 39, Uppsala: Institutet för personal- & företagsutveckling, 1998.

Modéus, Martin. *Mänsklig gudstjänst Om gudstjänsten som relation och rit.* Stockholm: Verbum, 2008.

Montin, Stig. *Moderna Kommuner*, 3rd ed. Malmö: Liber, 2007.

Morris, Michael H., and Foard F. Jones. "Entrepreneurship in Established Organizations: The Case of the Public Sector." *Entrepreneurship Theory and Practice* (1999) 71–91.

Mühlenbock Ylva. *Inget Personligt. Om entreprenörskap i offentlig sektor.* Göteborg: Förvaltningshögskolan, 2004.

Myers, Paul, and Teresia Nelson. "Considering Social Capital in the Context of Social Entrepreneurship." In *Handbook of Research on Social Entrepreneurship*, edited by Allain Fayolle and Harry Matlay, 271–285, Cheltenham: Edward Elgar Publishing Limited, 2010.

Nicholls, Alex. "Social Enterprise—At the Forefront of Rethinking Business?" *Journal of Social Entrepreneurship* 2 (2011) 1–5.

Nordlund, Therese. *Att leda storföretag: En studie av social Kompetens och entreprenörskap i näringslivet med fokus på Axel Ax:son Johnson och J. Sigfrid Edström, 1900–1950.* PhD diss., University of Stockholm, 2005.

Nyström, Harry. *Visionärt, entreprenöriellt och strategiskt ledarskap: företagsledning i ett kreativt perspektiv.* Sandvika: Handelshøyskolen BI, 1996.

Palmås, Karl. "Socialt entreprenörskap. Ny sektor eller rehabilitering av ideellt arbete." In *Perspektiv på förnyelse och entreprenörskap i offentlig verksamhet,* edited by Anders Lundström and Elisabeth Sundin, 259–74, FSF 200:1. Örebro: Forum för småföretagarforskning, 2008.

Petersson, Olof. *Statsbyggnad: Den offentliga maktens organisation.* 6th ed. Stockholm: SNS, 2007.

Philips, Åke. "Eldsjälar. En studie av aktörsskap i arbetsorganisatoriskt utvecklingsarbete." PhD diss., Handelshögskolan, 1988.

Pinchot III, Gifford. *Intraprenörerna. Entreprenörer som stannar i företaget.* Stockholm: Svenska Dagbladets förlag AB, 1986.

Pinchot, Gifford, and Ron Pellman. *Intrapreneuring in Action. A Handbook for Business Innovation.* San Francisco: Brett-Koehler, 1999.

Rochester, Colin, and Malcolm Torry. "Faith-Based Organizations and Hybridity: A Special Case?" In *Hybrid Organizations and the Third Sector,* edited by David Billis, 114–33. New York: Palgrave Macmillan, 2010.

Sahlman, William A. "Some Thoughts on Business Plans." In *The Entrepreneurial Venture,* edited by William A. Sahlman et al., 138–76. Boston: Harvard Business School, 1999.

Schumpeter, Joseph. "The Theory of Economic Development." In *Schumpeter: Om skapande förstörelse och entreprenörskap,* edited by R. Swedberg. Ratioklassiker. Stockholm: City University Press Stockholm, 1994.

Selznick, Philip. *Modern organisationsteori.* Stockholm: Prisma, 1968.

Shockley, Gordon E., and Peter E. Frank. "Schumpeter, Kirzner, and the Field of Social Entrepreneurship." *Journal of Social Entrepreneurship* 2 (2011) 6–26.

Skaug, Jan Edvard. "Affärsstrategiskt ledarskap En studie av samband mellan ledarskap, konkurrensstrategi och prestation i logistikintensiva handelsföretag." PhD diss., University of Gothenburg, 2000.

———. *En förstudie om entreprenörskap: en kartläggning av tidigare forskning och utredningar om entreprenörskap, entreprenöriellt arbete och ledarskap.* Forskningsrapport 2000:1. Uddevalla: Institutionen för Arbete, Ekonomi och Hälsa, Högskolan Trollhättan/Uddevalla, 2000.

Stensmo, Christer. *Vetenskapsteori och metod för lärare—en introduktion,* Uppsala: Kunskapsföretaget 2002.

Stålhammar, Bert. *Kyrkoherdens ledningsvillkor.* Stockholm: Verbum, 2002.

Sundin, Elisabeth. "Slutkapitel." In *Den offentliga sektorns entreprenörer,* edited by Elisabeth Sundin, 143–50. Stockholm: Kommentus förlag, 2004.

Sundin Elisabeth, and Malin Tillmar. *A Nurse and a Civil Servant Changing Institutions: Entrepreneurial process in public sector organisations.* Department of Management and Engineering, IEI. Linköping: Linköping University 2008.

Wijkström, Filip. *Svenska organisationsliv, Framväxten av en ideell sektor.* Särtryck Civilsamhällets många ansikten: en samling essäer, 1995–2010, EFI. Stockholm: Handelshögskolan, 1999.